# WALKING POINT

★

# WALKING POINT

## FROM THE ASHES OF THE VIETNAM WAR

### PERRY A. ULANDER

North Atlantic Books
Berkeley, California

Published by
North Atlantic Books
Berkeley, California

Cover photo courtesy of National Archives and Records Administration, United States Department of Defense, U.S. Marine Corps and Real War Photos.

Cover and book design by Howie Severson

Printed in the United States of America

*Walking Point: From the Ashes of the Vietnam War* is sponsored and published by the Society for the Study of Native Arts and Sciences (dba North Atlantic Books), an educational nonprofit based in Berkeley, California, that collaborates with partners to develop cross-cultural perspectives, nurture holistic views of art, science, the humanities, and healing, and seed personal and global transformation by publishing work on the relationship of body, spirit, and nature.

North Atlantic Books' publications are available through most bookstores. For further information, visit our website at www.northatlanticbooks.com or call 800–733–3000.

Library of Congress Cataloging-in-Publication Data

Names: Ulander, Perry A., 1948- author.
Title: Walking point : from the ashes of the Vietnam War / Perry A. Ulander.
Description: Berkeley, California : North Atlantic Books, [2016]
Identifiers: LCCN 2015022372| ISBN 9781623170127 (trade pbk.) | ISBN 9781623170134 (ebook)
Subjects: LCSH: Ulander, Perry A., 1948- | United States. Army. Airborne Brigade, 173rd. Bravo Company. | Soldiers—United States—Biography. | Vietnam War, 1961–1975—Vietnam—Central Highlands. | United States. Army—Military life—History—20th century. | Soldiers—Drug use—Vietnam. | Vietnam War, 1961–1975—Personal narratives, American.
Classification: LCC DS559.5 .U43 2016 | DDC 959.704/342—dc23
LC record available at http://lccn.loc.gov/2015022372


1 2 3 4 567 8 9 Sheridan 21 20 19 18 17 16

Printed on recycled paper

*I would like to dedicate this book to all the people who, having put their faith and trust in social, political, or religious institutions, discovered that their faith had been misplaced and their trust betrayed.*

# ACKNOWLEDGMENTS

I would like to thank Dennis and Jo Eberl for introducing me to Roshi Philip Kapleau's style of *zazen*; Betsy Ruth Dayton, Donna Carey, Dr. Xue Zhong Wang, and Dr. Michael Phillips for their expertise in various healing arts that helped me survive the transition from a war zone into a world gone mad; and my wife, Jayne, for accepting me as I am.

I would also like to thank the people who were involved in a sequence of events that made this book possible. I'd like to thank Brenda Peterson for sensing that there were memories I'd rather not share and creating an atmosphere that allowed me to put them on paper; Stan Sales for his preliminary edit and encouragement; Dr. Larry Dossey for his time and encouragement; Robert Phoenix for his insight and wise counsel and for introducing me to Richard Grossinger and Tim McKee, who took the time to read my rather raggedy rough draft and present it to North Atlantic Books for consideration. I would also like to thank Jennifer Eastman and Vanessa Ta for their editorial skills and willingness to work on a difficult project.

# CONTENTS

# 1  INTO THE UNKNOWN

**Fort Lewis, Washington, December 1969**

The rain changed to snow as I walked, aimless and alone, around the post. On the wall of the barracks labeled "Transient Personnel," the duty roster had been posted for the day. Under the heading KP (the army's acronym for Kitchen Police, which included details like scrubbing pots and pans and peeling potatoes), there was my name: Ulander, Perry. It might have been possible to hang around the barracks and read or play cards, but that would have been asking for extra duty, such as polishing door knobs with Brasso or cleaning latrines.

I opted for the snow. When your mind is numb, you don't really feel the cold.

Memories of the previous couple years passed through my mind as I walked, trying to justify my plight. I recalled a fateful but seemingly logical decision: get some on-the-job experience after two years of studying structural engineering. There were companies in Milwaukee that would hire people with less than a bachelor's degree, and I thought that after working for a while, it would be easy to see how all the math, physics, and chemistry were applied, making it easier for me to discipline myself for the next two years of course work.

In college, no one was being drafted. I was nineteen; my world revolved around assignments, exams, and parties. There was news of this small war somewhere on the fringe of my narrow, self-centered perception, but it seemed that it should have been nearly over any day. So it was, with what seemed to have been a well-thought-out game plan, that I dropped out of school and accepted a junior position at one of the local firms.

Things seemed to be going quite well. The head of the engineering department gave me a project that one of the full-fledged engineers had left behind when he returned to school to get his master's degree. My brother and I were sharing an apartment, and even though I occasionally stumbled over the engine block of the sports car that he was overhauling in the living room, it was better than living in the dorm. Ignorance is bliss.

I remember breaking into a cold sweat reading the letter that told me to appear for a preinduction physical in Chicago. A few sleepless nights later, there I was, in my jockey shorts, following the yellow line painted on the floor, hoping the army would find something wrong with me. But it seems that when one is up for a major life transition, there's nothing that will hold it back. Still, after reading yet another letter, this one starting out "Greetings from the President," I couldn't help but wonder why, out of all the people in this country, they wanted me.

As I continued to wander around the military base in the snow, as if on autopilot, my mind raced through the memories of the months that followed my greetings. There was an image of me on a bus with a group of equally anonymous recruits, pulling in to Fort Polk at two in the morning. We were ordered to march in an orderly fashion to some bleachers to receive our orientation talk. Drill sergeants took two-hour shifts telling us, in a high-speed, mechanical monotone, what we were expected to do. Most of it didn't make much sense; it seemed to be designed to keep us awake all night rather than to inform, so we would be groggy and malleable for the indoctrination to come. At the first light of dawn, processing started, with the traditional haircut. The army barber held the back of my head with his left hand and brought the heavy-duty electric clippers in for a crash landing just above my forehead. Four or five strokes across the top and a few scrapes up the back, and I was nearly bald. A heavy thump on the shoulder meant I was done, ready to be herded to another building for shots. Anyone who hesitated wound up on the floor doing push-ups while a sergeant informed him that he was in the army and that his present status was *trainee*. In case you didn't know what a trainee was, he'd let you know that it was lower than whale shit, and that was on the bottom of the ocean.

It was clear that phase one, mortification, of the military's psychological remodeling job was already in full swing. The programmed dissolution of one's identity had begun. Any indication of valuing or identifying with our previous identities was met with swift punishment and humiliation. It was clear that we were no longer jocks or eggheads, streetwise city kids or ol' boys from the country; to the army, we were nothing, worthless, useless. For two months, we were confined to the post to ensure that contact with the civilian world wouldn't remind us of our former selves.

Phase two, reconstruction, began to blend subtly with phase one after a couple weeks. As one's new identity was introduced, those who conformed most readily were referred to as *troop* or *trooper*. Guys with the shiniest brass and boots were no longer at the bottom of the ocean, but were, by virtue of a new name, suspended a few feet off the ocean floor. The osmosis of the new value system in some of the guys was so complete that they began to compete for a string of carrots that was dangled before the now-eager horses. With a little effort, one could become a trainee squad leader, platoon leader, or company commander.

These were honorary positions. One's actual rank and pay grade remained the same, but guys fought for a new name. Pushing for a front-row seat on a hell-bound bus. Insanity within insanity.

The power of naming was evident on the rifle range as well. At first the targets were targets—a black bull's-eye within concentric rings. Later they were silhouettes of the head and trunk of a man, and finally they were animated silhouettes that would pop up from behind rocks and bushes. The form had changed, but the name remained the same— targets—so that, with a large but not illogical leap, future targets would be flesh and blood.

Even hypnosis found its way into the reconstruction process. After being roused at dawn and gathered in formation, we'd be double-timed around the post, chanting:

> *I wanna be an airborne ranger.*
> *I wanna live a life of danger.*
> *I wanna go to Vietnam.*
> *I wanna kill ol' Charlie Cong.*

The early morning grogginess and the force of a hundred men chanting together made it easier to pump the message into the subconscious, where it would eventually become — apparently — one's own thought, one's own desire.

Over the weeks, there had also been a progression in rank of the people addressing us. At first, it was just a drill sergeant, then, occasionally, the company commander would deign to say a few words to the men. Finally, on graduation day, amid the bands playing and the bleachers full of proud parents and relatives, they managed to pry this overweight, alcoholic bozo of a general away from the officer's club long enough to tell us what great fighting men we'd become.

Even the gloomy sky and cold drizzle couldn't keep me from laughing to myself at the absurdity of the pageantry of our graduation from basic training. It seemed barely possible that the actors in the play would be able to keep straight faces through it all, and yet, though also tragically funny, they were serious.

I remembered a queasy feeling setting in after basic training; it made me think of the kid who thinks he's on top of the bargaining with a slick used-car salesman and drives off in a new "cream puff" with the bad transmission. I wanted out, but at this point, the options weren't very appealing. Out-and-out rebellion could get you a few years of being sodomized in jail — or if you could conjure up a convincing case of lunacy, you could get an undesirable discharge that would follow you around for the rest of your life, as we were regularly reminded. But perhaps there was something to the rumor that the only openings for airborne personnel were in Germany.

Grabbing at straws, I signed up, and after three weeks of jump school, I was officially authorized to be the only thing besides bird shit that comes out of the sky. After jump school, I was assigned a military occupational specialty for the next phase of training. It came up 11B—infantry, light weapons—and I was sent back to Fort Polk for eight more weeks of double-time and rifle range. A few new variations on the theme were introduced, such as cordon and search, infiltration of enemy territory, and war games with blanks. The weeks flew by, and at the end, a sergeant read the list of our names and new duty stations. The list only occasionally featured the names of stateside bases or Germany, but still, when he read, "Ulander, Perry, RVN," I was stunned. I remembered listening to his voice when he announced RVN (Republic of Vietnam) after other names. It sounded sad, sickened, apologetic. And recognizing the combat infantry badge sewn above his shirt pocket, I saw the reason—he'd been there.

And now I was standing out in the snow, a duffel bag full of jungle fatigues lying on my bunk in the transient personnel barracks. The cold must have awakened me from the dreamlike reflections. I felt a fiery rage as I realized that the army didn't care if you caught on to some of the propaganda and deception. The program undoubtedly allowed that some of the guys would catch a whiff of what was going on. The bottom line was even most of those would be a half step behind and willing to get on a plane heading west.

A feverish heat went from the top of my shoulders up the back of my neck; the blood seemed to be draining from my face and brain. I found the mess sergeant and told him, "My plane's leaving in the morning, and I don't feel too good." I gave him five bucks and got out of KP.

The next morning, after an hour of filling out some last-minute paperwork, I wandered back to the barracks to find Hank, who usually confined himself to the bunk above mine, digging through his duffel bag.

"Hey, Ulander," he called, "check out what my brother sent me for the trip."

He fished out a one-pound coffee can and took off the lid.

"He cleaned it and everything." He beamed as he showed me the contents: brown, spicy-smelling pot.

It was clear that Hank was one of those guys who had developed a "give a shit" attitude early on. It was a common phenomenon; almost everyone experienced it sooner or later. It was accompanied by a sudden release from the fear and tension that had been implanted as part of the program. A sergeant would walk in the barracks, and you'd notice that the intimidation-by-rank factor was gone. When guys reached this point, most of them would still go through the motions, just being grateful that the release from the tension made the situation much more tolerable, but people responded to this sense of relief in differing degrees, and Hank's was an extreme case. When the pressure lifted, he'd become completely heedless. So I wasn't too surprised when he pulled out a pack of rolling papers and casually rolled a dozen joints. He stuffed them in his shirt pocket, looked up, and said, "Make sure you find me when we stop to refuel, and we'll get high."

"You bet," I replied, hoping that the other guys in the barracks hadn't picked up on what it was that Hank had been doing.

A half hour later, we boarded the bus for the airfield. Once there, it pulled right out on the runway, where a large Flying Tiger Airlines jet was warming up its engines. I boarded the plane in a state of emotional numbness. There were times in the military when I'd be too stressed or exhausted to think or care. My mind would be on hold, leaving my body to function on autopilot. This was one of those times. It wasn't until I heard the aircraft door being secured that some realization of what was happening returned. But then the engines whined, the G's increased, and when the plane's nose lifted, I returned to my mental coma.

All too soon, we were in Alaska. Hank and I stood just outside the terminal passing a number back and forth. He jabbered merrily away while I glanced nervously around to see if we were being spotted.

At Osaka, Japan, the scene was repeated, and the last leg of the long flight was underway. The stewardesses passed out another round of brown-bag lunches, and I dozed off for a while. When the plane's change of elevation brought me to, a stewardess announced that the no-smoking light was on, and the plane assumed the steepest imaginable landing approach for a civilian aircraft. Reality again asserted itself, as the steep descent was no doubt an attempt to reduce the plane's vulnerability. My heart started pounding, and I looked around to see if I could glance at somebody's watch to check the time. As if somehow it mattered what time it was. I spotted a watch — it was some god-awful time. I imagined that there must be an army regulation stating, "Any time enlisted personnel are to report to a new duty station, it shall be at some god-awful time in the early morning — if possible, between 0200 and 0400 hours."

## Cam Ranh Bay, December 1969

The plane rolled to a halt and sat there. An hour passed, and even in the predawn darkness, the heat and humidity seemed to seep into the plane to mix with the smell of nervous sweat. Every one of those asthmatic little cone-shaped air-conditioning vents was wide open, and they were losing ground. Finally, the stewardess's voice came over the PA system and announced, "We have arrived at our destination, Cam Ranh Bay, Vietnam. We're sure the army has some various and sundry things for you boys to do here, and we hope you will enjoy your tour. We'll be back in about a year to pick you up."

I couldn't believe what I'd just heard, especially since it was delivered in that saccharine, singsong style that was usually used to announce the arrival at destinations like Honolulu or Acapulco. "Various and sundry"? Here we were, supposedly trained to hate and to kill, and she's got to come up with something like that? It was all too much. "We'll be back in a year." What of those who would be dead or maimed in a year's time, but who were surely at this moment on board? I felt flooded with a nearly uncontrollable rage and wished she hadn't said anything at all—but then the thought occurred to me that the situation might also be pretty hard on her. That cooled me enough to be able to walk past her as I exited the aircraft without making some caustic comment. I made it a point to avoid eye contact with her as the line of soldiers ahead of me disappeared around the corner of the aisle and went out into the thick, warm air and glaring white lights of the airstrip.

We were herded into buses and then, after a short drive to the base, were prodded into some semblance of a formation. After another classic list of instructions, we were allowed to retire.

When I woke the next morning, I was disappointed to find myself there—in Cam Ranh, that is. During the last six months, I'd become somewhat accustomed to the uncertainty of knowing where I was for the first few seconds of each day. Dreaming of home, I'd wake up in boot camp; thinking that I was in jump school, I'd wake up and find myself at home on leave. This time, though, the reality was Cam Ranh Bay.

The other guys in the barracks were shuffling about as I got up; some had already left. I quickly put on my boots and headed for the door, not wanting to be snagged by some non-commissioned officer (NCO) who might be looking for a crew to pick up trash and cigarette butts. When I made it to the door, the guy in front of me said, "Hey, let's go to the PX." And so I tagged along with a few other guys, thinking it was as good a choice as any.

There were four of us. In the facile friendships of transient personnel, the fact that we didn't know each other wasn't considered the least bit relevant. We were all new there, but finding the PX—the post exchange, the post's store—was no problem. Even ten thousand miles from the States, military uniformity prevailed, and the PX would be found in a logical, central location.

Once we were inside, I was confused by the almost instant revulsion I had for the place. The other guys had already started to dash about, checking out the bargain-basement prices on the usual PX fare. I wandered off, hoping that my emotions would, at some point, be translated into thoughts. All the stuff there—watches, cameras, stereos—glittered under the bright fluorescent lights, and it all seemed so worthless. Then it struck me that none of the items could even begin to ease my mind or guarantee a safe tour of duty. Under the conditions, it all seemed ridiculous. I was amazed that before this day they might have had some appeal. I was feeling hungry and figured that it might shake the mood to find the mess hall and have some breakfast.

There was a clearly marked enlisted men's mess not far away, and the short line in front of it was reassuring — they were still serving. It also had a familiar uniformity about it, but once inside, I briefly lapsed into a civilian habit and pushed open a door on one side of the serving line, expecting to find the men's room. It turned out to be the back sink area, and I almost stumbled over a dark form on the floor, only knee-high, before I realized the mistake. Looking down, I saw a scraggly mass of black hair, streaked with gray, and two arms reaching into a plastic pan of dirty dishwater. The disheveled head lifted as my boots came into view, and the face of an ancient Vietnamese woman looked up with a big open grin. The teeth she had, about half of the normal issue, were stained the color of dried blood from chewing betel nut, the Vietnamese version of a caffeine buzz. She had deeply wrinkled, nut-brown, parchment-paper skin and glassy, laughing eyes. In shock and pity, I stumbled backward, groping for the door, as a chorus of laughing and Vietnamese yammering erupted in my ears.

After breakfast, I wandered around, musing about future probabilities. Perhaps they needed replacements in Cam Ranh; it seemed safe enough. Occasionally there was the sound of artillery in the distance, but none of the "permanent parties" showed concern. They hadn't even been issued helmets, much less M16s, and the beach wasn't far off. The place did have a PA system, however, and my name, toward the end of a list of others, came across loud and clear. We were to report immediately.

In the transient-barracks formation area, we were given orders to report to jungle school, which was "up north somewhere." We were taken back to the airfield and loaded on an air force plane. It was a twin-engine turboprop of some kind, with a row of nylon web seats running down each side, facing the center aisle. With very little crosswind, the thing seemed to fly about 15 degrees askew of the direction of flight. Although the beach at Cam Ranh was literally out of the picture, I took some consolation in the fact that jungle school was supposed to last a week. For a draftee with fifty-two weeks to spend in Vietnam, a week was a week.

Prior to boarding, I took a look at my personnel file, which had been expanded during processing "in country." Apparently the army had given most of us a promotion to reflect the fact that we were now officially in a combat zone. I had climbed the ranks one step, from private first class to Specialist 4. My base pay had increased from $155.00 a month to $214.20. I flashed momentarily on the lyrics of an old WWII song, "We'll never get rich diggin' a ditch. We're in the Army now."

The plane landed at a medium-sized air base, complete with a military-style terminal of concrete block and tile floors. Another Spec. 4 was there to meet us and told me and two other guys to hop in his jeep. This was to be, among other things, our introduction to driving, Vietnam-style. It seemed that drivers here knew only two speeds: full blast and screeching halt. Any complications caused by the limited speed control were compensated for by intense, sudden manipulation of the steering wheel. A flick-of-the-wrist swerve was all the driver granted a Vietnamese man or woman who was on foot or riding a Honda motorbike in the driver's lane.

We came up on a village. The highway was somewhat narrowed by the village, as buildings were set back only a few feet and some of those had tables and stalls set up in front of them. There were children playing and women—mama-sans, as the GIs called them—quickstepping along with twin shopping bags or burdened with a balance pole that had baskets hanging from either end. I looked to see if the driver showed any indication of slowing. He didn't. The jeep blasted through; it was miraculous how the pedestrians, bicycles, and Hondas parted in front of the jeep, like the Red Sea before Moses, and closed as we passed.

Even this quick flash of village life caused me to feel pity for the Vietnamese. Here, a Honda 90 was a Cadillac, and a two-room, mud-walled, thatched-roof hut was their version of a house in the suburbs.

From the smell of the village, it was clear that indoor plumbing was for the elite.

It was a relief when the jeep finally skidded to a halt in front of the headquarters at the jungle school. It was a small compound with four permanent buildings: a classroom, a snack bar, a communications office, and the headquarters, which doubled as a mess hall. In the center of the compound were four OD tents, twenty feet by forty, each with rows of cots. Each tent was surrounded by fifty-five gallon drums filled with dirt. I knew immediately where we'd be staying—hello, cot.

Since no specific orders had been issued for the rest of the afternoon, we were free to roam about. I claimed a cot by throwing my duffel bag on it. When I turned around, I saw Rodrigez grinning at me.

"Let's check the place out," he said.

Rodrigez was one of the guys who had been with me on the wild jeep ride from the airstrip, and although the open jeep hadn't allowed much conversation, we'd already sized each other up—a couple of fuck-offs, for sure.

There really wasn't that much to check out, but we learned that they showed movies at the snack bar at night. So after an afternoon of lounging on my cot and watching a high-powered Korean Bible salesman trying to convince a few of the manically depressed guys in the tent to buy huge $50 deluxe Bibles to send to their folks at home, I went to the snack bar and waited for the show. I'd just bought a Coke and lit a cigarette when Rodrigez appeared, eyes shining.

"I was over at the transport battalion across the street," he said. "One of the dudes over there gave me some pot. Let's go get high."

As we walked off, Rodrigez proudly produced a nearly microscopic joint, fired it up, took a toke, and passed it to me. I was amazed to find myself getting high while I held the first hit. In the time it took to finish the joint, things were going in slow motion; my body felt like it was floating. My mind went blank, but my senses were amplified. We'd pretty much made the rounds of the small compound, and in front of us was the headquarters building, which was illuminated by small floodlights aimed at its façade. It was beautiful, shimmering and shining, surreal, translucent, like … the Emerald City. Evidently, Rodrigez wasn't nearly as impressed; he grabbed my sleeve as I stood gawking. "Come on, man, let's get the hell out of here. There might be lifers hanging around."

Even though the snack bar was only fifty yards away, it seemed like a miraculous feat of navigation to get there. Each step was a surprise in itself. I was considerably relieved when each foot, in turn, finally touched the ground. I felt like a child just learning to walk, and when we reached our destination, I found it, too, was transformed. The movie was already half over, and between the indecipherable sound track, the din of the people talking, and my newly discovered sensitivity to ambient emotions, it was almost unbearable to be there.

Rodrigez must have felt the same, because with very little hesitation, he said, "Hey, man, this place is too heavy for me. Let's split."

The oppressive feeling lifted quickly as we headed for the tent. Most of the guys had already crashed for the night. Only one guy was still awake; he smiled knowingly at us, watching us straining to be cool. After a few minutes of conversation, we relaxed, recognizing a kindred spirit.

His name was Calendar. In spite of his boyish face, he was a couple of inches taller than me — and I was six feet two. There was also an ironic contrast between his cherubic looks and the mischievous sparkle in his eyes. As he told of his two years at Purdue (also in engineering), I found it easy to imagine him amiably loaded on beer at weekend parties, chasing women, and getting rowdy with the boys. He'd discovered an enlisted men's club across the street and suggested that we check it out. It sounded okay, but I remembered that at the orientation we'd been given on our arrival, we'd been told to stay in the company area. I mentioned this.

As if on cue, Calendar and Rodrigez looked at me and said in unison, "What are they gonna do? Send us to Vietnam?"

The enlisted men's club — the EM club — was easier to deal with than the snack bar, particularly after the first beer. Calendar seemed to be thoroughly enjoying himself playing the slot machines for tokens, and Rodrigez wasted no time in trying to put the make on the Vietnamese bar girl who was delivering drinks. But for me, it soon seemed to be too chaotic, so I wandered back to the tent to crash.

The next morning, after chow and formation, I found myself on trash detail. There were three of us in the cab of a big two-and-a-half-ton truck, known as a "deuce and a half" in country, as it headed out of the compound and down the highway to the dump. I felt edgy; the driver had brought along an M16. The notable absence of weapons in the bases I'd been in so far had been an indication that we were in a relatively secure area. The dump was only a couple of miles down the road, and we were greeted by three grubby Vietnamese boys who were obviously familiar with the procedure. As the truck backed up to the pile of junk, the kids positioned themselves directly behind it. They clambered barefoot over the cans, cardboard, and smashed crates to get dibs on the stuff from the new load. The driver dropped the tailgate, and the other newbie and I began shoveling the stuff off the back end. The other guy took no notice of the kids, and occasionally the garbage would land right on them as they scrambled for unopened C-rations, broken shoelaces, and mess-hall scraps. I tried to get them to move back but got no response, and when I tried shoveling stuff over the side, one of the kids moved to the new location.

"Don't bother about those kids," the driver said. "They won't move." He was right.

Shortly after we returned to the compound, another formation was called. Classes were about to begin. The first class was about the dangers of drug use among the troops. It was given by a CID (Criminal Investigation Department) major, who, from his puffy face and red nose, looked as if he must not have been listening too closely to the class he was teaching.

After giving us a description of the no-nos that the medics carried in the field, he showed us vials of the French speed that was sold by the Vietnamese and some blobs of opium. For the grand finale, he pulled out a large plastic bag containing a basketball-sized tangle of Vietnamese reefer. To make sure we could identify its "characteristic smell," he took out a huge flower top and torched it thoroughly with his Zippo. He handed it to the guy in the front row to pass around the class. About every fourth guy in the class took an extra-long, slow smell of the smoldering bud before passing it on, while the CID officer was saying, "If you see anyone smoking this stuff, report it to your nearest NCO or officer immediately, and let him handle it from there."

For me, the whiff of pot was a welcome relief, as the lingering emotional impact of seeing the Vietnamese kids showered with garbage seemed to have stuck somewhere in my system. The scene in itself was bad enough, but seeing how eager the kids were to get something to eat or trade made it all the more piteous. I was beginning to realize how lucky and sheltered I had been.

For the next bit of training, we were marched to the edge of the compound to a tent that had been sealed and filled with CS gas—tear-gas. I couldn't help but wonder what sadistic son of a bitch had set this up. We'd all been through this once in basic training, where, after being herded into a room full of gas, we were required to remove our gas masks and recite our name, rank, and serial number. The test had been designed so that we'd be out of breath and sure to get a lung-full of gas as we stumbled blindly for the door, eyes tearing, nose running, and skin and lungs burning. This time it was easier—all we had to do was don our gas masks and walk through. Thank God.

That was it for the day's classes, and I'd had enough. After a few relatively free days of floating passively in transit, the "Green Machine" was clamping down again. It was back to taking orders again. Do this; do that; report to XYZ at 1200 hours. It was a drag, but there was no turning back.

After chow, I went back to the tent to rest a bit. There were a few guys there, but nobody was talking. It seemed they all had retreated into their private worlds, thinking of home or wondering *Why me?* To counter the gloomy atmosphere, I decided to numb out for a while, but soon Rodrigez came in. He was really straining to look nonchalant as he sat down on the empty cot next to mine. He looked around rather nervously for a while and then confided that he'd scored some more reefer. As we left the tent together, my mood lightened. It was nice to have found a friend, and the prospect of getting stoned was appealing. It wasn't quite dark, so we strolled to an unoccupied end of the compound.

Rodrigez looked like a shifty-eyed actor in a cloak-and-dagger mystery as he lit a joint. "I'll smoke the first half, and you can have the rest," he said. "After that rap the CID gave us today, we can't let anyone see us pass it back and forth." When we finished the joint, I ate the roach, and then we could relax a bit; the evidence was gone.

We sat quietly for a long time, mesmerized by the pink clouds that hung over the lush green mountains. A sense of peace and contentment settled over us as we watched the clouds turn to slate gray. In the east, a deep purplish-blue was creeping up from the horizon, and a sprinkle of stars appeared.

Rodrigez gently broke the silence. "Nice, huh?"

"Yeah," I replied. "Never really noticed before."

As the spell of the sky and mountains faded, I realized that my mouth was dry. My body was screaming for something sweet. It was the stoned munchies in the worst way.

"Hey, let's head to the snack bar and get a Coke," I said. "Somebody said they had ice cream."

Rodrigez was grinning as he wobbled to his feet. "Iiiice cream! Let's go."

We staggered to the snack bar, laughing at how well the army provided for the needs of stoners. After a Coke and an ice cream cone, we headed back to the tent to find Calendar. We'd floated down the hill and were nearly there when I caught some movement out of the corner of my eye. I turned to see four guys running for the tower on the perimeter of the compound.

Almost simultaneously, the lights inside the compound went out and the perimeter floodlights went on. A sergeant came running up to us. "We're under red alert!" He pointed at me and said, "Report to the communications building." Then he turned to Rodrigez. "*You.* Come with me."

I nearly peed my pants. *God*, I thought, rushing toward communications. *Here we are, under the threat of attack, and I'm stoned.*

The NCO in charge of communications seemed reasonably calm as he informed me that I had first watch. Our code was *Hotel Quebec*, and I was to rouse the lieutenant in the next room if there were any calls. I sat nearly paralyzed in front of the radio, hoping that it would stay quiet. I could hear bits and pieces of conversation coming from the room next door.

From the sounds of it, our perimeter was surrounded by a much larger circle manned by Korean troops, about a thousand meters out. They had spotted some Viet Cong but hadn't exchanged fire. The NCO in charge doubted that the VC could penetrate the Korean defense, even at night.

I'd already heard of the ROKs, as the Koreans were called. They were generally considered much more effective than most American units. Tough and highly trained, they were fueled by an ancient hatred of the Vietnamese and had little regard for the Geneva Convention. Stories had it that if they passed through a village, they would kill a few villagers, in case they might have been VC, line a well-traveled path with the bodies, and dare any one to try to bury them.

The news from the next room wasn't the worst, but still, my fear was barely controllable as I stared at the radio, not knowing how well I could function. Time crawled by. Finally a replacement took over and told me to find a place on the floor to sleep for the night. I tried to relax by reminding myself that the blast from mortars was cone-shaped and that unless you were standing, chances were that most of the shrapnel would go over your head. I lay on the floor, feeling electrified, for what seemed like hours, but finally fell asleep.

The night had passed quietly enough, but I was in a pretty sober mood in the morning, almost glad to be herded around again, as it kept my mind from dwelling on my condition the night before. The first order of the day was to report to headquarters, where we were told to take turns standing at parade rest in front of an American flag while an NCO took each man's picture with a Polaroid camera. It seemed a strange thing for the army to do, but orders were orders. They gave us our pictures, evidently to send to the folks at home. I looked at mine and didn't like what I saw. I was scared, and it showed.

The class for the day was about booby traps, and I found myself listening quite intently as the diagrams of the most commonly used ones were explained. We were then divided into five-man teams and taken on some well-established trails that had been booby-trapped with harmless but near-deafening explosive charges. As the exercise progressed, each team proceeded to blow themselves away five times. None of the simulated traps had been discovered before it exploded, and even afterward, it was hard to find what had caused it to go off. The point was driven home that in the jungle, any rock, root, vine, or overhanging branch could be used to trigger a land mine and that if we traveled by established trails, it would take incredible attention and discrimination to avoid being maimed. The trails we used in the exercise had also been marked in the ways commonly used by the North Vietnamese Army or the VC to keep their own people from taking them accidently. Their method of warning was to place three small rocks at the trail's edge — or perhaps a few twisted blades of grass or a knife-cut twig pointing toward the booby-trapped area. Amid the dense vegetation, it wasn't much warning, and obviously we'd missed even these.

The days slipped by, and all too soon it was our last day of the training. We were issued M16s, ammunition, and one meal of C-rations and divided into squads again. I could see that our team leader, who was leaning on a radio pack, was sizing us up, so I went into my "Incredible Shrinking Man" mental routine. It involved imagining myself shrinking and projecting an image of someone who looked like me but was much smaller.

"You." The sergeant pointed at me. "Take this." He handed me the radio.

I was kicking myself as I adjusted the straps of the twenty-eight-pound radio pack, thinking, *Should have done the "Invisible Man." You know you're better at that one.*

Or so it seemed. The "Invisible Man" was an exercise I'd started to practice the first week of basic training in the States. It seemed that if I let my mind go blank and tried to suspend my emotions, the drill sergeants would quite often pass me by when they were looking for someone to demonstrate rifle drills or spar with them in hand-to-hand combat. They would often pick the bigger guys, especially if they felt the need to humiliate someone, and my being six feet two and 190 pounds required whatever evasive tactics I could muster.

We left the perimeter of the compound through a gate in the barbed wire and followed a trail along the base of one of the small mountains. The sun was blazing, and the humidity that hung in the vegetation that crowded the trail from either side seemed just short of a fog. The trail gained elevation and, inevitably, it seemed, led to the top of the mountain. At the peak, we rested a bit, ate our Cs, and sent a message to headquarters that we'd arrived at our destination. The patrol might have been more intense if we had been outside the area that was guarded by the ROKs, but even so, there was pressure to stay alert; we weren't all that safe. The return to the compound was uneventful, and now there was only the waiting.

As I lay in my cot that night, part of me was still hoping that there was a chance of being assigned to something other than an infantry outfit. With each step, the prospects became bleaker, but the die had not yet been cast. For me, that meant that there was still hope.

The following morning, when travel orders were passed out, I knew. I stared at the paper, hoping that I was misreading them or that perhaps they were someone else's. But there was no way around the way they read: "LZ Uplift, 173 Airborne Brigade, Company B." Calendar and Rodrigez had been assigned to the same place but were in Charlie Company.

Feeling as if I'd heard the judge say, "And you shall be hanged by the neck until dead," I asked Calendar, "What's this LZ business, and where's Uplift?"

"LZ means *landing zone*; it's a base camp," he replied. "And Uplift is in II corp; it's the second division south of the border between North and South Vietnam.

Bad news. My sinking heart sank some more. The farther north you were, the hotter the action was, and to be in an airborne unit was almost as bad as being in the marines.

My voice cracked a bit as I spoke. "I hope they're not too gung ho up there."

"Hey, man," Rodrigez said, smiling. "Don't sweat it. At least we can travel together, and maybe we can score some weed."

It was beyond me how Rodrigez could be smiling, but it seemed—in a way—that he was right. Why get all upset till you're there? We still had a day or two of travel time and, with luck, a few days hanging around Uplift. We might as well enjoy it. I was grateful to have Rodrigez as a friend. With his spunk and a few choice words, he saved me from sinking into the depths of depression.

One of the NCOs approached us just then and said, "Let me see your papers."

He studied them for a while and said, "You three, get your duffel bags and report to headquarters on the double. Your plane leaves in an hour."

It wasn't any easier to get four people and three overstuffed duffel bags in the jeep this time than it had been before. I was still looking for something to hang on to as the jeep lurched onto the highway. The little four-banger under the hood was running red line all the way. Settling in for the ride, I was amused at how Calendar and Rodrigez were handling the situation. Here we were with orders for "up north somewhere," and they were as playful as a couple of kids who had just been let out of school for summer vacation. Rodrigez was hanging off the side of the jeep, giving the peace sign to Vietnamese kids as we roared by and laughing when they gave it back.

Moments later, Calendar grabbed my shirt and hollered above the noise, "Did ya see that? There were four gooks on that Honda!"

I nodded, also laughing at the sight. A small child—a *baby-san*, as a little kid was called—sat on the gas tank in front of the driver, and two people sat behind him. If it had a motor and wheels, the Vietnamese would load it till you could barely tell what was under the heap to make it go. Even their little buses would wind up piled high with luggage, crated chickens, and a few extra people on the roof.

We made our connection at the airstrip with time to spare and, after about an hour's flight, landed at Phu Cat Air Force Base. There was a driver waiting when we arrived, and after another jeep ride, we were at the headquarters of LZ Uplift.

A mean-looking sergeant took us across the street to our quarters. It was one of several single-story plywood buildings with tin roofs and rows of cots. He took our paperwork and after glancing at it a bit, said, "Bravo and Charlie Companies are in the field. They'll be back in three or four days. In the meantime, you guys will be staying here. I want you to stick around the company area till they get back."

That was our cue, of course, to leave as soon as he was out of sight and make ourselves as scarce as possible. The place had much more of a combat-zone feel to it than the jungle school. Helicopters, both Hueys and Cobra gunships, flew over the place constantly, and instead of just concertina wire, this place was circled with sandbag bunkers at fifty-meter intervals. As we toured the place, we realized that there wasn't much to see. There was an aid station with a landing pad near by, a mess hall, an ammo dump, and the EM and NCO clubs. The PX was a trailer with some steps going up to the side door, and behind it was a big sheet of plywood that had been painted white and nailed onto some four-by-four posts, which, along with a few bleachers, served as the movie theater.

The place was pretty deserted, which made our main occupation of dodging "Sarge" pretty difficult. He snagged me for KP one afternoon, and as I was scrubbing pots, one of the other guys mentioned that it was Christmas Eve. I hadn't realized it. It might seem that it'd be hard for someone who had been assigned to an infantry unit to feel sorry for himself because he had to scrub a few pots on Christmas Eve, but I managed.

Bravo and Charlie companies showed up for Christmas dinner the next day. Even after they cleaned themselves up, they were the motleyest bunch of guys I'd yet seen in uniform. Some had their helmets on backward, and most of their helmets had peace signs or FTA (which stood for *Fuck the Army*) drawn on them — or both. They wore sunglasses and bandanas. One guy had sunglasses with purple lenses, and a few had pierced ears with gold peace-sign earrings. Their boots, aside from being muddy, were so badly scuffed up that they looked like they had gray suede toes and heels. I was beginning to wonder if there had been some sort of breakdown in military discipline.

Later that evening, Rodrigez and I happened to wander by Bravo Company's barracks. The door was open, and we could see three guys sitting on cots nearest the doorway. They just sat there staring at the floor under the harsh light of the bare bulb above them. Suddenly, a blond-haired sergeant, who was sitting nearest the door, broke the tense silence when he violently threw his bayonet, sticking it in the floor, and yelled, "That goddamned, cock-suckin', motherfuckin' McDouche! Somebody ought to blow his shit away. Somebody ought to frag his ass!"

His body was shaking with rage. He reached into the pack behind him and pulled out a fifth of Jack Daniel's.

At this point the man behind the sergeant spotted Rodrigez and me, bolted out the door, and led us away from the barracks. "You guys better not hang around here for a while," he said quietly. "Sarge is real pissed off, and it would be best to leave him alone."

Rodrigez asked, "What's the matter? What happened?"

The man let out a drawn-out "ohhh" and hesitated, as if wondering whether or not to say. "We were out on this mission, and the lifers in the rear are pushing these tacks in the map and saying we're supposed to get from here to there in so much time, see? Well, the point man sees signs that the trail was booby-trapped and wants to cut around it, but then we'd be late. So McDouche, our lieutenant, tells him to take the trail anyway and to be careful, but they hit it. The point man got blown away, the guy behind him got a leg blown off, and the third guy back got peppered with shrapnel. When the medevac chopper came, the guy with one leg tried to help them get the point man loaded on. He didn't know his buddy was already dead."

Rodrigez and I were speechless, to say the least. The man seemed to go into a daze for a while, as if he hadn't yet come to grips with what he had just related.

"Well, hey," he said, regaining his composure. "My name's Tennessee."

We introduced ourselves, and after a few clumsy attempts at conversation, Tennessee excused himself and went back to the barracks, leaving Rodrigez and me standing there, shocked and dumbfounded. We decided to call it a night.

As I lay back on my cot and reflected on the scene, I couldn't get over how eerie it seemed. What struck me was that with only a brief glance at the men sitting under the bare bulb, it was clear that they were different from anyone I'd ever seen. Imagining the scene in my mind, I realized what it was. It was their eyes—something in their eyes almost made me shiver. There was anger, pain, and sadness, but beyond that, there was a depth that spoke of something incredibly intense and unknown to me. Then, almost reflexively, my mind started calculating odds. I'd been at Uplift three days, and during that time, one of the men in my new company had been killed and two seriously wounded. There were one hundred men in a company and over 350 days left in my tour. The mathematics didn't work out too well, not to mention the possibility of my new platoon leader meeting with an untimely demise.

"Welcome to Company B," I thought.

They had a name for trying to be invisible while in transit or in the rear. They called it "ghosting." Floating around, waif-like, sometimes guys would be forgotten for days or even weeks while their company commanders thought they were at the aid station and the medics thought they were in the field. The next morning, I figured that if I got good enough at ghosting, maybe I could float around the rear for a whole year and then become visible when it was time to go home. Things worked out fine for the better part of the first day until I made the mistake of stopping by the barracks after evening chow. Old Sarge snagged me for guard duty, and so at dusk, I got an M16 from the supply sergeant and headed for bunker number nine.

Having already seen what the men of Bravo Company looked like, I couldn't help but feel awkward about my new fatigues and shiny boots, but that was the reality of the situation. Green as a gourd and scared to death.

"Is this number nine?" I asked.

"Yeah, this is it." The man who spoke had sergeant stripes on his sleeve, and after he confirmed that I was a replacement, he began to question me about my use of drugs.

"Ever smoke any dope?" he asked.

"Well, once or twice in the States," I hedged, trying to figure out what was going on.

Suddenly a gruff voice growled from the bunker's dark interior, "Hey, Ski, give the man a bomber."

There was a slight pause, and with a flick of the wrist, Ski handed me this long twist of lumpy paper. I looked in amazement; it was as big as a fountain pen and, without a doubt, the biggest joint I'd ever seen. As I stood there gawking, Ski stepped out of the bunker, reaching into his pocket for his Zippo.

"Here," he said with a big grin. "Let me give you a light."

While I was puffing away trying to get the thing lit, a big black dude came out of the bunker and stood next to Ski, eyeing me carefully. When the bomber was finally going, I tried to pass it to Ski, who looked at me and smiled as he held up his own. With mild desperation, I glanced at the black dude. He had one too.

*Well,* I thought, *when in Rome.* I was already pretty stoned, and the thing was still five inches long. Bombers, I soon realized, were not only huge but also highly opiated.

"This is 'The Creeper,' " Ski said, introducing me to the powerfully built black man at his side. "He's our slack man."

That term was new to me, so he explained. "The point man is the first guy down the trail, and since he's busy hacking through the bush and looking for booby traps, the slack man stays close behind and watches for anything else. He picks up the slack."

My mind said *Nod,* and a few seconds later, I nodded to indicate I understood.

There was a childlike innocence about Ski that seemed untarnished even by the present situation. He had an all-American-boy look about him, and you just knew he played Pee Wee League baseball as a kid and was into sports in high school. Creeper, on the other hand, had an air of seriousness, strength, and street smarts about him, and it was apparent that he'd been exposed to some of life's harsher realities early on. He was quiet most of the time, but when he did say something, it was brief and direct, and there was a lot of gut-level power in his voice. His eyes were cold and penetrating, and he frightened me a little — not because of what he might do, but because of what he knew.

While Ski was telling me that McDouche would be by later in the night, the sounds of rustling paper came from inside the bunker.

"What's that?" I asked nervously.

"Jus' the rats," Creeper replied.

"Yeah, it's the rats." Ski smiled. "They run dirt-track races in the bunkers at night. Guys don't always clean the food scraps out after guard duty, and the rats come in and clean up what's left. Don't worry about them. They'll crawl on ya while you're sleepin', but they don't bite."

The conversation was getting so bizarre that I was beginning to have my doubts about its reality, but then the scratching started up again. I hoped, at least, that Ski was pulling my leg about the things crawling on you at night, and while I was tying to figure a way out of my dilemma, I realized that the Vietnamese reefer had already put the thinking part of my mind on hold. To make matters worse, I began to realize that another pattern of sounds I was hearing was footfalls, and they were coming up from behind us. I desperately hoped it wasn't a lifer, because by now I was nearly speechless.

Ski was quick to pick up on my fear and said, "It's cool, man. Don't sweat it. It's only Tennessee."

And so it was, with an armload of Cokes, french fries, and fried chicken from the EM club, to boot. A real godsend, because besides being incoherent, I had what was known as the "electric tongue," a fat, dry tongue that craved sweets.

Tennessee instantly surmised the situation and, noting that I'd been initiated into the cult of the Bong Son Bombers, laughed and said, "Here, man, have a Coke."

The cool, bubbly Coke eased the dryness in my mouth and throat, and Tennessee's presence eased my mind. I was relieved to meet someone in the company who I felt would give me a hand. Everyone would help in his own way, but Tennessee's gentleness and sincerity was something I desperately needed.

Things were looking up, in a relative sort of way. The bomber was getting short, at last — it was now about the size of a cigarette filter — and as I took a second long drink of Coke, Creeper grabbed what was left of the bomber and threw it on the ground, saying, "You're in Vietnam, man, and that's a roach."

Ski, Creeper, and Tennessee split the night into four shifts, giving me, the newbie, first watch so they could keep an eye on me. It was definitely for the better, as I was in no shape to function dependably. Tennessee and I climbed on top of the bunker and manned the pair of lawn chairs that were there. Not wanting to blow it on my first night with the company, I scanned the area in front of the bunker intensely and was dismayed to find that the bushes on the edge of the perimeter seemed to be moving. I'd forgotten what they'd said in training about using your peripheral vision, as it was more sensitive and less apt to cause the illusion of movement, as would one's focused gaze.

Tennessee was watching me with amusement. "Don't worry about the VC coming through the wire. They haven't tried that since the Tet Offensive of '68. The main thing you need to remember tonight is to not do much talkin' when McDouche brings the coffee around later on. He'll probably be able to tell you're stoned if you say much."

We sat quietly for the rest of the watch, and just when it was about time to rouse Creeper, Tennessee spotted the headlights of McDouche's jeep across the LZ.

"You might as well grab a cup of coffee and a doughnut if ya want," Tennessee suggested. "He's gonna do a head count anyway."

I agreed, and the four of us stood by the road as the lights of McDouche's jeep swept over us. Ski covered for me before McDouche had a chance to talk to me directly.

"We're all here," he said. "The new guy made it, too."

"Okay," McDouche responded. "Did you get your Claymores out before dark?"

"Yes, sir," Ski replied.

In the meantime, I was doing my best to stay out of sight by hiding behind the big spigot-type thermos can that was strapped on the back of the jeep. I hadn't been there early enough to help set out the Claymores, but I remembered them from training. They looked like an old-model Polaroid camera before it was unfolded. They held three and a half pounds of plastic explosive that would spray 750 eighth-inch steel balls over a wide-enough range to stop anything coming up a trail.

Satisfied that things were in order, McDouche ordered the driver to continue on. The jeep roared off, bouncing down the rough dirt road that circled inside the bunker line, but just as my system started to relax a bit, the jeep made a quick U-turn and headed back toward us. There was barely time to panic. In seconds, it flew right by and back to headquarters.

Tennessee was laughing. "Did ya see that? They must have talked Moody into setting up his Claymore in the road!"

It had been aimed at the jeep, with its control wires leading back to the bunker. It was hard to tell if it had been merely a warning or if McDouche had been saved by his driver's quick reflexes. Either way, it was a not-too-subtle hint that the guys in Company B weren't fond of McDouche's tactics in the field.

Creeper, Ski, and Tennessee definitely enjoyed the sight of Second Lieutenant McDouche and his driver speeding past in the jeep. They laughed and joked with delight, while I just stood there stunned, half expecting a load of big brass to arrive en masse and grill us all for information.

Tennessee came to the rescue again and led me to the entrance of the bunker. "You can go ahead and crash if ya want. Your guard is over anyway."

With great relief, and a thoroughly short-circuited mind, I groped in the darkness for a cot and, finding one, fell into a deep, dreamless sleep.

## THE MAGIC PONCHO LINER

IT MUST HAVE TAKEN ME A WHILE TO WAKE UP THE NEXT MORNING, because Tennessee sounded kind of anxious as he shook my shoulder and said, "Come on, man, get up. The mess hall closes in ten minutes."

We made a mad dash across the compound and slid into the line just before the mess sergeant locked the door. When we sat down, I realized I was still pretty stoned from the night before, because the rubbery bacon and powdered eggs tasted pretty good.

We'd just returned to the barracks when a lifer stuck his head in the door and said that all the new guys were to report to supply. There we were issued packs, canteens, ponchos, and helmets, and then we were escorted to a bare plot behind the barracks where the rest of Company B was already milling around. Cases of C-rations, ammunition, grenades, and Claymores were divided into squad-sized piles. Following instructions, each of us newbies loaded into his pack a case and a half of Cs, a poncho and poncho liner, a gas mask, hand grenades, a Claymore, an entrenching tool, and ammunition. Since I was assigned to carry a grenade launcher, I was told to load up on fifty-two rounds of HE (high explosive) grenades — each weighing a half pound — a couple CS gas grenades, a couple signal flares, and a few buckshot rounds, all of which were designed to be fired with my launcher. Since the rounds were pretty bulky, I was given a gas-mask bag in which to store the surplus. My pack was bulging, and as I tried to figure out what to do with the two "fat-rat" (half gallon) canteens and two standard quart ones, McDouche arrived on the scene.

Befitting a man of his rank (after all, he was a second lieutenant), he wore crisply starched fatigues and highly polished boots. Beneath his army-issue glasses was a cleanly shaven face that leered with an unmistakable air of superiority. Beneath that was fear and insecurity. On his helmet, instead of the FTA or peace sign of the common soldier, was the neatly printed Latin motto COGITO ERGO SUM (I think, therefore I am). It was implied in his demeanor that we didn't, therefore we weren't.

When we'd finished packing, he stood on an empty crate and announced, "All right men, saddle up. We're going to march in formation down to the chopper pads."

At that, I grabbed the shoulder strap of my pack and gave it a yank, intending to swing it on my shoulder. Nothing happened; the pack sat there as if rooted to the ground. Embarrassed, I looked around. The old-timers used an entirely different method. They sat on the ground in front of their packs, slipped on both shoulder straps, rolled to their hands and knees, and then stood up. Imitating the move, I wobbled to my feet. The pack hadn't grown roots; it weighed a hundred pounds.

I followed the mob, which in no way could be considered a formation, to the chopper pad a hundred yards away. Halfway there, two guys passed me, and one of them was saying, "Did ya see that newbie back there? After only fifty yards, he sat down and cried." I couldn't help but pity whoever it was, knowing that a couple of the new guys would be trying to carry two-thirds of their body weight on their backs. By the time we reached the chopper pad, my hands felt puffy and were starting to tingle. These military packs, unlike their civilian counterparts, had no waist belt to transfer most of the weight to your hips, and the thinly padded straps would grind the outside end of your collarbone into your shoulder and cut off the circulation in your arms. The choppers were already fired up, engines whining and blades churning up a cloud of dust.

Sgt. McCoy pointed to a group of six of us, and following his gestures, we hunched over and ran for one. The Hueys had had their side doors removed and so, following the example of guys who were loading onto another chopper across from us, I sat on the edge of the floor and grabbed part of the frame at the edge of the door. Another guy sat toward the rear, and a third squeezed between us. Our legs from the knees down dangled in the breeze, and as the chopper lifted off and began to pick up some airspeed, they were blown to the rear. It felt good to have something to hang on to as the Huey banked into a turn. For whoever wound up in the middle, it was an exercise in trust; he had to depend on his buddies to keep him from falling out.

In a land and time that offered few pleasures, flying this way was always a joy to me. I was starting to learn that here, the past had to be left behind quickly and completely. The future could not even be considered. There might not be one. And so, with these irrelevant and worrisome considerations set aside, there was only now. If now one was floating over endless lush green mountains, there was nothing to do but enjoy it.

The ride ended as the Huey swooped down into a grassy clearing and hovered momentarily with its skids still five feet off the ground. It paused only for an instant, and as I felt it beginning to rise again, someone hollered, "Jump!" So I jumped, and when I hit the ground, my knees buckled, and I fell on my face. Scrambling to my feet, I saw McCoy motioning me to head for the tree line. So I ran as fast as possible under the weight of the pack. I stepped in a depression, fell again, and staggered back up to my feet. Finally at the tree line, I crouched, panting and sweating, intensely searching for "Charles" in the tangled mass of green before me.

When the whine of engines and the sound of slapping blades subsided, the company regrouped into platoons and squads and slid into the dense jungle like a snake, single file. We moved at the pace of a slow walk, occasionally stopping while the point man hacked through vines and branches. At times, the vegetation was so thick I'd have to crawl on hands and knees. After the first half hour, my fatigue shirt was wringing wet, as were my pants from the waist to the knees. In two hours, I was totally exhausted and started prodding myself, thinking, *One more step, one more step, one more step.*

The order came down the line, whispered from one man to the next: "Break in place, take five." I squatted, leaning my pack into a clump of brush, slid out of the straps, and unsnapped a canteen for a long drink of lukewarm water. My fingertips looked like prunes from the constant bath of sweat. Lighting a cigarette, I leaned against the pack and managed to get half of it smoked before the sweat dripping off my face put it out. My heart was still pounding when the next order came: "Saddle up." For the rest of what seemed to be an interminable twelve hours, the company pushed through the jungle. At twilight, the commanding officer (CO) decided that we would spend the night in a wide valley. Unfamiliar with the routine, I imagined that we'd be able to eat some Cs and sleep at least part of the night, but each squad was to dig a foxhole and hack a line of sight between positions in the large circle. While that was being done, a few guys from each squad would patrol the company's position with wide, half-mile, cloverleaf loops. Somehow my fear squeezed a few more drops of adrenaline from my system to prod me to follow Ski and four other guys away from the company and into the marshy valley. Our loop took us through waist-deep water before we could turn back toward the company's encampment. When we reached high ground, I imagined that if there were any VC or NVA in the area, they'd probably be laughing, because even though the squad was moving like a cat on the prowl, our boots squished loudly with each step.

When we arrived at the company's position, there was barely enough light to read the painted labels on our Cs and to find a large-enough clearing to sleep. After the night was divided into shifts for guard, I found my spot and slept.

It seemed like only a few minutes before Ski was pushing on my shoulder, "It's your guard," he whispered, handing me a watch. It was midnight. "You've got from now till 0130 hours."

I found my way to the position, sat on my helmet, and pulled the poncho liner over my shoulders. Through the trees were stars, but in front of me, only darkness. I listened intently to the sounds of the night birds, lizards, and insects. Occasionally, I'd close my eyes for a time and, focusing more carefully, I discovered that there was a pattern to the sounds. The different calls had a strange, tranquilizing effect, and it seemed to require considerable effort to stay alert for sounds that didn't belong — snapping twigs or metallic clicks. Part of me sensed that there was something behind me. Hoping to dispel the notion that it was possible to sense something without seeing it, I slowly turned to check it out. About ten paces away, there was the silhouette of a man standing as still as a cigar-store Indian. When he knew he'd been spotted, he seemed to glide slowly toward me. I knew he was one of the company, but I wondered who and why he was joining me.

When the man crouched beside me, I realized I'd seen him around before; the guys called him Captain Speed. He was the company's point man and had a reputation for being impeccable in the field. The story about him was that he'd arrived in Vietnam after graduating from Special Forces (Green Beret) training as a staff sergeant, but he couldn't keep up the pretense that he didn't smoke pot. He lost stripe after stripe until he was transferred to our unit as a private, where the lifers, who respected his ability, ignored the habit. If our officers decided to bust him, they'd lose his services, because the army required troops in the field to have at least one stripe — without any stripes, they were considered incompetent. One stripe was all that Speed had, and he liked it that way.

"You're one of the new guys, aren't you?" He was whispering.

I replied in the affirmative and watched him pass me a lit joint in cupped hands from beneath his poncho liner. It seemed like a dangerous thing to be doing, but something in me trusted Speed, so I took a few tokes. After passing it back, I asked, "Won't the gooks smell it?"

"Sometimes, but if they do, they'll know we're awake and on guard. If they're anywhere in the area, they already know we're here, but if they smell this, they'll stay away."

It sounded remotely logical, and not being in a position to argue, I helped him finish the joint.

"How long you been here?" I asked.

"It's my second tour."

Having expected an answer of eight or ten months or something, I felt stunned. The army required only one year in the field, even from career people. The idea that anyone would volunteer for a second tour was incomprehensible to me.

We sat quietly for several minutes, and I felt comforted by Speed's obvious concern. As the pot took effect, I focused again on the nocturnal sounds. It was as if someone had turned up the volume, and it was easier to tell the direction and range of individual calls. I also realized that if there was a break in the pattern, it could possibly be a clue that VC were prowling about, with the void in the sounds indicating where they were. After a time, my thinking quieted, and forgetting my damp fatigues and still-soggy boots, I became immersed in the subtle, beautiful, almost musical rhythm of the sounds.

Speed allowed me to indulge in the experience for quite some time. He seemed very loose and relaxed. From the corner of my eye, I could see he was smiling. There was something about the old-timers that was beyond my understanding. They were comfortable being whoever they were: Tennessee with his giggly, maternal concern; Creeper with his blunt directness; and Sgt. Ski with his childlike innocence. But they all had a sort of warmth and kindness beneath the surface. And they all, like Speed, found it easy to smile.

Speed leaned closer and asked, "Did anyone ever tell you about these poncho liners?"

"What do you mean?" I would have thought that there wasn't much to be said about them. They were well suited for the jungle — two layers of finely woven nylon with a half inch of Dacron insulation quilted inside, printed with camouflage blotches of various shades of green and brown.

"Well," he continued with a grin, "most people don't know this, but these poncho liners are bug-proof, snake-proof, and bullet-proof. I've never heard of anyone being killed at night while wrapped up in one."

It was hard for me not to laugh out loud. It was such a ridiculous thing to say, but having been anxious to ask one of the old-timers for hints on how to survive, I realized that here was the most experienced man in the company sacrificing his own much-needed sleep to give me a clue.

His words sank into my being like pennies tossed into a lake, sinking slowly and steadily till they hit the bottom. Something inside me knew that even though, at face value, what he'd said wasn't true, I should take it as being true—completely and without reservation. What Speed was saying was that here in the Central Highlands, in Charles's land, there were two ways to retire at night. You could be anxious and fearful about your throat being slit or a mortar round landing on your head, or you could retreat into the warm womb of your magic poncho liner and feel secure that you would get a deep, revitalizing night's sleep.

Speed was watching me carefully, and somehow he saw that I got what he was trying to say. He nodded. He doubled his poncho liner over his head and lit a cigarette, demonstrating how it was done in the field at night, and then offered me the glowing end in cupped hands. I pulled a soggy Camel from my pocket and took the light, realizing that I had been incredibly tense all day. Now, though, sitting with Speed in the humid cool of the night, something in me relaxed, and something smiled.

The entire company was awake before dawn to pull guard in the dangerous and deceptive moments between night and day. At sunup, we were allowed a few minutes to eat and then were ordered to fill in the grave-like trenches we'd dug the night before and get our packs in order. Soon we were on the move again, struggling up hills, crossing streams, and wading in muck. We followed the routine for several days, moving for miles through trackless jungle. Wherever we were (only God and the officers were privy to such heady information), there were no roads, no villages, and not even so much as a trail, except for the one we were cutting ourselves. Luckily, there weren't any NVA either—or if there were, they had chosen not to reveal themselves. One could never be certain which was the case.

During the day, few words were spoken. The occasional breaks offered a chance, but rarely did anyone have the wind or the desire to talk. At night, guard was a silent, solitary vigil. For me, the days were full of subtle lessons that had to be gleaned from careful observation of others in the outfit. I noticed that when we were climbing the steep hills, the man in front of me was always careful not to lose elevation. If there was a depression in the trail, he'd lengthen his stride rather than step down, then up again. Going up some of the steeper places, I watched how he'd dig in with the side of his Vibram-soled boots. On the downhill trails, he'd ski a few feet at a time with amazingly good control. In addition to what could be learned through observation, I experimented with techniques of my own. It seemed to help, when climbing an unusually steep slope, if I coordinated my breath with each step. After a time, this became a habit. Since some of the guys were so occupied with keeping up that they didn't seem very alert, I forced myself to follow a systematic routine. The first part was to scan the edges of the trail for booby traps and signs; then the bush at eye level and below, left then right, for Charles; and finally the treetops, for snipers. This became a habit that I repeated over and over again.

Each day seemed like a week of real time. The intensity of concentration and the exertion of constant movement made each step — every moment — a challenge to one's attention and stamina. There could be no slack, nothing sloppy. Something the old-timers said scared the bejesus out of me and made me try to give it my best: "Charles waits and watches. These gooks have an altogether different sense of time. When your stuff is tight, you'll never see him, but when you're flaky and fuckin' up, somehow he'll come out of nowhere and kick your ass."

We'd been out six days when the CO ordered us to make a landing zone on the ridge where we had spent the night. In an hour, we had hacked down enough small trees and bushes to make a clearing big enough for a Huey to land. We formed a perimeter around the LZ and waited. When there was the faint sound of helicopters in the distance, one of the radio operators popped a purple smoke grenade in the center of the clearing. The tension mounted as the first chopper settled into the clearing, stirring up a cloud of leaves and chopped brush. This was one of those moments that Charles was particularly fond of — fragile Hueys hovering within easy range of an AK-47. It paused for an instant, like a hummingbird at a flower, then rose quickly above the trees and disappeared with a squad of grunts trying to hang on. The pilots were well aware of their vulnerability, and usually a guy could consider himself lucky to get one cheek on board before taking off.

After a half hour of chaos, the last sortie of Hueys arrived to pick up our platoon, the last to leave the area. McDouche waved at Tennessee and me, indicating that we'd be on the next lift. We scrambled to catch it, and soon we were above the trees, rapidly gaining speed and elevation. When we'd climbed to about two thousand feet, my system relaxed some, since we were no longer an easy target for small-arms fire. Although we didn't know where we were going any more than where we'd been, there was time to enjoy the ride and spectacular view. After about fifteen minutes, an unusually large mountain appeared on the horizon, and even at a considerable distance, we could tell that there was something unusual about its peak. By the time we started to lose elevation, we could see that sandbag bunkers ringed its bulldozed top. A river curved around its base. It was clearly our destination, and I was surprised when we landed at what seemed to be a relatively well-defended small base. The pilot was still reluctant to bring us any closer than a few feet from the ground. We leaped once again and headed for a bunker where McCoy, our platoon sergeant, had gathered the rest of the platoon.

Feeling edgy, I took the cleaning kit out of my pack and tried to get some of the grit from our landing out of the works of my grenade launcher. McCoy nodded with approval when he noticed what I was doing, but it seemed to have little effect on the wave of anxiety that suddenly overwhelmed me. Without the constant pressure of being in the field, my mind started reminding me how green and perhaps fatally inexperienced I was. It was also disturbing to realize that even after almost a week in the field, I knew only a half dozen of the guys in the platoon by name. Traveling silently and in single file hadn't offered much of an opportunity.

I studied McCoy at a distance. He was second in command under McDouche and shared responsibility for the platoon. He was a rather short black man whose arms seemed a little long for his height. In contrast to the by-the-book rigidity of McDouche, he appeared to be relaxed and competent. His facial expression changed from a smile to one of concern as he briefed the squad leaders on the roof of a bunker a few yards away. At one point he burst out laughing, shoulders shaking and head bobbing up and down. It made me feel good to see that he hadn't alienated himself from those in his command, as McDouche had done.

The meeting broke up, and Ski came over to where I was sitting. "Come on, man, grab your pack. I'll show you where we're setting up."

*Bunker guard!* I thought as we walked across the bare hilltop. Not exactly the Ritz, but after a few days in the field, it seemed like it.

Tennessee, Creeper, and Speed were already settled in and were wasting no time getting stoned. As soon as I'd ducked out of the bright sun into the cave-like cool of the bunker and leaned my pack against the wall, Speed handed me a joint. I'd wanted to get to know these guys, exchange a few words after having been in the field with them, but after the third toke, I'd become a mute witness. Speed pulled a small transistor radio from his pack and tuned it to the army's AM station. To my surprise, the station played the standard rock and roll that was popular in the States at the time. The little radio sounded great as the Beatles song, "Come Together" came through loud and clear.

Creeper sat next to me on the cot with his eyes closed, completely absorbed in the music. His upper body rocked fluidly back and forth to the rhythm. Tennessee was busy making a stove out of one of the cracker cans that came with our Cs. He punched holes around the sides of the can and dropped in a heat tab (a small tongue-shaped slab of solid fuel). Once it was burning, he began making a deluxe version of the instant hot chocolate that also came with the Cs by adding three packages of coffee creamer to the brew. Ski was lying on his back, blowing smoke rings, and Speed, after looking out the door toward McDouche's bunker, was digging in his pack for more weed.

In spite of the scene of domestic tranquility, I was still edgy. As usual, when we were on bunker guard during the day, no one was really on guard. The firing ports of the bunker were completely unattended. The main concern seemed to be whether or not any lifers were in the area.

Speed passed around another round of bombers, and though I felt no need, I accepted one. Things seemed to be settling down when Tennessee took a look outside.

He quickly popped back in. "Stash the pot — Sarge is coming!"

There was a brief scramble to get things out of sight. Curious, I looked out of one of the bunker's side ports and saw the man, who must have been Sarge, waddling toward the bunker.

Sarge was also the only guy under the rank of E-6 who wore his fatigues according to army regulations. Evidently, carrying the platoon's radio for McDouche had reinforced the streak of lifer in him.

"Hi, guys!" he said, amplifying the bullshit mission he was on by trying to effect some semblance of friendship.

He insinuated himself into the bunker. Ski and Speed talked with him for a while, but it was easy to tell from the brevity of their remarks that Sarge wasn't particularly welcome. The visit passed uneventfully, but when Sarge left, he had the information he wanted: Ski's squad was stoned to the max.

"Somebody ought to slap him upside the head," Creeper growled. "Jus' might wake his ass up."

"There's no need," Speed replied. "They can't do anything. What are they gonna do? Send us to 'Nam? And if they want to bust everybody who smokes dope, they'll have to fight the war by themselves."

Speed was right, of course; 60 percent of the company was getting high with some regularity. If the army suddenly decided to bust people, they'd have a mutiny on their hands. Besides, the big brass didn't want to admit that there might even be a problem.

At sundown, Ski sent me over to an unoccupied position "next door" to pull guard till nightfall. It was pleasant to sit on the bunker alone and watch the sun as it slowly slipped below the horizon. Reflecting on what Speed had said about the lifers and the ubiquitous pot, I felt I had one less thing to worry about.

"What are ya doin'? You on guard?" The voice came from behind me.

"Yeah," I replied. "Come on up."

At that, a small, thin Mexican guy climbed on top of the bunker. His name was Shorty, appropriately enough, as he was only five feet five. It took him only seconds to notice my new boots.

"You're new, aren't ya?"

I nodded. In the conversation that followed, I discovered that Shorty had been scouting around the rather limited confines of the hilltop. He'd come across a bunker that was manned by some guys from the 101st Airborne, who were more or less permanently manning the position. They'd turned Shorty on to some opium, and it was easy to tell.

"You should have seen 'em, man," he said. "They were some real heavy dudes. They had a real stereo in their bunker—with big speakers and everything—and a whole quart jar full of opium."

At that we both cracked up, laughing at the increasingly strange position we'd found ourselves in with Bravo Company. All the gung ho bullshit from training in the States—"I wanna kill ol' Charlie Cong"—was thoroughly lost in the translation from someone's patriotic and militaristic ideal to reality. Only the lifers, whose careers and pensions required a somewhat convincing performance, were into the war. For the rest of us, it was a long year of hoping and praying for a trip home with our bodies intact.

Shorty and I compared notes. Speed had visited us both in the night, as he had two other newbies Shorty had talked to. "And what about that pack they gave us?" Shorty asked. "It's really kicking my ass! Really, man, I don't think I'm gonna make it."

I suddenly realized how small Shorty was—slender as well as short. The same huge pack was issued to everyone, regardless of their size. And if it was killing me, I couldn't imagine how Shorty had gotten this far. He outweighed the thing by only about thirty pounds. Fumbling to come up with some kind of reassurance, I suggested that maybe we'd get used to them after a while, and I kept my doubts to myself.

"Hey," I said, remembering the joint in my pocket, "I've got half a bomber left from this afternoon. Let's smoke it."

Soon we were floating away on a fresh cloud of euphoria, laughing and joking. During a pause, I noticed that Shorty was studying my face. I turned and watched his expression. Suddenly it changed to one of great surprise.

"Wow, man!" he exclaimed. "You look like my brother!"

He was serious, but somehow it cracked us both up again, and we found ourselves laughing without reservation. By the time we'd caught our breath, he was looking at me intently again. "Wow, man! Now you look like my *seester*."

This surprised me as much as it did Shorty, because I wasn't trying to look like anyone, and we both wound up rolling on top of the bunker, laughing uncontrollably. Shorty worked through the rest of his family until at last he said, "Wow, man — now you look like my grandmother!"

This was the most ridiculous of all, and for a time we were absolutely hysterical. My side hurt, and I was almost crying by the time we settled down. Had Shorty been one of the old-timers, I might have suspected that he was goofing on me for sport, but there was little doubt that he was actually seeing his entire family superimposed on me. We sat quietly for a time, and then, remembering that I had some Life Savers (which always tasted good on a fat, dry tongue), I opened the package and offered one to Shorty.

He looked at the package wide-eyed and said, "What are you trying to do, man — blow my mind? Hey, man, this is too heavy. I gotta go." With that, he slid off the bunker and wandered off into the darkness.

Alone again, I chuckled to myself and pondered the bizarre incident. It was all so weird, but with a little reflection, it seemed easy enough to conclude that Shorty probably had a warm and supportive family at home, and beneath it all, was incredibly homesick. His longing for his family, mixed with copious amounts of opium, seemed to have projected their faces onto the nearest available screen — me. For a moment, I felt sad, but then I realized that it had been dark for some time and that it was past time for me to return to my squad.

Not quite ready to crash, I climbed on top of the bunker where Tennessee was pulling guard. My system relaxed as we sat quietly together, watching the faint silhouette of the mountains and the patches of starlight between the clouds. When Ski came to relieve him, he mentioned that the lifers had put out an order that there was to be no indiscriminate firing at midnight.

"Why'd they say that?" I asked.

"You've probably spaced it, but tonight's New Year's Eve," Ski replied. "By the way, the 101st is having a party on the hill back there. You guys ought to check it out."

Tennessee turned to me and asked, "We're not gone yet?"

We climbed off the bunker and trudged up the hill looking for signs of a party. As we approached a bunker near the top, we could hear a radio playing and saw a dozen guys standing in line. We took our places at the line's end, and two others soon came in behind us. While we stood, joints and pipes traveled continuously from one end of the line to the other and back again. At times, we'd be caught with a joint in one hand and a pipe in the other. All the while, the line itself moved toward two people at its end (one of them being Captain Speed), who were administering "shotguns" with a grenade launcher.

A grenade launcher is similar to a single-shot, breech-loaded shotgun, except that its barrel is one and a half inches in diameter and only two feet long. Speed had a standard-sized tobacco pipe full of pot, and placing the stem into the weapon's breech and sealing the leaks with his hand, he blew through the bowl of the pipe. One by one, the guys in line stood in front of the barrel and inhaled the huge cloud of smoke that came rolling out of the muzzle. This "shotgun" process intensified the effect of the already potent Vietnamese reefer to the point that it would render one almost unconscious for a second or two. After three trips to the end of the line, my body felt almost nonexistent and my mind no longer produced thoughts. A light rain started to fall, so Tennessee and I headed back to our own bunker.

I lay on a cot feeling simultaneously electrified and numb. While my mind was definitely on hold for the time being, my senses seemed to be incredibly amplified. I could hear the soft rain falling on the sandbags overhead. My entire nervous system seemed to be charged with energy and sensitivity. There was a pleasant sense of security in being wrapped in the warmth of the poncho liner — and knowing that there were two feet of earth and timbers between myself and whatever was out there didn't hurt a thing either.

After a half hour of quiet reverie, I heard a muffled pop, and bright white light came streaming through the firing ports. There was the sound of panicky voices outside, and an instant later Ski stuck his head in the door. "Everybody up! There's gooks in the wire!"

*God help us!* flashed through my mind as I groped around in the darkness for my grenade launcher. By the time I found it, leaning in the corner, Creeper and Tennessee were already at the firing ports with their M16s. Two click-clacks indicated that they'd each chambered a round. Grabbing a bag of rounds for my grenade launcher, I fingered a round of HE, slid it into the breech, and snapped the barrel closed. Staring into the darkness from a firing port, I could occasionally glance at Tennessee and Creeper out of the corner of my eye. They'd obviously been in this situation before. Creeper moved from one side of the port to the other — back and forth — to widen his field of vision, while Tennessee was simultaneously keeping watch and arranging the detonators of the Claymores neatly in front of him. Both were very businesslike and intense.

Long minutes passed as we watched and waited. Remembering stories of the Tet of '68, I halfway expected to see droves of VC crawling through the wire any minute. A human wave, as it was called, would attack — hundreds of VC would attempt to infiltrate en masse. Most would be sacrificed for the few who managed to penetrate the defense, but those few would really raise hell. They carried satchel charges with them and would make a beeline for the ammo dump, fuel storage, or lifers' quarters, and light them up. The old-timers said that when they cleaned up afterward, they found that many of the VC and NVA had a plastic pouch of opium taped to them, with a plastic tube leading to a needle in their arm.

In the electrified minutes of silence, I figured that a trip flare had been set off. The entire outermost perimeter of a position like the one we were manning was usually marked with flares (each the size of a small can of foot powder), which were filled with bright-burning magnesium. Thin, olive-drab trip wires were strung across trails and gaps in the bush, which would set off the flares. Between the area that would be illuminated by the trip flares and the bunkers, there were Claymores, so that most of the illuminated area could be sprayed with one mine if there was visual confirmation that the flare had been tripped by the enemy.

Outside our bunker, chaos abounded—indecipherable hollering of orders and the sound of GIs running to position machine guns and stock extra ammunition. If this was it, I thought, the dinks were in for a bad time, having blown the element of surprise.

"It's not gooks," someone hollered, "only a couple of monkeys in the wire. At ease, everybody, at ease."

In a couple minutes, the official word was passed from bunker to bunker: false alarm.

My body sank, sliding down the bunker wall, but it took some time for the rest of my system to adjust to the news. Gradually, my heart returned to its normal rhythm and my body chemistry accepted the "at ease" command. Exhausted, I took the round out of my grenade launcher, found my poncho liner, curled on a cot in a fetal position, and tried to sleep. I was almost asleep when a horrendous explosion shook the bunker enough to send dirt sprinkling down from its sandbag roof. The electric jolt to the nervous system lasted only seconds. A loud whistle announced the source of the explosion: outgoing, as opposed to incoming, artillery. The 101st had started working out with the 155mm howitzers they manned on the hill, and they were to continue through the night. Even in the relative security of the bunker, the night was long and nearly sleepless.

Early in the morning, Ski, Creeper, Tennessee, and I were sitting on top of the bunker again, passing a bomber and waiting for the sun to rise. Perhaps because of the false alarm the night before, the valley and hills in front of us seemed particularly beautiful. When it was light enough, we could see that a fog had settled in the deepest valleys, and as the sun warmed the earth, clouds of misty vapor rose slowly above the tree-covered hills. The wonderland before us stopped abruptly at the concertina wire that circled the hilltop, displaced by bunkers, artillery, and bulldozed earth. It seemed as if we were cut off from the flow of life and creativity that surrounded us.

We spent the morning lounging around the bunker. Tennessee was thoroughly enjoying the slack time, playing gourmet with his C-rations. He was thoroughly familiar with the twelve different meals of the rations. Each box contained an entrée, such as beans and wieners, spaghetti and meatballs, ham and lima beans, chicken and noodles, ham slices, beef slices, or scrambled eggs. Along with the main dish, each box contained a small can of fruit, a can of crackers, a small can of cheese or peanut butter, a pouch of hot chocolate mix, a small envelope of the most god-awful instant coffee ever created, a plastic spoon, a pack of four cigarettes, a pack of matches, and a small roll of toilet paper. He slowly warmed a can of "eggs, *scrambled*" and added a can of cheese, topping the gooey blob with several drops of Tabasco sauce. On the side, he fried a piece of "ham, *sliced,*" which was the entrée of one of the other C-rat meals. It was his second tour, and having eaten the twelve different meals almost daily for the past eighteen months, he knew how to make the best of what he had. It amazed me to watch our squad's point man, who could be so intense and alert in the field, orchestrating the timing of his breakfast in such a relaxed and casual way, as if he had been temporarily transported to his back porch in the hills of Tennessee.

Around noon, Sarge waddled up to our position to let us know that McDouche had okayed a swimming trip to the river. Somewhat surprised, we gathered our weapons for the short hike. There was a well-beaten path from the hilltop to the river's edge, where a "lifeguard" from the 101st manned a machine gun. Squinting through sweat-stung eyes, I surveyed the situation. The river was forty yards wide, lined with thick underbrush on the far side. On our side was a wide area of short grass and a four-foot embankment above the river. If there were sniper fire, we'd be scrambling out of the water and up the bare riverbank. It seemed to be a classic case of fucking up to be hanging Charles a pale moon to snipe at from the bush, but Speed, Creeper, and Tennessee were already in the water, and it was too inviting to pass up. The water was cool and refreshing, the closest thing to a bath any of us had had in a week. The rest of the squad was enjoying themselves with complete abandon, laughing, screaming, and doing daring dives off of the riverbank, but I never lost a nervous edginess and often scanned the bushes.

When we returned to base, as I was passing McDouche's bunker, Sarge appeared and told me that Sgt. McCoy wanted to talk with me. McCoy was sitting on the hillside a few yards from the bunker, and from the look on his face, I guessed that the "talk" was going to be an ass chewing of some kind or another. McCoy didn't look angry, but his expression was one of fatherly concern and disappointment.

I approached reluctantly and squatted next to him. For a few long seconds, he just looked at me. When he talked at last, he came right to the point.

"I hope you haven't been smokin' dope with Speed and those boys."

My heart sank. I liked McCoy already and appreciated his fatherly concern. I hated to lie.

"No, Sarge," I replied, knowing myself well enough to know that by now guilt was written all over me.

"Don't get me wrong," he continued. "Those boys have been with me a long time, and they're damn good troops, but we've kind of had our troubles lately. Smokin' that shit ain't nothin' to be doin' in a combat zone, and I don't see any good in you doin' it. Ya got me?"

"Yeah, I got ya, Sarge," I replied, relieved to have gotten off with a reprimand, but disappointed that after only a week in the field, I'd received one.

"Well, okay, then," McCoy said as he stood up. "You keep yourself out of trouble."

"Okay," I agreed. I felt pretty sad as I turned to walk up the hill toward my position.

I wondered what "our troubles" meant on the walk back to the bunker. Evidently, the word of threats on McDouche's life had gotten back to him, and Moody's Claymore in the path of his jeep had been taken seriously. It was hard for me to tell how serious these threats were, but it was clear that the guys figured that, for a shot at a set of captain's bars and a Bronze Star, McDouche had pushed the point man right into a booby trap. And the guys weren't about to allow any more lives to be sacrificed for his career. Even after the incident with Moody's Claymore, some of the guys had been saying stuff like, "In the next firefight, it'll be two shots at the VC and one at McDouche" or "Hand grenades don't leave no fingerprints." They were pissed. I found it hard to believe that they would actually murder McDouche, but then I didn't know the guys who had been wounded or of the man who was killed — or anything about what they'd been through together.

Mid-morning the next day, the platoon was called together and ordered to get our stuff together for another trek in the boonies. We loaded up and met near one of the 155mm howitzers on the hilltop. McDouche was conferring with the 101st about the local terrain and appeared shortly after the platoon had been gathered. We started through the barbed wire single file, and from the start, the point was chopping through thick brush. It was a nearly vertical descent that required a combination of side-stepping and carefully chosen hand-holds on trees, roots, and rocks. The trail, after the first squad went through, turned into treacherous, slippery mud. We'd move a few yards and stop, move a few more and stop. After a longer halt than usual, McCoy decided to check on the problems at point. He worked himself around the people who were sitting along the muddy trail, walking upright with the help of a short stick.

"Watch Ol' Sarge strut his stuff," he said in passing. But after a few more steps, there was the sound of breaking branches as he tumbled ass over teakettle down the slope, pack and all.

The point element had come to the edge of a sheer cliff and was trying to find the best way around it. At this point, I began to suspect that someone in the 101st had given McDouche a bum steer about the terrain for spite. After a twenty-minute delay, we were on our way again, moving carefully along the edge of the cliff, then dropping into the valley below.

The jungle this time of year was thick and steamy. It rained with regularity just after sunset, as it was late in the winter monsoon season. Usually it was a sprinkle at first, but when the air cooled, it would come down in sheets for a couple hours. It would clear before morning. During the day, the sun would push the temperature to about 100 degrees, and at night it would cool to only 75 or so, but that would seem cold to an exhausted, rain-soaked body. The rain, sun, and fertile soil of the Central Highlands created what was known as triple-canopy jungle. There were three layers of vegetation between one's head and the sky—brush and two sizes of trees.

Now that we were out in the field again, the platoon fell back into the familiar routine: up before dawn for watch and filling in bunkers and on the move shortly after sunrise. Its members were also back in their private worlds of silence and struggle. For me it was the mental chant, *One more step, one more step,* after the first hour on the trail. The incredible heat and heavy pack were still barely manageable. In the hours of silence, I began to notice how lapses in concentration seemed to increase the pain and blur my attention. If I fell into thinking of home or worrying about fucking up in my first ambush, fear would squeeze its way in and sap my energy. I soon found a way to break out of that emotional mire. When passing under a low branch or crawling through a tunnel of thick brush, I would tell myself that I was entering a whole new world, and for a time, it seemed that I could maintain a fresh and concentrated attention. It was clear to me that I could increase the chance of surviving by staying awake and alert, and I was determined to do my best.

My duty at the day's end was to dig the squad's overnight position, so while the other guys were setting out trip flares and Claymores, cutting firing lanes, and making tents out of ponchos, I'd be digging in. We needed a hole that was waist-deep, thirty inches wide, and six feet long.

More than once, staring at the hole in the dim twilight, it had occurred to me that I might be digging my own grave. The dirt from the hole went into sandbags that turned the hole into a miniature bunker. Some sandbags were stacked on the narrow ends of the hole to support four long poles over the hole, and two layers of sandbags lying across the poles provided overhead cover. Creeper or Tennessee would give me a hand if they'd finished their work ahead of me, and usually by the time we were set up, we'd have to go "fish" for whatever we were going to eat that night, because it would be too dark to read the labels on our Cs.

The morning of the sixth day, the routine changed, and we were told to hack an LZ for resupply. A single Huey arrived, kicked off a few cases of Cs and a bundle of clean fatigues, and flew off while we exchanged our greasy, overripe fatigues for clean ones. It returned for a quick dip into the LZ to pick them up and was gone. While we were stuffing our packs, McCoy made the rounds with the mail that had been relayed from the rear. To my surprise, he handed me a letter from home. I stashed it in the button-down leg pocket of my fatigues, and in less than an hour after the chopper had landed, we were beating the bush again.

Several hours later, we made our way up a steep hillside and picked up a well-used trail that ran along its ridge. The trail was wide, and in spots, it had even been paved in stone, a relic of the French, who had pulled out years before. It was easy going—too easy, I thought—and it was a sort of terrain I'd never seen before. There was no need for me to remind myself that this was a whole new world, because it was. Huge trees shaded the trail, but instead of the usual two layers of plant life between us and the high trees, there was only bare earth, moss, and rotting leaves. It seemed to be a great place for the NVA to set up an ambush. They could have easily hidden half a company of men behind the trees and had a turkey shoot with us. I wished for a moment for a second set of eyes, but then I remembered the old-timers' adage, "Wish in one hand and shit in the other and see which one fills up first." I tried to maximize the two that I had.

McDouche must have been in hog heaven, as we made great time following the trail. He also got carried away in our quest for point B.

By the time we stopped for the night, it was too dark to dig in, so we were ordered to form a perimeter, set out Claymores, and let it go at that. One of the guys in the platoon was only a few yards off the trail when he crashed through the lid of a spider hole and was chest deep in it before his boots hit bottom. Closer inspection of that side of the trail uncovered six other spider holes. This was indeed an NVA ambush site. They'd crouch under the camouflaged lids of the holes until a platoon or squad of GIs were centered in the kill zone, then pop up and clean up. Usually, when they abandoned the holes, they'd line the inside with sharply pointed bamboo spears angled upward — pongee stakes — that they'd dip in their own fecal matter to ensure that any puncture would become meanly infected. Luckily, this time that wasn't the case.

When Ski woke me up for guard late that night, I was surprised to see that the entire floor of the jungle was aglow with a pale blue-green phosphorescence. The forms of sleeping people and their packs appeared to be black holes in the light. Ski led me to where the detonator of the Claymore had been set up, handed me his watch, and left quietly to get some sleep. Sitting there alone and uneasy about the openness of the place, I slowly relaxed enough to allow my mind to go into a "data search" mode. The many hours of enforced quiet had created an atmosphere conducive to introspection, and it seemed that the situation pushed everyone to explore and draw on internal and previously unknown resources. In the data search mode, I would quiet my mind and emotions and trust that my mind was searching for relevant information. While in this relaxed and totally receptive mode, my attention sank through outer layers — like tuning past static on a radio — and finally images of my childhood appeared. I remembered that when I was a child and had committed a "wait till your father comes home" offense, I could feel my father's anger well ahead of his approach to my room. I could also tell when his feelings were in contradiction to his verbal reprimands. Sometimes I knew that he felt duty-bound to try to chastise me when he actually felt said offense was cute, and other times I knew that he was straining to be reasonable in spite of his anger. It dawned on me that in a place where the ambient emotional energy was nil, the NVA had—through their considerably extended experience in guerilla warfare—probably developed their own emotional radar, and that this might explain their seemingly magical cunning and efficient tactics. I played with tuning my mind to the tranquility of the place and found that for short periods of time, I could feel the harmony and quiet soaking into my being enough to feel that I might be emotionally transparent. The exercise was refreshing to me and seemed to be of definite survival value. I was determined that this was another area that I would work on (or let myself go to) whenever possible.

The practice also brought an awareness of the strange beauty of this particular spot. A nearly full moon sent shafts of light through the trees, which lit the already glowing jungle floor with pools of milky white light. I felt grateful for the time to sit and quietly observe, but then I remembered the letter in my pocket, and my curiosity prevailed.

Quietly I slit the envelope and found that it contained another sealed envelope inside. The inner envelope had been addressed to my mother's house in the familiar handwriting of a girl I'd dated after graduating from high school almost three years ago. I recalled another world and another time—the summer that we'd spent together before she'd gone off to college. She was a pretty, petite woman-child, standing five feet two and weighing just under a hundred pounds, with soft, tiny hands and large blue eyes. I remembered how strange it seemed that the warm emotional current between us somehow got tangled up when we tried to talk and how, after she'd left for college, the letters faded away with time and distance. In her letter, she talked about the dorm at Northern Michigan University, but the general tone of it said that she was sad and lonely.

After considering a reply for a few moments, I started to write, but all that came out was a translation of my perception of the moment. Time in the jungle had narrowed my perception to the here and now, so I wrote of the cool breeze and the soft night sounds of the animals, the tall, still trees, and the patches of moonlight. I managed in the end to relate how strange it seemed that in a place as tranquil and beautiful as this, a war was going on.

 **INITIATION**

IN THE MORNING WE CONTINUED ALONG THE TRAIL FOR SEVERAL MILES into what seemed to be an extremely remote area and were surprised to find the remains of a Montagnard village. They had cleared a half-acre plot for some primitive farming, and there was evidence that there had been several bamboo-and-thatch huts. It was not unusual that the tribe had abandoned the site, as it was the custom of these independent jungle nomads to keep on the move. What was strange, however, was in the center of their clearing was a table that was definitely factory-made, and sitting on the table was a finely crafted wooden box, only slightly smaller than the table itself. In the midst of miles of jungle, the table and box had an eerie and magnetic draw, but the chance that it was booby-trapped far outweighed curiosity, so giving it a wide berth, we left the mystery alone.

For the next several days, we traveled through miles of jungle, and although the going wasn't getting any easier, there was one consolation—there hadn't been any sign of Charles. McDouche seemed to have found a way to squeeze a few extra miles out of each day by not digging in at night, and now it was becoming common practice to push on till almost dark. When the platoon was running out of water, he'd keep us moving as we crossed clear, cold mountain streams, and then after going dry for a day or two, we'd be forced to fill our canteens in a swampy bog. One evening we were moving across the face of a steep mountain when darkness fell, and we wound up spending the night all strung out single file — not exactly what could be called a strategic defensive position. I was beginning to see why McDouche hadn't been winning any popularity contests among the men and why McCoy, when he'd given me a talking-to, had said that he considered Speed, Tennessee, and the others to be damn good troops, in spite of the fact that he knew about the pot smoking and the guys' threats on McDouche. McCoy was a soldier's soldier and cared about the men in his charge, while McDouche was concerned only with his career. We were all aware of the situation, but McDouche was the senior officer in charge, and he had his commission and his ambition.

The platoon stopped on a hilltop for resupply. It was pretty much the same routine, except that two new men were added to the platoon along with the rations. One of the men, a medic, was exchanged for our platoon's medic, who was going home at last. Most of the guys were glad about the exchange, as it was common knowledge that our medic had taken to shooting up with the morphine from his aid bag and replacing it while we were in the rear by buying stuff of questionable quality from Vietnamese civilians. The practice was tolerated by the men, but not appreciated. The new medic's name was Mock, a thin, wiry little guy from Kansas. He carried an aid bag that was bulging at the seams, and when he strapped it to his regular pack he was dwarfed by the bulk of it all. The new rifleman, Bruce, was from Massachusetts. He seemed a little shocked to be dropping in on us like this, but he was a welcome member to our shorthanded squad. He cracked us up right off the bat with his heavy Boston accent, and when introductions went around, Creeper turned to Ski and asked, "Hey, what is it with this mutha? Don't he know how to speak English?" It cracked us all up, because neither was obviously familiar with what my dad referred to as "the King's English."

In the midst of this, a pair of Phantom jets screamed over our heads, and each, in turn, took a practice run at the hills across the way. They started flying opposite each other in a large circle with their target on the circumference. After the first run, they alternated dropping HE bombs and napalm on a rocky outcropping in the middle of the hillside. McDouche stood in the center of the perimeter with binoculars, and after several loads were dropped, he said something into the headset of Sarge's radio, and the pair of jets disappeared. He claimed to have spotted some NVA among the rocks, which seemed very unlikely, because from where his head usually was, the most likely thing for him to spot would be a case of hemorrhoids. Odds were that he was just toying with the firepower at his disposal.

We saddled up and were on the move again. The platoon dipped into a valley and up onto a ridgeline that gained elevation for several miles and then merged into a huge, cone-shaped mountain. We headed for the top, and with each few hundred feet of elevation gained, the vegetation became more stunted and sparse; near the top, we were sliding through tall grass. They called it "elephant grass," which was a good name for it, because it was like crabgrass, only seven feet tall. By the time we reached this elevation, everyone was exhausted and drenched with sweat. It didn't take me long to discover that the edge of each tough blade was like the teeth of a saw. One quick and surprisingly deep cut on my arm convinced me to roll down my shirtsleeves. We reached the peak an hour before sunset and found it was dotted with small lavender orchids.

McCoy, who had been only a couple of guys ahead of me on the climb, immediately slipped out of his pack and let it drop.

"That's another motherfucker I'll never have to climb again," he said as he took off his shirt. He stood on the peak holding his arms over his head and turned his body this way and that to let the breeze cool his overheated body.

Ski slipped up behind me and said, "That ol' McCoy is one tough son of a bitch, man. See that big scar on his back? He said they took a big chunk out of one of his lungs after he'd been shot in Korea, and he's still out here humpin' these hills with the rest of us."

My respect and admiration for McCoy grew as I watched him from a distance with Ski. After cooling himself, he let his head hang down, and as he shook it back and forth, we could hear him chuckling to himself. Why he'd decided to be a lifer was his business, as far as I was concerned. Somehow, in spite of his chosen career, his humanity was still intact, and unlike other lifers, who had just grown old and cold, with hearts of stone, McCoy's concern for the members of his platoon was nothing short of fatherly.

We formed a perimeter around the peak and dug in, with time left over to eat, make some coffee, and watch a spectacular sunset. To the west, the view took in thirty or forty miles of ridges and valleys of various and vibrant shades of green. Here and there, sections of a river reflected the sun's changing color, as did the clouds that had banked up in horizontal stripes as far as the eye could see. Speed had dropped by our position earlier with a supply of bombers, and even before the sun's rays had changed from yellow to orange, the five of us were mutely mesmerized by the beauty and wonder of the scene before us. In the silence of the high mountain, we watched as yellow changed to orange, orange to pink and then lavender, and then the sky quietly faded to shades of gray.

Besides the view, the hilltop was about the most strategic location we'd been in yet. A ground attack of our dug-in position would have been nearly suicidal for the NVA, and although it might have been possible for them to lob a few mortars in on us, that was unlikely. Everything the NVA had to fight with had to be carried by hand over two hundred miles from the border between North and South Vietnam, and they used it sparingly, though very effectively. Their AK-47s and booby traps were primarily for ground troops. They tried to save their machine-gun ammunition for helicopters and jets (although they could bring down a Huey with their AKs as well), and their mortars were usually zeroed in on ammo dumps or highly concentrated troops in the rear. As far as equipment was concerned, the situation was like the muscle-bound ape kicking sand in the face of the ninety-seven-pound weakling in the Charles Atlas ads, except that the ninety-seven-pound weakling here was a karate expert. At any rate, insofar as our position was concerned, this was clearly a situation where Charles would employ one of the most effective weapons in his bag of tricks: he would wait.

Speed returned to our position with a fresh supply of bombers and good news. He'd overheard McDouche saying that we were going to man the position for two days. Considering the options, it was almost like a reprieve from the governor. Knowing that the next day was likely to be one of lounging and napping, the party was on. Tennessee, Creeper, Bruce, Ski, and I dug in our packs for sweet stuff, the canned fruit and candy bars that came with our rations, and sat in the grass behind our foxhole, each of us toking a bomber in the luxury of the moment. Bruce was amazed that the guy he'd been told to report drug use to (Sgt. Ski) had given him a light. He was about halfway through his bomber when a seed popped.

"There goes another problem," Tennessee said.

"Really?" asked Bruce.

"For sure," Tennessee continued, with his own version of the bullet-proof-poncho-liner routine. "Everybody knows that when you're smokin' a bomber and a seed pops, one of your problems has just disappeared. Don't ya feel better?"

"Well, yeah," Bruce replied, straining against the powerful reefer for a thread of rationality.

Tennessee couldn't keep a straight face and started giggling at Bruce's trust and gullibility. Waves of giddiness passed through the group. It was a real struggle to laugh quietly. Tennessee's game with Bruce was one of an endless variety of ways that the old-timers goofed on newbies. Making use of Bruce's openness and somewhat vulnerable state, Tennessee had created a moment of doubt that allowed him to inject a new way of perceiving reality into Bruce's experience. During the few seconds that Bruce had actually believed that a problem had disappeared, he had felt a measure of real relief. In the context of a joke, Tennessee had allowed Bruce to feel the effect of a new idea on a relatively mundane event and demonstrated the relationship between one's perspective and one's experience of things. This principle had many applications, but what both Speed and Tennessee focused on — either knowingly or intuitively — were mentally created negative emotions. Not only did dwelling on "problems" and worrying short-circuit your energy and distract your attention, but also—for the experienced and highly sensitive North Vietnamese guerillas—emotions were as palpable as the glow of a cigarette at night or an unmuffled cough.

The sound of a prop-driven plane grew louder as we sat looking over the now almost completely darkened abyss. It sounded more like a window fan than a plane, even as it came closer to our position. As the sound grew louder, it became apparent that the plane was flying without displaying navigation lights of any kind; only its quiet hum revealed its approximate location.

"It's Puff," Tennessee offered quietly to Bruce and me. "Bet you guys have never seen him work out before, have ya? It's an old air force cargo plane specially outfitted for night work. You'll see."

As the sound moved from behind us to nearly overhead, Bruce and I followed it, but saw nothing. Then, as it started to fade away in front of us, the blinding beam of a powerful searchlight created what looked like a glowing white amoeba that slid over hills and into valleys. The eerie light crawled along a ridge for a few seconds and suddenly went out. The hum stayed in the same general area, and a few seconds later, two silent streams of red tracers poured from the sky, followed by the chain-saw sound of miniguns and the frying-bacon sound of bullets as they cracked through the air. It made for a terrific light show, which would have been hard to enjoy if it had meant that scores of NVA were lying dead and wounded in its wake, but that was highly unlikely. As with most of the actions taken by the United States in this war, the awesome display of force was full of sound and fury, signifying nothing—except frustration.

While Puff was making a large circle for another go at the ridge, Tennessee spotted a lone figure coming across the hill from behind us. As the figure approached, he recognized our new medic, Doc Mock. How Doc negotiated the lumpy ground in the dead of night while wearing his dark-lensed granny glasses was beyond me, but he did manage. One of the disadvantages of being the platoon's medic was that he was required to travel in the center of the platoon. This supposedly offered more protection, but it also meant that at night, he wound up camping out with the lifers. Undaunted, Doc had slipped off to party. Ski passed out another round of bombers, and the party continued.

While Doc was talking to Ski and Tennessee, I was amazed how our new medic seemed to fit right in. Here he was, fresh from the States, yet seemingly knowledgeable about being in the boonies. As a medic, he had a couple of advantages. One was that it was less likely that he would have to ponder the personal repercussions of blowing some-body away in a firefight, and the other was that no one in his right mind, lifers included, would dare piss off a medic in a combat zone, for obvious reasons. Yet he was as liable as anyone to be killed. If he had any fear of this, it certainly didn't show. Puff made it around for his second display of fireworks, and after another quiet round of *oohs* and *aahs* and *wows*, the party broke up, and people wandered back to their positions for some sleep.

Even before dawn's early light, we were up, and the squad witnessed the birth of a new day. The horizon to the east became pale gray, then blue, and color returned to the hills and valleys below. The jungle itself reflected the changing light of the sky; misty grays and greens were transformed into lush shades of green, yellow, and brown. I wondered if it would have been possible to appreciate the beauty of it without the sense that my own life, at this point, was just as fragile, delicate, and temporary. As the sun floated slowly above the horizon, once again the ghost-like vapors rose through the canopy of green, revealing the presence of rivers and bogs below. Of all the army regulations, the one that required us to man our positions at full strength during sunrise and sunset was one that I actually was grateful for. It served as a daily reminder that, in spite of the absurd situation we were in, a greater sys-tem existed, one of beauty, harmony, tranquility, and joy.

With the sun clearly above the horizon, people started moving freely between positions, catching up with buddies who weren't often seen when we were on the move. Doc Mock returned to our position with a guy known as Orville. There were two black dudes in the platoon who had the same last name, Wright, and as black guys were usually referred to as "brothers," one of the Wrights was nicknamed Wilbur and the other Orville. Ski welcomed Doc and Orville with a bomber, and after the usual backslapping and handshaking, Orville took off his helmet and found a place in the circle that the squad usually formed when there was slack time to party. He took a couple of long draws on his bomber and, after a thoughtful moment, decided to speak.

"Man, getting up this hill was one son of a bitch, but the worst thing was that I had to hump it right behind that fuckin' McDouche. When we were about halfway up here, even McCoy wanted to stop and take five, but McDouche wouldn't hear of it. So here I was, draggin' ass all the way up here and havin' to stare at McDouche's shrunk-up little pack all the way. He don't carry shit—no Claymores, no grenades, no 60 ammo, nothin'—jus' Cs and water, a couple maps, and that fuckin' Ranger's Handbook stickin' out his shirt pocket. Half the time, he's bummin' Cs off of Sarge, and you know how that sorry motherfucker is. He's saying, 'Yes, sir. Got ya covered, sir. No problem, sir.' In the meantime, he's runnin' us into the dirt." By this time, Orville's head was hanging down, and tears were welling up along his lower eyelids.

"Don't you worry about McDouche," Creeper said. "Somebody's gonna frag his ass before this is all over, and it jus' might be me."

Tennessee and Ski jumped into things, consoling and gently razzing Orville. Soon he was laughing, no doubt glad to have sincere and sympathetic buddies. Although complaining and self-pity were generally not encouraged, with Orville, it was different. The platoon allowed Orville his right to be, which always seemed to be given precedence over any other consideration. The grief and frustration he expressed were real, not only for him, but for all of us. It seemed to help to have someone let it out. In consoling him, we had the opportunity to look at ourselves and know that, emotionally, we weren't alone. For me, the scene was particularly helpful, because no matter how hard I'd try to deny the pain or distract my attention from it with a forced focus on Charles or booby traps, the pain was there. But now it felt like it was flowing into the communal pool, which seemed to evaporate as it was acknowledged to be a part of us all. Everyone in the platoon, it seemed, had a deep affection for and appreciation of Orville exactly as he was.

The party continued as people started breaking out Cs, digging for candy bars or leisurely brewing some concoction or another. Tennessee wowed the squad by warming a can of peaches, breaking up a highly prized can of pound cake into the brew, and pouring over it several packets of coffee creamer that had been warmed with a bit of water. When it was done, he passed it around the circle, keeping an eye on it to make sure no one bogarted it by forgetting to pass it on. Speed dug his radio out and tuned it to the army station, where a DJ who called himself Sgt. Pepper played music, most of which was inspired by the peace movement that was going on in the States. How the army lifers allowed Santana, the Beatles, Jimi Hendrix, and others to come across the airwaves was a mystery, but for the ragtag bunch of draftees on the hill, it offered support and hope that not all the folks back home were oblivious to what was going on.

The day slid into night, and the new dawn found us on the move again. After several miles of easy going, down the gradual slope of the ridge, we were into the ups and downs of steep terrain and cutting through dense jungle. It was nice to have had a rest, but after only a few hours, the demands of being on the move had me digging deep for reserve energy and concentration. For me, each day that passed without a sign of Charles made it seem more likely that he would pop up the next, and I was determined to stay alert. We pushed on until dark and were up and on the trail with the sunrise the following morning. We moved as quickly as possible and were allowed to slow only when the density of the plant life required time-consuming chopping at point. Toward the end of the day, after a few hours of slow going — much chopping and crawling through the tangled underbrush — the trail suddenly opened, and we made a traverse across a steep hillside of gravel.

There was a path of sorts, after the first squad had passed across the area, but it amounted to only a boot-width plateau. The few plants that grew on the hillside offered only occasional and iffy handholds.

Halfway across the fifty-yard stretch, I came across Speed, who, from the looks of him, was on the verge of heatstroke. His eyes were glassy, and his face was red and flushed. His whole body was as wet as if he had fallen into a stream. Although he was still conscious, his speech was slow and somewhat slurred. I noticed that he was carrying a can of two hundred rounds of belted ammunition for the machine gun, which was an unusual thing for the point man to do. Usually the extra rounds were carried by the assistant gunner, who stayed behind whoever was carrying the 60, but evidently McDouche had requested extra ammunition and allocated a can to Speed. There were several reasons having the point man carry extra ammo was an incredibly poor decision. The point man usually carried a machete in one hand and an M16 in the other, and although this was awkward, it was necessary. If he had to carry a can of ammunition for the 60, it would have to be in the same hand as his weapon, which made for a needlessly complicated situation should he suddenly break into a clearing full of NVA. Instant access to his weapon was critical, and not only would he be hampered by the clumsiness of the ammo can, but also the fatigue of carrying around an extra seventeen pounds in his "free" hand was absurd. McDouche also had the option of replacing Speed with one of the platoon's other experienced point men, which, considering all the hacking Speed had done that day, would have been a logical and prudent thing to do. Instead, he pushed Speed to the breaking point—an irrational and dangerous thing for all of us.

I had been behind Wilbur all day. Orville's barrel-chested, strong-as-an-ox "brother." He always moved at a steady pace with never so much as a grunt or groan, no matter what the terrain. We were all exhausted, as it was getting toward sundown, and even Wilbur passed Speed without a hint of taking on the extra weight. I grabbed the ammo can and, after noting a nod of thanks from Speed, saw that the trail had grown even more treacherous. I realized that I'd lost my much-needed free hand for clutching roots and rocks. Army regulations required that grenadiers load their weapon, but keep the breech open, but since it was impossible to carry the ammo can with my grenade launcher open, I snapped it closed and freed up three fingers so as to be able to carry the ammo can and my weapon in the same hand. This worked well for a time, but just as the trail entered the thick brush, my foot slipped, and I felt the ammo can slipping from my sweaty hand. Reflexively, I clutched at the handle of the can, making my hand slip on the stock of the grenade launcher. The web of my thumb slid, flicking off the safety, and my index finger pulled the trigger.

There were three very slow-motion seconds that followed. Wilbur, who was facing me at the instant my weapon fired, seemed to have been paralyzed. His eyes were huge as he looked down the smoking barrel of my weapon; he fell backward into the embankment behind him and slid into a squatting position. At the same time, I was trying to tear my eyes from his gaze long enough to see if there was a gaping hole in his chest. Slowly, we both came to realize that the round had somehow missed him; he regained his composure and struggled to his feet. I was so relieved to see that Wilbur was okay that I'd forgotten that somewhere in flight was a high-explosive grenade, and a muffled explosion ahead of us precluded any wishful thinking about a dud. From the sound, it had landed near the top of the hill where the trail seemed to be heading, and another wave of terror, helplessness, and anxiety jolted my nervous system. It was still possible that someone had been killed or wounded.

When he was standing, Wilbur looked me calmly in the eye and said very slowly, in an even tone, "Hey, man, you ought to be careful with that thing."

How he kept his cool, I'll never know. After nearly getting his head blown off, he responded instantly to my fear and guilt. At a time when a harsh word would have torn me to shreds, he had calmly reminded me to be careful, turned, and moved up the trail to keep pace with the still-moving platoon. Feeling only marginally functional, I heard a radio call from another platoon in the company; the man behind me was carrying the radio. They were doing recon in the same area and wanted to know if McDouche had heard an explosion. He denied it, and another load of anxiety fell away. No one had been hurt. Considering the options, the idea of being considered a bungling idiot had great appeal. The idea that there might be some unfinished business about the matter was almost completely displaced by my sense of relief.

We stopped almost an hour before dark and, not wanting to look a gift horse in the mouth, I started digging in immediately. The hole was about knee-deep when I looked up to see McDouche standing over me. His usual air of cocky superiority seemed to have worn pretty thin, and even though he maintained a leering grin, there was as much fear in his eyes as there must have been in mine.

"Ulander," he asked, "was that your weapon that went off today?"

"Yes, sir," I replied, still thinking of the possibility of a court-martial and leg irons at Long Binh Jail.

"I'll tell ya what," he said. "Why don't you start heating up some Cs for the squad while Creeper finishes digging in."

I agreed, climbed out of the hole and started digging in my pack, confused about McDouche's strange request. When I returned to the foxhole and set up a couple of cracker-can stoves, Creeper put an end to my bewilderment.

He looked at me with a big grin and said, "That dumb son of a bitch thought you was tryin' to fire his ass up."

Ski agreed with Creeper's deduction and was slapping me on the back and laughing.

"Good show, guy," he said. "Maybe it'll loosen him up a bit."

I couldn't help but join in with their laughter at the irony of having inadvertently become a hero of sorts in the eyes of most of the squad—everyone but Wilbur and me. To me, it had been a regrettable error in judgment, and the reaction seemed to me to be all out of whack with reality. Even more absurd was the fact that from that day on, McDouche treated me with embarrassingly obvious deference in an attempt to ward off a second attack.

The night passed uneventfully, and for the next several days, the platoon covered miles of jungle during our dawn-to-dusk marches. McDouche quickly slipped back into the habit of pushing us until it was impossible to dig in, and we went back to spending more and more nights in hastily set up, half-assed positions. One afternoon we were moving along a river's edge when someone spotted movement on its opposite shore. Word was swiftly, quietly passed down the line, and we set up one hellacious blast of firepower to send across the river. The machine gunners found guarded positions behind rocks and trees, and the three guys who carried the army's new disposable bazookas had uncorked their end caps and were ready. In less than a minute, riflemen and grenadiers, along with the rest, were ready for action.

Suddenly someone hollered, "Don't shoot! It's GIs!"

We'd come within seconds of exterminating another platoon of our own company. One thing about this business of war was that mistakes were deadly. In this situation, it could have been deadly for us as well as them, and we were both on the same side. There had been rumors circulating for some time that one of the reasons that we were always in a hurry was that McDouche frequently had us off course and occasionally lost. If that was the case this time, no one knew, but the old-timers said that if there had been a firefight between platoons, it wouldn't have been the first. They said that another danger of being lost was that, with all the firepower the United States was throwing around, it wasn't unheard of that a platoon would be on the receiving end of our own artillery. Some of the more cynical old-timers said they wondered why the NVA were fighting the war at all; given time, we'd wipe ourselves out.

We repacked ammunition, regrouped, and pressed on. It had nearly been disastrous, but there was no looking back. Only occasionally would there be time for reflection — on a hilltop, at a minibase, or in the rear. In the meantime, it was one moment to the next, wondering *when* — when we might run into the enemy. For several more days, we pushed on, with still no sign of Charles. I was beginning to realize that trying to hunt down the NVA was as futile as a snorkeler trying to swim after fish or a five-year-old trying to catch a robin by putting salt on its tail. The NVA didn't slog along with heavy packs. Once they were in the area of their choice, they'd hide out in tunnels and caves and scout the area, traveling light, with just a weapon and a bag of rice.

They could travel quickly, and without large, unwieldy packs, they rarely needed to hack through the jungle. When they did make trails, they were waist-high tunnels through the foliage that they could move through quickly in a bent-over position. This protected them from aerial reconnaissance, and the tunnels were too small for a GI with a pack to use. Compared to their cunning and finesse, we were the circus coming to town.

Days blended into what seemed to be an interminable blur of time. For me, the only reference to time was sunrise and sunset. There were no Saturdays or Sundays, and it had been a long time since I'd considered what day of the month it was. There was no way of telling even what month it was; it was irrelevant and not worth the bother. Time seemed to be a relative phenomenon in Vietnam, and it was generally agreed that with the intense concentration and exertion required in the field, each day seemed more like a week. There might have been a connection between one's sense of time and the amount of information one took in, and surely it related to whether or not one was experiencing pleasure or pain. We just kept moving on.

One day Yaqui, our squad's radio operator, and I had been "pulling drag," which meant that we were the last two guys in the long column. It was late afternoon when we came across Shorty lying along the trail, looking deathly ill. Doc Mock was taking Shorty's temperature. He said that from Shorty's fever, chills, and fainting spells, it was clear that he had malaria. But the platoon, like ol' man river, jus' kept rolling along.

"Why aren't they stopping?" Yaqui asked.

"I told McDouche that Shorty was sick," Doc replied. "I told him that he wasn't faking. Look at him. He's red as a beet, and if his fever doesn't come down, he's gonna be in trouble real soon. He needs a dust-off so they can cool him back at the aid station." A dust-off was emergency removal by a medevac helicopter.

"Jesus fucking Christ," Yaqui growled. "What in the hell are you supposed to do here by yourself?"

"I don't know," Doc replied. "He said we were to catch up later, 'cause he wasn't stoppin'."

Doc had a wet towel on Shorty's forehead and was pouring water from his canteen onto his chest. It was certain that—come hell or high water—Doc wasn't about to leave a sick man behind alone.

"Well, fuck McDouche. I'm staying with ya," Yaqui said. "Ya gotta have a radio. What if it gets dark, and ya can't find the trail?"

The last man in the platoon had already disappeared around the bend and the four of us were alone. While Yaqui kept the rear guard, in case any NVA were keeping tabs on us by following at a distance, I fanned Shorty with my shirt as Doc continued to dribble water on his chest and wrists. Needless to say, we were in an extremely vulnerable position. After a time, Shorty became coherent enough to recognize me and eked out a faint smile before moaning and fading away again. My mind flashed back to our night together on the bunker at the mini-base, when he told me that he didn't think he was going to make it. There were guys who consciously opted for malaria rather than being in the field by not taking their daily antimalarial pills, and I wondered if this had been the case with Shorty. Doc Mock would deliver the pills individually every morning, but our other medic had been pretty haphazard about it, so it was hard to tell.

Yaqui got on the radio and called McDouche for assistance. Once again we were told that we'd have to catch up later. Luckily, Shorty was showing signs of improvement. In another half hour, he was on his feet, though still terribly weak. The sun was already casting long shadows, and our chances of being able to follow the trail were dwindling with every passing minute. Shorty said he'd try walking. While Doc helped Shorty, Yaqui and I took turns with the extra pack. It was slow going, and the newly cut trail we were following intersected an established trail several times, followed it for a few hundred yards, and veered off again. As darkness fell, each intersection became more difficult to recognize, but Yaqui (nicknamed after the Indian tribe he belonged to) was an excellent tracker. When we found the platoon, it was totally dark, and thanks to McDouche's relentless marching, they were still setting up.

In the morning, we moved on, and after we'd found an open spot big enough for a Huey, McDouche relented to Doc's persistent nagging and called for a dust-off. In fifteen minutes, a Huey appeared, and in seconds, Shorty was loaded on—gone, never to return. Malaria was a chronic condition, and symptoms could recur without warning. In no time, we were on the trail again, and although the situation once again called for my utmost attention, occasionally the memory of the four of us fumbling in the darkness would return, and a seething hatred would distract me. I'd stayed behind by choice—I wasn't the one McDouche had abandoned on the side of the trail—but his consistent disregard for the welfare of his men was continuing to generate intensely negative emotions. I was beginning to understand the bitterness and passionate hatred most of the men had for him. In my more generous moments, I'd think of him as a man who, one day, would realize that his Faustian bargain with the army had left him holding the short end of the stick, because in many ways, the script for the role he was playing had been drilled into him in Officer Candidate School. Occasionally there would be a crack in his veneer, and the frightened and lonely man who he was could be seen, but it seemed that when this happened, he'd push his rank even more for a while and be even more of an ass than the army required.

During the next few days, I tried to determine what Doc's response had been. In the course of several brief conversations, he hadn't revealed so much as a hint of anger or hatred, and even under close observation, his eyes and tone of voice showed nothing but a light sense of humor and a feeling of bemused centeredness. As with Captain Speed, Doc seemed to possess a type of understanding that, to me, was mysterious, alien, and sometimes frightening. Doc was able to accept bizarre and bewildering chaos with unperturbed equanimity and was able to act with clarity and compassion in the midst of confusion, anger, and fear. At some point, I realized that, unlike even the most seasoned old-timers, men who had proven their courage, Doc seemed to have mastered his ego and anger as well as his fear. After leafing through my memory bank, I couldn't recall a single incident in which Doc had spoken ill of any individual. Even when McDouche was being grilled on the fire of collective hatred, Doc maintained, seemingly without strain or repression, an innate understanding and pity for the man. I had been studying Doc closely for a long time, waiting to find a chink in his armor—a crack in the facade of the man who, it seemed to me, couldn't possibly be as he appeared to be. During the weeks we'd spent together, I found myself as mystified by him as I had been by the "magical" gifts my grandfather had given me as a child—a gyroscope and a radiometer. The gyroscope would stay upright as long as it was spinning, and the black-and-white squares on the spinner inside the glass globe of my radiometer would spin indefinitely, as long as there was light. They, like Doc, appeared to demonstrate the validity of laws and forces that functioned consistently whether they were understood or not, even though the source of their magic remained a mystery.

If the platoon was allowed to take five, Doc's aid bag would seem to spontaneously explode, and in whatever time was available, he would work his way up and down the trail, cleaning cuts and boils, giving antibiotics for jungle rot, and bandaging raw and bleeding feet. Most often, he'd still be sitting amid a pile of gauze pads and Q-tips, trying to squeeze in a few extra minutes when McCoy would start nagging him in increasingly loud whispers, "Get your shit on, Doc. We're heading out."

Although I greatly appreciated being with Doc, Creeper, Tennessee, and Speed, there was something about them that made me aware of my own inadequacy. I'd heard them say "cut him some slack" enough times to know that harsh criticism was one of the few taboos among the people in the platoon, and yet what seemed natural and self-evident to them was still an ideal to me. They seemed to be clearheaded, smooth, keenly sensitive, and yet relaxed, while I felt awkward, strained, and painfully self-conscious. They seemed to be willing to help me make the transition, but they offered teaching mostly by way of demonstration, which, considering the situation, was about all that could be done. In the course of a normal day, we'd have a total of only about an hour for conversation, but it wasn't an hour straight. It was a few words in the morning over Cs and in the evening after we were dug in for the night. The rest of the time was spent being "alone-together," struggling silently through the jungle, each man left to find his own method of survival.

I continued to practice telling myself that each low-hanging branch was the gateway to a new world, always trying to keep my attention fresh, and I began to adopt new strategies as well. I had discovered that if I coordinated my breathing with my steps during some of the steeper climbs, that it lessened the fatigue. At night, if we were on a hilltop, I got into the habit of staring at the stars for a few minutes before falling asleep, as it seemed to relax and refresh my mind. If we loggered-in under a canopy of trees, I would try to relax and imagine what would be left if my body were gone. I reasoned that if my mind was quiet and my breathing slow, this was the direction of death and that whatever awareness that was left would also survive my body's destruction.

In spite of the fact that my sense of time was, by now, something other than linear, time had been marching on, and after three months in the field, Bravo Company convened in a grassy valley deep in the Central Highlands. A large perimeter was set up, and amid much speculation, the official function of the gathering was announced. We were to be extracted from the field for a few days of stand-down in the rear. It would allow the company some time to rest, replace leaky canteens and shredded jungle boots, and get medical treatment at the aid station. A purple smoke grenade exploded in the center of the perimeter, and the first sortie of Hueys landed in front of a man who was holding an M16 over his head with outstretched arms. The tension on the perimeter rose as the Hueys dipped into the circle, loaded a platoon of GIs, and rose slowly, rotor blades slapping and straining for speed and elevation. Minutes later, another smoke was popped and Tennessee, Creeper, Speed, Bruce, Doc, and I made our crouched dash for a Huey. Soon we were once again grinning with relief as our machine rose above the range of AKs.

We landed at Uplift in a cloud of dust, and after turning our packs in to supply and trading our steel pots — our helmets — for OD baseball hats, we made a dash for the showers. The cold water in the fifty-five-gallon drums overhead created its own sort of water conservation as the showers filled with whooping, hollering, laughing, and cussing, and though the water was numbingly cold, no one was about to bitch about taking a shower with real soap. The atmosphere of celebration lasted through evening chow and was only slightly dampened by McDouche's lifer act during evening formation, when he assigned the squads of his platoon for bunker guard.

Just before dusk, Ski, Orville, Tennessee, Creeper, and I headed out to bunker number nine, relieved, refreshed, relaxed, and ready to party. To be inside a heavily fortified perimeter, circled with barbed wire and mines, allowed us to relax in a way that was hard to come by in the boonies, where the only barrier between one's physical existence and the great beyond was the thin and questionable metal in one's steel pot. Ski wasted no time in handing out a sunset round of bombers, and as we sat, quietly agog at the changing hues of sunset, the Beatles were coming in clearly over Armed Forces Vietnam Network (AFVN). They were playing an old song about "Fixing a Hole" and it seemed to be right on time.

As the twilight gave way to darkness, the crew of bunker nine quieted some. The guys were either quietly talking or allowing themselves to float away with the tunes from Ski's radio. Doc Mock appeared and had been talking to Orville for a time when Orville went into his rap: "Ya 'member when we were stateside, and we had those drill instructors makin' us holler, 'I wanna kill — I wanna kill'?"

The other conversations stopped, and everyone was focused on Orville, as his voice was raised in passion.

"They thought they were makin' badasses out of us and gettin' us all fired up to come over here and kick ass on Charles. Since I been here, I haven't met anybody who bought that jive ass shit, have you?"

"Look at him!" he said, pointing at me. I sat there grinning, thoroughly delighted by his feeling and sincerity. "Does that motherfucker there look like a killer, or what?"

At that, the crew roared with laughter, and I found myself falling on my side, twitching with spasms of hilarity.

When things settled down, Ski and Creeper started working on Tennessee.

"Man, my mouth got dry from all that laughing, didn't yours?" Creeper said to Tennessee, straight-faced.

"Well, yeah," Tennessee replied, puckering his lips and clicking his tongue against the roof of his mouth, testing its dryness.

Then Ski moved in on him, saying, "Ya know all that time we were in the field? I didn't say anything, ya know, but I kept thinkin' about fried chicken."

"Fried chicken ... yeah," Tennessee replied. "Yeah, that sounds good."

"And french fries," Creeper added. "Ya know, we've been in the field so long, I forgot about the Steak House back here." The Steak House was the EM club.

"Oh yeah!" Tennessee said. "The Steak House!"

Ski moved in for the kill, got real close to Tennessee, and confidentially said, "Ya know what? I'd buy if we could find someone to go over there and get the stuff."

Tennessee burst out laughing at the punch line of their ploy and said, "You're fuckin' with me. I knew you were fuckin' with me. Well, all right, cough up the cash, Ski, I'll go."

He grabbed a handful of crumpled bills and asked if I wanted to go along. I agreed without hesitation, and we slid off the bunker's roof and strained in the darkness to stay on the road. The combination of the potent Vietnamese reefer and darkness made it seem as if we'd stepped into another dimension. The cool, moist night air seemed to be more a liquid than gas, and the rubbery quality of stoned legs added to the surreal quality of our moonwalk to the Steak House. Occasionally one of us would stumble as the rough road would rise or sink abruptly. As we laughed and stumbled our way across the LZ, I had a flash about some stories I'd heard about Tennessee.

There had been a time, before I'd arrived, when the squad's radio operator had asked to trade places with him for a day. Tennessee agreed, knowing that the guy was probably looking for some respite from his heavy load—the radio operator had to carry the twenty-eight-pound radio in addition to his pack. The guy Tennessee had traded with had missed the signs of a booby trap (if there had been any) and was killed instantly. Months later, another guy volunteered to fill the squad's canteens in Tennessee's stead from a nearby stream after the platoon had been loggered-in for the night. This man ran into a squad of NVA at the stream and was killed. So now, even more than before, Tennessee — who had been equally blessed and cursed by these events — would jump at the chance to serve his fellow troops. Although he'd stuck his neck out at point for the platoon for eighteen months, no one could tear him from his post. He was a trustworthy, sensitive, and steadfast friend, consistently selfless — a fine man, whose only "fault" was that, at times, he felt guilty for being alive.

For a time, it seemed that we had each journeyed into the cool, moist darkness of ourselves. As our eyes and bodies adjusted to the light and the road, we walked quietly, rhythmic and silent, content with each other's company, and content to be without words. The road took a turn, and we found ourselves on a beeline path to the illuminated windows of the EM club. Faint sounds of music drifted from the building.

The last stretch was uphill, and I allowed myself to be mesmerized when Tennessee said, giggling, "Hey, check this out. If ya stare at the lights, they'll pull ya right up this hill."

I discovered that with a slight shift of mind, I could suspend my normal disbelief, and it seemed that we floated effortlessly up the hill.

When we made it to the door, he noticed my reluctance to go in, as the place was incredibly loud and rowdy. Turning my way, he said, "Don't sweat it, man. Ya don't have to talk or anything. Jus' follow behind and help me carry stuff."

And we entered yet another world, which was in screaming contrast, literally, to the quiet walk. The crowd was mostly made up of REMFs (rear-echelon motherfuckers, those hapless dudes who had to spend their tours with the lifers in the rear). They were trying to ease the pressure of their own unenviable situation (i.e., the lifers who nitpicked them to death with army regulations) and were getting sloppy, stumble-down drunk. Not to be outdone by the blaring music, they were hollering above it, screaming, babbling incoherent profundities, and they were wearing about as much beer as they were drinking.

Tennessee cut point for us through the semiconscious mob and hollered his request to the barkeep for a half a case of Pepsi. He slid it over for me to carry and, relieved for a sense of focus and purpose amid the nearly intolerable din, I snatched it up and bounced behind him to the food counter, where the "spoon" behind it slopped gobs of french fries, fried chicken, and a few steaks on paper plates and loaded them into a cardboard flat from the many empty cases of canned beer. At long last, the screen door slammed behind us, and it seemed to take the better part of the return trip for my nervous system to settle down.

Ski and company welcomed our return, and the ravenous crew made short work of the heap of food and drinks. After dinner, a round of bombers was passed around, and as we sat in quiet contemplation, I mused how these men (or boys?—we were all under twenty-one) had shown more concern for me than I'd ever known. Even though I'd occasionally revert to my mistrustful "what are they selling" mentality, I knew that their kindness and sincerity was beyond question. The old-timers all seemed to tolerate my reticence without condemnation or condescension, and I sensed that they knew that if they cut me enough slack, a time would come when I could express myself without fear, hesitation, or apology. A seed in my bomber exploded, showering the front of my shirt with sparks.

Tennessee slapped me on the back, saying, "There goes another problem! Pop!" And he let loose with his contagious giggle.

The thick stone wall of my personal isolation was showing signs of erosion, and here and there a crack appeared. Although parts of me feared what seemed the inevitable exposé of my secret thoughts and fears, another part of me welcomed the process and urged me to trust these old-timers. After all, they were still very much alive.

The morning routine was short and sweet. After breakfast at the mess hall, a company formation, and a head count, we were left to our own devices. The crew grew quickly restless after an hour of lounging in our tin-roofed hootches, and soon Tennessee approached and said, "Hey, we're going to Linda's. Wanna come along?"

"Who's Linda?" I asked.

"You'll see."

I looked up to see Ski, Creeper, and Captain Speed waving us on. They were already heading out. We made it to the asphalt road that cut through the base camp in no time and spent a few nervous minutes standing along the road in strained nonchalance. We were about to commit two punishable offenses at once: leaving the compound without a pass and arriving at an off-limits destination. Soon a deuce and a half came roaring down the road. It skidded to a halt as Speed flagged it down, and in a flash, the five of us clambered over its side rails, and we were off. Ski and Tennessee stood behind the truck's cab, catching the rush of air and celebrating our temporary escape. We'd only traveled a few miles when Ski started pounding on the cab's roof, signaling the driver to stop. The driver jammed on the brakes and brought the truck to a halt in the midst of a grove of coco palms. The village there was a small cluster of primitive mud-walled houses with thatched roofs. We jumped off the back of the truck and ran down a footpath that went through the village. The fifty-yard dash ended at the door of one of the small houses, and ducking the shoulder-height eve of its thatched roof, we entered the "living room." The room was sparsely furnished, with simple, unupholstered wooden beds the size of their doors, a couple of aluminum and plastic lawn chairs, and a small table. A tiny, moon-faced girl in her late teens welcomed us and told us to sit down. Ski introduced us and explained that my nickname was Babe.

"What do you mean — 'Babe'?" she asked sharply.

"You know, same-same Baby-san," he replied.

"Him? Baby-san?" she inquired, looking at me incredulously.

Ski explained the nickname to her in Vietnamese, while I sat there growing increasingly embarrassed and uncomfortable.

"Oh! Oh! I see," she said smiling. She turned to me. "Hello, Baby-san."

I managed a shy hello and was quite relieved when her attention turned back to Ski. While they were talking, I was drawn to the details of the room. It had two simple wood-frame windows with slatted shutters. The room had no ceiling and revealed the pleasingly aesthetic weave of vine-tied bamboo that supported the layers of thatch. From around the corner, another girl appeared. She was pretty and even younger than Linda, and even at a glance, I could see she was of a somewhat different nature. She viewed the scene with wide-eyed innocence and entered with quiet grace.

"Sit down, sit down," Linda ordered, and Ski and Creeper sat on one of the beds and leaned against the wall.

The girl who had entered the room opened a package of bombers that had been wrapped in red paper and ceremoniously extended the package to each of us with both hands. Her serenity seemed to request quiet while the ritual was performed, and only when we were all smoking did talking begin. After a few tokes, I became a mute witness to the surreal scene. The atmosphere was comfortable and calm, and I was content to relax and enjoy listening to Ski and Tennessee playfully bantering with Linda. Speed, in the meantime, set his radio on the table and tuned it to the AFVN station in time to catch the disc jockey who called himself Sgt. Pepper spin one of the platoon's favorite cuts. Noticing my withdrawal, Tennessee leaned across and waved twin peace signs in my face in sync to the music while the Beatles sang "With a Little Help from My Friends."

His goofy smile cracked me up—another crack in the wall of loneliness I didn't know I had. The party took off to dizzying heights.

Katy, the girl who had passed out the bombers, quietly left the room and returned with a porcelain bowl and gave us each a white washcloth that had been dampened with ice-cold water. Following the others' lead, I pressed the cold cloth to my face and wiped my hands and the back of my neck. She quietly made the rounds again, collected the used cloths, and left. We sat for a time, absorbed in the music of Speed's radio, when she returned with a large hookah. She placed it gently in the center of the floor, kneeled in front of it, and handed the hose to Speed. She lit a wooden match, glanced at Speed—who started puffing on cue—and waved the flame slowly across the pot in the pipe's golf-ball-sized bowl. Speed handed the hose to Creeper and, exhaling a huge cloud of smoke, settled back against the wall. In a short time,

Creeper had the bowl glowing brightly, and Katy calmly rolled a marble-sized ball of opium and nestled it carefully in the center of the bowl. The ball bubbled and crackled on the hot, well-toked pot, and Creeper filled his lungs deeply with the thick, sweet smoke. He nodded as he held the long draw, handed the tube to me, and exhaled slowly and completely. I puffed a couple of times and took a draw. Halfway through the toke, time became suspended, and my body and mind relaxed more and more deeply. It took all the presence of mind I could muster to pass the tube to Tennessee. I was aware of smiling as I closed my eyes and sank back into the peaceful womb of mindless euphoria. The only sense of bodily awareness was of my slow, deep breathing. The radio faded to a faint reminder of another realm. A strange sensation in my right arm caused me to open my eyes, and I saw that Creeper was tapping me gently and handing me the hose. I stared at the red glow of the pipe's bowl and took another draw. The gurgling of the pipe became an incredible, sensual throbbing. Passing the pipe to Tennessee, I gazed in wonderment around the room. In the soft glow of the shuttered windows, the walls and furniture seemed to have lost their density and were now translucent, glowing, ephemeral. Ski and Speed were staring at the bowl. Creeper was leaning back against the wall, looking comfortable and serene. Katy was standing in the corner, watching peacefully with gentle, compassionate eyes. After its third circle, the crew needed to remind each other to pass the hose, as the effect of the opium caused us to drift further and further from "reality." I leaned back against the wall, barely conscious — no thoughts, no fear, no time. Slowly a thought percolated up from a source deep inside of my being. I observed how an impulse was translated into words and how the words spoke to another level of awareness and were given meaning, and yet another layer of consciousness made a decision to act or not act.

The message at the level of words was "open your eyes"; slowly I opened my eyes. From a place of utter tranquility, the image of the room and its occupants appeared. It was now a dream-like hologram, glowing and vibrating with exquisite beauty. The heavy material stuff no longer existed. Its reality seemed to exist as an idea rather than the solid masses of mud and bamboo, flesh and bone, which at other times seemed so absolute and unquestionable. The room felt as if it had been transported to the rarified atmosphere of a mountaintop in Tibet, to some remote and uninhabited land, secure amid crystal blue sky and crisp, clean air.

It seemed as if time had lost its grip. We were going to exist forever in a place of beauty and harmony, until I noticed that Speed was looking at his watch with concern.

"We'd better be heading back," he said. "I'll go flag us a ride."

We said our farewells to Linda and Katy and ducked out of the door into the still-bright sun. Speed waited near the road while the rest of us hid behind a nearby hut, and when he hollered that a truck was coming, we all dashed to the road and jumped on when it stopped for us. It roared off abruptly, leaving us with only one concern—getting back to the base camp undetected. The dash had reanimated us somewhat. Creeper and Tennessee were standing behind the truck's cab smiling and nodding as they shouted to each other above the wind and the engine's roar. Speed was content to lean against the wooden side rails of the truck and watch the scenery flow behind us. I was happy enough to watch them all and wonder how they'd come to be the men they were.

Soon Tennessee was slapping on the truck's canvas roof, and the deuce and a half made a brief stop. It was barely enough time for us to jump off, but we were inside the wire at Uplift. A few steps toward our hootches, and we were indistinguishable from the rest of the company who had been listlessly hanging around the barracks all day. Later, as I took my place in evening formation, I began to realize something of how Speed and the other old-timers had learned to cope. To some degree, they'd internalized and maintained a sense of opiated detachment from the drama around them. To them, the drama was only valid to the degree that, through conditioning or choice, one aligned with that perspective. So far as they were concerned, the army—its structure and purposes—was a strange and pathetic sideshow they viewed with amusement and, at times, outrage. To them, what was really real was that life and energy permeated everything—everywhere. For them, the validity of this perspective was demonstrated continuously by sunrise, sunset, clouds, stars, and the rain, and it was reinforced by their beings' response, to the degree that they could resonate with these subtle, eternal rhythms. In front of us, the CO barked assignments for the night, strutted, and saluted, but how many glazed eyes stared from behind sunglasses in amusement at his playacting? "Only the Phantom" knew for sure.

In the morning, we were told that those who wished could go on an escorted trip to LZ English and visit the larger PX there. I was curious and, along with about half the platoon, opted to go. In humorous contrast to the previous day's outing, we were herded onto a waiting deuce and a half, and a scrupulous accounting of personnel was taken. McDouche followed the truck in his jeep to make sure that there wouldn't be any unauthorized stops or off-limits adventures. The fifteen miles of countryside on the way to English was entirely new to me, and I was surprised to see rice paddies and sizable villages where the local population was carrying out business as usual. After three months in the field, I had started to think of Vietnam as a country consisting mostly of jungle inhabited by invisible companies of NVA.

LZ English, on the other hand, was no surprise. As soon as we passed through the main gate, I recognized the layout and lifelessness of yet another army installation. The PX, although larger as billed, had nothing of interest, so Tennessee and I went to the EM club for something to drink.

It was the policy here to have all enlisted personnel check their weapons with the Army of the Republic of Vietnam (ARVN) soldiers, who were posted outside the club by a tin shed. I felt uneasy but complied with their demand, and Tennessee and I entered the dreary, nearly deserted club. The trip seemed to have been a bad choice, but we tried to make the best of it and ordered a steak. Somehow, neither Tennessee nor I could shake the dark atmosphere of the place, and after eating, we decided to find the rest of the platoon and possibly some excitement.

When we sorted through the weapons in the tin shed, I noticed that mine was gone. Tennessee immediately deduced, no doubt correctly, that the two ARVNs who were supposed to be guarding the weapons were VC in disguise and had conspired to steal it. He knew enough Vietnamese to accuse them of it, and they, of course, angrily denied it. There was really no other possibility, and in spite of their denial, they gave us arrogant and challenging looks, as if to say, "Yes, we stole it, but now you have to prove it." Things were getting increasingly hot, and Tennessee was getting intentionally careless as to where he was pointing his M16 when Sgt. McCoy arrived with the rest of the platoon. Even before I could say anything, he took Tennessee by the arm and led him a few steps away for a conference. He had come to the same con- clusion as Tennessee had, but hoping for a lucky break, he had the guys fan out and search the area in case the ARVNs had stashed it nearby and were waiting for a more opportune time to get it off base. It was one of the few times I'd seen McCoy get upset. The frustration of the situation was really getting to him, because with his experience in Vietnam, he knew the ARVNs were not only of questionable allegiance, but also, in the field, they had proven to be unpredictable and cowardly. Had we been off base, he might have had more options, but on a military base, the official status of the ARVNs was that they were our allies. After a futile search, we filed a report at headquarters and left.

Back at Uplift, we discovered that another replacement had been attached to Bravo Company. His name was Cowan, and seeing his face, I couldn't help but sympathize with the barely disguised terror in his eyes. He didn't have much to say but when he mentioned he was from a small town in Nebraska. Something clicked, and I could see him in a poorly fitting suit on Sunday afternoons after church, passively sit- ting suffocating in the living room with the old folks. He seemed to be altogether too innocent and tender to be where he was, but the draft, obviously, had made no such distinctions.

Bunker guard that night offered the day's only respite from tension and frustration. Tennessee and I were relaxing on top of our position when a guy from the next bunker came running over in a panic.

"Cowan's stoned to the max, and he's got a gun!" he exclaimed in a shaky voice.

I didn't particularly appreciate the guys' lack of sensitivity in their hurry to initiate Cowan into the cult of the Bong Son bombers. I suspected that he had acquiesced, as I had done, not wishing to offend anyone, but in my own case, I felt sure that there had been more choice and desire. Tennessee and I left our position and ran to the bunker next door. We slowed as we approached, seeing that a crowd had gathered and that they were cautiously trying to cajole Cowan into giving them his M16. No one was inclined to get too close to him, because he had an angry and confused expression on his face, and when anyone got near him, he would level his rifle at his midsection. He had his finger on the trigger, and it was hard to tell whether or not the safety was on.

Tennessee told the crowd to be still for a while, and sensing that Cowan had begun to feel less threatened, he approached him slowly, talking softly and steadily in a reassuring tone, "You don't have to be afraid of me. I'm your friend. I know that you're probably pretty high, but it'll be okay if you give me your M16."

Tennessee was trying to diffuse the situation as quickly as possible and was approaching Cowan as fast as he could without causing him to panic. Still, the process seemed painfully slow. Cowan's rifle eased its aim from Tennessee's gut to his feet, and when Tennessee finally put his arm around Cowan's shoulders, Cowan looked sad and ashamed. They went into the bunker for a talk, and whether Cowan could understand his words or not, he responded to his kindness and agreed to try to sleep for a while. I had little doubt that Cowan had meant no harm. He had just become severely disoriented because of the incredibly strong pot. Tennessee's cat-like sensitivity had come to the rescue once again, and I was more than content to return to my own bunker and crash.

The next morning we were packing our packs, and after the events of three short days in the rear, I almost welcomed returning to the field. We were alerted that we were landing in a "hot" LZ—which meant that intelligence had reported that a company of NVA had been spotted in the area—and that we were going to land as close as possible to their position. Supply had issued me an M16 to replace my grenade launcher, and I inherited Yaqui's job as radio operator for the squad. He had been shuffled to another squad, as an old-timer in that squad had returned to the States. My pack was full, and I still had the twenty-eight-pound radio to deal with. I had seen how some of the other RTOs (radio telephone operators) had strapped the beast to the outside of their pack and gave it a try. It worked well enough, except that it threw the pack off balance. The heavy radio had leverage on the pack and wanted to pull the top of the pack away from my body. When I turned in my M79 and the numerous rounds it required in the field and picked up the radio, an extra battery, an M16, and a bandolier of ammunition, my pack was not only a net fifteen pounds heavier but also way more awkward.

I thought that I could manage with the unbalanced pack until I could find a better way to carry everything. And then McCoy came up to me and said, "Where's your smokes? An RTO has gotta carry smokes. Jus' stay here. I'll get ya some."

He returned with seven smoke grenades, each the size and weight of a can of beer, and set them by my pack. "Don't forget your squad's call letters are Delta Foxtrot. I don't want you sleepin' at the wheel."

"Gotcha, Sarge," I replied and joined the already moving mob that was heading for the chopper pads.

Despite the confusion of getting ready for a new mission, I'd been trying to survey the company's response to the information that we were landing in a hot LZ. It seemed to be a mixed bag, as far as I could tell. Some of the guys had responded with noticeable nervousness; others showed no effect. In making the survey, I'd been reminded that there were many people in the company who I didn't know very well, if at all. Outside my own platoon, some of the faces were familiar, but that was about it. In the field, these people were either scouting a nearby grid square or were on the other side of our perimeter, and although I'd followed in the footsteps of most of them for days at a time, their character was unknown to me. I decided to err on the safe side and considered a hot LZ to require even more than usual concentration.

Our platoon was the last to leave the base camp, and it seemed that, even from my limited experience, things were unusually chaotic. Our platoon had grown together as an organic unit. We knew each other's most likely response to a variety of situations, as well as each other's skills and weaknesses. There was an ebb and flow of attention and energy between us that, regulated by need and circumstance, maintained the stability and efficiency of the group. These exchanges came spontaneously in response to the series of crises we were subjected to and were motivated by compassion for our fellow sufferers and by the knowledge that the survival of the whole depended on the health and well-being of its parts.

An inevitable conflict arose when our mission was not about merely surviving a recon mission but about descending into forced and often less-than-strategic contact with the enemy. The majority simply wanted to go home in one piece, but our officers, because they were required to serve only six months in the field, had a relatively short time to advance their careers. This advancement, they hoped, would be the result of their brilliant strategic maneuvers, which, they believed, the rest of us would be willing to kill and die for. Wrong.

We loaded on the last sortie of Hueys and were again floating over the jungle. The usual few minutes of present-centered enjoyment abruptly ended when we came over a ridge and headed toward a ribbon of green smoke in the middle of a small, grassy valley. My gut wrenched, and unlike before, I couldn't wait to get off of the vulnerable Huey. Our squad was ordered to defend the position at the tree line and to wait for further instructions. Although I was relieved not to have landed in a hail of small-arms fire, I crouched nervously and wondered what tactic Charles was ready to use. Drenched with sweat, I tried to fulfill the impossible order by scanning the dense jungle in front of me. I couldn't see three feet.

Someone hollered, "There's gooks in the tree line. There's gooks in the tree line."

My personal threshold of tension reached an all-time high as I scanned the jungle and flicked off the safety on my M16. I needed a quick glance at it to be sure that the selector was set on auto (fully automatic), made a mental note to know the selector's position by feel, and continued to scan the area in front of me with grim determination.

"Don't shoot! GIs in the tree line! GIs in the tree line!" came another call.

Confused and irritated, I relaxed a bit and put my weapon back on "safe." The company commander had started a point element into the bush, and it was at last clear that we were going to eventually follow the other platoons. As we approached the trail, the story of the conflicting orders circulated among the men. It turned out to be a simple, but nearly fatal, miscommunication between the captain and two of the platoon leaders. The first two platoons to land were under the impression that they were to form a perimeter by positioning their men ten yards inside the tree line. The other two platoon leaders thought that the perimeter was to have been formed at the tree line. Only a miracle and the density of the jungle had saved the company from cutting itself in half.

We began another company-sized reconnaissance patrol. Almost one hundred men clanging and banging, hacking and chopping, grunting and groaning their way into Charles's territory—an absurd maneuver by any standards. I was beginning to agree with Speed in that the NVA would soon discover that we were in the area. As a company, we'd almost certainly forfeited the element of surprise. And if we didn't have it, Charles soon would. The terrain of the Central Highlands was ideal for hit-and-run sniping, which, in the battle of attrition that Charles was waging, was an effective tactic. One hundred men who had blown their position were also great candidates for booby traps, which, once your presence and general direction were discerned, could be set to welcome you whenever it was considered expedient. A hundred or a thousand men were no more effective at fighting booby traps than Don Quixote was at fighting windmills. The only "advantage" we had was that if Charles decided to fight the war on our terms and from equal tactical positions, we carried sufficient firepower to survive till air support arrived. That supposed advantage, however, was more than negated by the fact that our adversary was well aware of how we intended to use our technological superiority. All of our weaponry could have been effective if Charles had played the role that our military intelligence had scripted for him, but this was an offer that he not only could but did refuse.

Our patrol continued for several uneventful days. The terrain seemed new, but the routine remained the same, except that our company commander, unlike McDouche, made sure that we had time to set up a decent defensive position at night. The company had, for the most part, been traveling through thick jungle when one night we found ourselves setting up in a valley near the ruins of a small village. The area had once been used for growing rice, and although the village had long been abandoned, the dikes of the rice paddies remained, creating a raised patchwork covering most of the valley. For some reason, the dikes had sprouted thick tangles of vegetation, while the once-flooded growing areas were covered with short grass. Our squad had set up behind one of these dikes. I was uneasy about the terrain, but I resigned myself to being content with what could not be changed. The short grass made one of the most comfortable sleeping positions we'd had in a long time, and all too soon, Speed handed me a watch for my turn at guard.

It was a strange position to defend, since we had no line of sight to the next position and couldn't see the area outside of ours. I put my trust in our trip flares and settled in for an hour of intense listening. From time to time, the moon would be eclipsed by clouds, leaving me in utter darkness. I heard a rustle to my right, followed by what sounded like footsteps. I replayed the sounds in my mind and was positive that I'd heard someone walking outside our perimeter. The noises abruptly stopped. During the few moments of silence that followed, I reviewed the situation, flicked off my M16's safety, switched it to auto, and aimed it in the general direction where I'd last heard movement. The facts flashed through my mind—someone was out there; we were in a free-fire zone, which meant that anyone in the area who wasn't a GI could be shot on sight; and anyone who was outside our perimeter wasn't a GI. There had been silence for fifteen seconds, which was long enough for me to realize that if a firefight was to start, I'd best alert the rest of the squad. Silently, I made my way to Tennessee, who had been sleeping a few yards away. Slowly, I pushed on his shoulder till his head turned, indicating that he was awake.

I got right next to his ear and whispered, "There's something out there. I heard footsteps."

Just then there was the sound of two more footsteps.

"Ya hear that?" I whispered.

He nodded and grabbed his weapon. He held up one finger, signaling me to wait for a second, and took a few steps in the direction that the rest of the squad was sleeping. I kept my rifle aimed in the direction of the footsteps and kept my finger on the trigger.

Tennessee slipped silently next to me and said, "Cool it. It's Cowan. He must have gotten up to take a shit."

"Outside the perimeter?" I shot back in disbelief.

"Must be," he said. "He's not where I saw him set up to crash."

I felt relieved, outraged, and guilty all at once. Relieved that it wasn't VC, angry at Cowan for being outside the perimeter, and guilty that I'd overlooked the possibility that one of our own men would be outside the perimeter. As my nervous system settled down, I could only feel grateful that I hadn't fired and that Tennessee had saved me from a lifetime of guilt.

"Stay here," he said. "I'll go and have a talk with him."

I was more than happy to sit quietly for the remaining twenty minutes of my guard. My mind was numb and my body exhausted from the day's trek through the jungle, so I let my system shut down except for attention to sound.

In the morning, the company pressed on. Once again, there could be no looking back, no regrets, no distractions from the job at hand. The monsoon rains were getting more intense, and from early evening on, the rain would come down in sheets. Our positions were compromised by the weather, and I hoped that Charles had enough sense to stay out of the rain. In an effort to stay dry, we made communal hootches out of three ponchos, using one for the floor and two for the roof. The system worked fairly well, and occasionally we would wake up nearly dry in the morning, only to be soaked again before we'd finished stuffing our packs.

When we finally had a couple of days without rain, I took off my boots to dry my socks. I was surprised to discover three fat leeches on the inside of my ankle, which, from the looks of them, had been there for quite some time. I grabbed the bug repellent from my pack and gave them a liberal dose, which caused them to retreat without hesitation. Mosquitoes were also a constant bother, and we joked about going to sleep to the sound of a stereo humming, as usually several would be hanging outside the two-inch barrier afforded by the army's jungle juice bug repellent, waiting for it to wear off. In my previous life, I would have been thoroughly grossed out by all of this, but in the context of the situation, the leeches, mosquitoes, and all manner of creepy crawly things that were at home in the tropics were only mildly irritating.

On the fourth resupply of the mission, two new guys were added to our platoon. A skinny guy from Texas, who quickly became known as Tex, and a guy named Carlson, who had been transferred from duty in Alaska. Tex was fresh out of "shake and bake" school, where the army created sergeants in only eight weeks' time. He was a likable guy with a typical Texas drawl, and I was relieved to find that he took his stripes with the appropriate grain of salt. I felt sympathy for the awkward position he'd suddenly found himself in. He had the rank and responsibility for directing and caring for a squad of men and knew he wasn't qualified in the least. He took Ski's place as our squad leader, and Ski went home for a well-deserved thirty-day leave before starting his second tour. Carlson was also likable and a cutup to be sure. He had harassed the lifers at his Alaskan duty station enough that they made good on the classic stateside threat and sent him to Vietnam. He was honest but probably a bit too outspoken. He rubbed some of the old-timers the wrong way right off the bat by saying that if the shit hit the fan, he didn't know how he'd respond or if he could stick his neck out for people he didn't know very well.

To me, it was a confession of sincere doubts — doubts I thought we all shared at times, but to some of the second-tour veterans of the war, it revealed an attitude they couldn't accept. Perhaps they had been in the field so long that the events they remembered as spontaneous, selfless sacrifice were foremost in their minds, and they had forgotten their own initial doubts and fears. As usual, there wasn't time for analysis or debate. We filled our packs with new rations and pressed on.

The company climbed a steep mountain and followed a trail on its ridge. Traveling as a company, although absurd in many ways, was relatively easy. By the time three platoons had trampled down a freshly cut trail, most of the trouble spots had been ironed out. Thorny vines had been cut, and loose rocks had already been dislodged by someone else. Also, for some reason, traveling as a company usually invoked more confusion at point. Although most of the company never knew the reasons for the periodic consultations between the CO and platoon leaders up front, we were content to rest along the trail while they settled their disputes.

By this point, I'd had time to reorganize my pack and found if I strapped most of my miscellaneous gear on the outside, the radio would fit in the pack's main compartment. This not only allowed for much better weight distribution but also concealed the radio, which was known to be on Charles's list of prime targets for snipers. After four months, I felt that some of my greenness was finally wearing off, and although there was still a long way to go, I could now start the day with some confidence that my endurance would hold out till evening. I could see that some of my energy-conservation measures were finally paying off and that a time was coming when, rather than just making it through each day, I would have extra energy to offer the platoon and its new members.

On the third day after resupply, we made our way into an area of single-canopy jungle. Now, without the cover of multiple layers of vegetation, we would occasionally pass through areas totally devoid of overhead cover and be met by the relentless tropical sun. To a company of men who were already pressing the limits of their endurance and rapidly running out of water, the change was significant. My eight-quart ration of water was almost gone, and my head felt like it was cooking in my steel pot when I came across Doc Mock and Carlson on the trail. Carlson was unconscious, and Doc had dragged him into the shade. Yaqui had already alerted the CO on his radio, and the company had stopped. Carlson's pasty-white Alaskan skin had turned a bright crimson. I could see that his tongue was bone dry and remembered from basic training that his symptoms revealed a serious degree of heatstroke, severe enough that it could lead to permanent injury or death. Doc readily accepted my remaining half pint of pee-warm water and mixed it with rehydration salts from his aid bag.

Bruce, meanwhile, had taken up a collection and had nearly a quart of water from the troops closest to us on the trail. Yaqui had a wet towel on Carlson's head and sprinkled water on his chest while I fanned him. Carlson slowly regained consciousness. It was an hour before Doc considered him fit to travel. Luckily, it was nearing the end of the day. All we had to do was move to the next decent place to stop for the night and set up a perimeter. We split up the heavier items in Carlson's pack and made our way to the CO's chosen spot. Patrols were sent out in search of the nearest stream so that canteens could be refilled. By morning, Carlson had recovered enough to be considered fit to stay with us in the field.

Two days later, after having hacked through miles of jungle, we came upon a small river. Approaching the river from a ridgeline, we could see that the river had left a half-acre deposit of sand and clay on the inside of a sharp bend, and although it was only late afternoon, it was here, on the sand, that the CO decided that we would logger-in. Had we been camping back in the world, the place would have had great appeal, but in the Central Highlands, the strategy of the move left much to be desired. Behind us was the ridge, and across the river in front of us, a steep hill followed the course of the river. The other members of the platoon were as baffled by the choice as I was, but my job was to dig in, so I just kept digging. The mix of clay and sand on our side of the perimeter made for easy digging, and my squad's position was finished before the men across the way had returned from their expedition to get poles to support their overhead cover. Since there was still an hour till sunset, I started to clean my M16—the weapons were notorious for jamming if sand got into their works. I had it taken apart, and after running a brush down the barrel, I decided to do a deluxe job and clean the inside of the bolt. I removed the little cotter pin that held the firing pin in place and was looking in my cleaning kit for the brush to clean the inside of the bolt when I heard the most horrifying of sounds.

*Gotcha.*

*Gotcha, gotcha, gotcha.*

It was the sound of AK-47 fire.

I jumped into the foxhole and scrambled for the pieces of my M16. Everything was there except for the little cotter pin that held the firing pin in place. In desperation, I grabbed a handful of sand from where I'd thought it had fallen, and as it sifted through my fingers, the flash of shiny steel caught my eye. It was there! The position was instantly crowded as Tennessee, Speed, and Creeper piled in beside me. During the seconds that it took me to reassemble my weapon, I heard the crackle of M16s as the people across the perimeter returned fire.

*Gotcha.*

*Gotcha, gotcha, gotcha.*

The attack intensified relentlessly. We were fucked.

From somewhere in the confusion behind us I heard someone yell, "There they are! In the trees across the river, in the trees!"

Reflexively, I pulled the trigger on my weapon and, in an instant, fired half a clip of ammunition across the river.

Creeper had curled up in the corner of our position and was frantically flipping the pages of the miniature Bible that the Gideons had given us when we arrived in country. Speed peeked around the sandbags to get a feel for what was happening and told me to hold my fire.

"We're drawing fire from across the perimeter," he said as he ducked back inside. "We can't shoot across, so just hold on and watch in front of us."

Overwhelmed with curiosity, I glanced across the perimeter and saw two wounded men lying, unprotected, in the middle of the perimeter and a crew getting ready to let loose with one of our machine guns. Orville shot a round of HE as well as his cleaning rag at the snipers, and I ducked back in our position as several AK rounds cracked over our heads. The M60 returned fire with a reassuringly long burst, and I concentrated my attention on the hill across the river from us. Hoping for x-ray vision, I could see nothing but leaves and dense brush.

Someone screamed, "Medic!" Another long burst of rounds roared from the 60.

Still scanning the hill, I heard someone shout at the 60 gunner, "There on the limb of that big tree. Fire his ass up."

Another long stream of red tracers issued from the muzzle of the 60 till another voice yelled, "Ya got him! I saw him fall. Now get the other one—to the right."

The return fire was prolific if nothing else, as rifles and grenade launchers joined the 60 and blasted the suspected area. Then suddenly it was silent—deadly silent. Charles had retreated; he'd had enough.

There was no way to gauge time in the minutes that followed. It was as if time had been suspended. In the distance, I heard the thumpa-thumpa-thump of a helicopter, and an instant later, one appeared, swooping low over the hill across the river and setting down hesitantly in the center of our perimeter. I could see the Red Cross on its side and knew its purpose. In seconds, it rose again, lifted its tail, and zigzagged down the river. It returned later for another load of dudes, men who had not been as badly injured as the first group.

It was a while before people got out of their positions, finished setting up, and started picking up the pieces. When I got the nerve to look for my pack to find something to eat, I noticed that our poncho hootch was riddled with bullet holes. The incoming shit had definitely been as close as it had sounded.

Orville spotted me and came over to talk. "That dumb mother-fucker — stupid son of a bitch — settin' us up in a place like this. Man, I felt like one of them ducks in a shooting gallery. I mean to tell ya that my shit was really hanging out there when we got hit."

"Yeah," I replied, "I saw ya dealin' with your thumper." A grenade launcher was called a "thumper."

"Was all I could do," he continued. "Man, I didn't have anywhere to go. We were still tryin' to dig in. There was a couple of sandbags for me to get behind, but from where they was shootin', that wasn't shit! Where'd we get that son of a bitch anyway?"

I shook my head.

"Ya shoulda seen Doc!" he went on. "His shit was *way* out there. I think the gooks were trying to get the ol' man [the CO], 'cause most of their shit was comin' down there in the middle, and they didn't have nothin' to get behind, either. Doc was right out there though — all his white bandages and shit — patchin' them up. And I mean to tell ya — it was *bad*."

Orville put his hand on his chin, looking as if he realized what had happened for the first time, and went on. "They said that four guys got fucked up pretty bad. And there were some guys who were outside the perimeter, and one of them was wasted. Three dinks did that to us. With all the shit we carry? Jus' three of 'em. And we got one of them. Ya know who was one of the guys who got shot?"

"No."

"Was that new dude. 'Member the guy who said he didn't know if he could get behind us if the shit hit the fan? Carlson. It was that Carlson dude from Alaska. I don't know why, but Doc went out there and fixed his ass up. And that's where he got shot, right in the ass!" He chuckled shaking his head. "Man, if that'd been me, I'd have let him lay there!"

I looked over Orville's shoulder to see the wide-eyed buck sergeant coming toward us.

"Get your shit together," Tex said nervously. "We're going to set up an ambush. The ol' man asked McDouche for a squad, and we're it."

"Where we goin'?" Orville asked.

"We're going to cross the river."

"Oh, man," said Orville, shaking his head in disbelief. "If that ain't the dumbest thing I ever heard of. First the motherfucker gets us all fucked up, and then he's gotta do something even dumber. What's he think — that the gooks are gonna come wading across the river and attack us at night?"

"I don't know," responded Tex apologetically. "But those are our orders, and we haven't got much time to set up before dark, so get your stuff."

I could barely believe it either. Not only was an ambush on the other side of the river strategically ridiculous, but it required us to wade across in full view of the high ground that had, only minutes ago, been used so effectively against us. I strapped my radio on a small cloth harness, grabbed a few grenades, a bandolier of ammunition, and my M16 and was ready when Tex and Orville returned. We waded across the river — an absurd transformation from sitting duck to swimming duck. It was as dangerous as anything could be, but fate was on our side, and Charles let us pass. It was twilight as we found a hint of a trail and followed it fifty yards or so to the first semblance of a flat spot. Tex set out a trip flare and a Claymore and returned to the small depression that Orville and I hoped would provide at least some cover. We waited.

In two hours, it was pitch black. It started raining. I had already called in our position, and there was nothing left to do but hope for the best. We had split the night into shifts, but being on Charles's side of the river, we were all too wired to sleep. Time passed. Since we were dependent totally on our hearing, I focused. There was a sound, sort of a *saloosh,* about twenty feet from our position, which I recognized from previous nights on guard. I knew the plant that caused it only because I'd seen it before during the day. It had large leaves that caught rainwater, and when a leaf was full, its stem would bend and empty the water. I had to admit that it did sound like a foot stepping on the soggy jungle floor, but if one listened carefully, the sound would always come from the exact same spot. Even though I had disciplined myself enough to keep my mind clear and keep it from descending into nightmarish imaginings, my arms, legs, and entire body shivered like a Chihuahua on the Fourth of July.

"Listen," Tex asked nervously. "Hear that?"

"Yeah," I replied. "It's a leaf that empties water."

"No—listen—it's gooks! I'm gonna blow the bush. When I blow the Claymore, you and Orville grab your stuff, and we'll head for the river. Got it?"

In what little light there was, I could see Orville giving me one of his "oh, brother" looks, but before we could respond, the Claymore's roar nearly blew our ears out. I grabbed my radio by the antenna, and Orville caught hold of the ammo for his thumper just in time to catch up with Tex as he stumbled down the hill in the darkness. After we'd gone about thirty yards, Tex realized that he might have left us in the dust.

"You guys there?" His voice was panicky.

"Yeah, we're here," Orville responded.

"Okay, then, we're headin' for the river."

We waded back across the river and rejoined the company. It had been a pretty funky ambush, but Orville and I were glad that it was over and were hoping to get a little sleep before the sun came up. I curled up in a fetal position, wrapped in my magic poncho liner, and tried to sleep. Just as I started to doze off, I heard Tex calling my name.

"Ulander, is that you?"

"Yeah."

"Well, get your stuff together. McDouche says we have to go back across the river."

"You gotta be shittin' me!" I replied incredulously.

"Nah, I'm not. Don't worry though, he said we could bring a 60 and a gunner with us."

"Oh, great—yeah, that's great," I replied, thoroughly pissed to be subjected to the ignorance of our command.

I got my things together and was relieved to see Sgt. Sam arrive with his 60. He was a dynamite 60 gunner on his second tour and was sure to lend some sanity and stability to an otherwise insane maneuver. We crossed the river, set up again, and at long last, I got a little sleep—very little.

It was just after sunrise when the lifers decided to let us cross the river and return to the perimeter. Plenty of light for Charles to blow the shit out of a vulnerable group of GIs carrying the weapon he hated most, the M60. But we made it. After a grumbling session with the rest of the platoon, I started to dig in my pack for some Cs.

*Gotcha, gotcha, gotcha.*

*Oh, God, not again,* I thought, making a dash for our position.

*Gotcha, gotcha.*

The AKs were firing from the same place. The platoon responded a little quicker this time, and the M60 was pumping out rounds almost immediately. Evidently the NVA had found—or made—a better-protected position to shoot from, because even after a hellacious blast of firepower from half a company of pissed-off GIs, they returned fire with a well-aimed volley. I scanned the hillside, hoping to spot an outlet for my rage. There was nothing. I knew there would be nothing, but I wanted to distract my attention from what I was hearing. The NVA let loose a few more rounds, and I knew that from their position and the rate of fire that they were well-placed shots. The company blasted away, hoping that luck would help their rounds find a mark. Again, someone hollered for a medic, and my worst fears were confirmed—they were kicking our asses.

The battle was still raging when our medevac chopper slid over the hill and landed in the midst of our perimeter. It was as if someone had called time out in the middle of a football game. Suddenly the only sounds to be heard were the slapping blades of the medevac chopper. The NVA had stopped firing and allowed us to haul off the wounded and dead. When the chopper left, the firing stopped altogether, and the NVA dissolved into the jungle to wait for another day. Though I vaguely remembered that "persons taking no active part in hostilities" were afforded protection by the Geneva Convention, I was amazed to see that our adversary actually followed the rules. When word came around about the damages, I wasn't surprised to hear that three more GIs had been wounded and that one was dead. I felt lucky that our patrol had crossed the river when we did, because in talking with the old-timers, I learned that the timing of the attacks had been well planned.

The NVA knew our routines: we cut hootch poles in the evening and rolled up Claymore lines in the morning. Both activities required a few guys to be outside our perimeter. The NVA attacked at these times, knowing that most of us were conditioned to return fire freely, particularly when we had established a perimeter. They knew that our indiscriminate firing could be added to theirs, further endangering the unlucky few who were outside the perimeter. The total effect was devastating, statistically as well as psychologically. With the army's policy of pulling officers out of the field after six months, and their usual lack of receptivity to lower-ranking but clearly more seasoned troops, the NVA could get away with this tactic indefinitely. Each new officer would ignore the reality of the situation and follow the tactics and strategies he learned in Officer Candidate School, which were, at this time, painfully and dangerously predictable.

Tex again was searching for his squad. Once more we were to cross the river and patrol the hill. Fear, anger, and sorrow were the emotions I felt as I packed up my stuff for yet another excursion across the river. It seemed that our commanders wanted desperately to even the score with the NVA—so much so, in fact, that they were willing to stick our necks out again. I knew that this was just the foolhardy response that Charles would anticipate. I had heard stories about troops on the move getting sniped, responding reflexively and emotionally, and charging toward the snipers into areas rife with booby traps. Our adversary was just too cunning to be muscled about.

As we crossed the river, I tried my best to clear my mind and focus on the job at hand. Mentally, emotionally, and physically, the members of our patrol had been severely strained, but I was amazed that when I dug even deeper for reserve energy, there was still enough, I thought, to see me through another dangerous mission. In spite of the vulnerability inherent in the crossing, I focused intently on the moment and let the cool, chest-deep water soothe and calm my shattered nerves. Once on the other side, we headed directly to the ridge where the NVA had been only hours before. Struggling with my fear, I tried to take a cue from Sgt. Sam, whose movements revealed clarity of mind and sharply focused present-centeredness. Each step he took demonstrated the fact that he had mastered the art of stalking. He was not too tight, too loose, too nervous, or too resigned. Three months earlier, I might have observed only a man carrying a machine gun, but now I saw that he was traversing a deadly abyss on a mental-emotional tightrope with grace, precise balance, and unselfconscious ease. While watching him, I wondered if he was motivated by some mysterious force of which I had no knowledge or experience.

My own ability to maintain any semblance of "cool" had worn extremely thin by the time we reached the ridgeline. There, to my dismay, was evidence that the NVA had intended to settle in. They had built several bamboo-and-thatch shelters and had camouflaged observation platforms built in the taller trees. I radioed back to the company that we'd located their position while Tennessee prowled around the hootches like a cat. He spied in the open door of one and, realizing he couldn't see the extent of its interior, pulled the pin on a grenade and tossed it in. The explosion actually calmed me, because it broke the intensity of the silence. It was apparent that the NVA had split, and after discovering a freshly abandoned cooking fire, it was clear that they had abandoned the site only that morning. We set fire to their thatched huts, and I requested permission for us to reenter our perimeter. It was granted, and greatly relieved, we again crossed the river.

We barely had time to get our stuff together before the company moved out. I now knew that Charles was indeed prowling about and that he more than lived up to his reputation. The simple mathematics of our exchange told the tale. He had wiped out 15 percent of a company of GIs and sacrificed one or maybe two of his own. A great trade in anyone's chess game. I forcibly wrested my attention away from the past and rallied new determination to focus on the present. It was a major chore to discipline myself again. I was beginning to doubt how effective my efforts might be in countering our CO's ineptitude. Yet I had no choice but to dig deeper and strive more diligently.

# HEAD ON

THE COMPANY SLOGGED ALONG FOR THREE MORE DAYS BEFORE WE moved into a wide valley and set up a perimeter. None of the enlisted men were told what was happening, whether it was resupply or extraction, and at this point, no one seemed to really care. A green smoke was popped, and a huge Chinook settled into the perimeter. I had never seen these flying buses in the bush before and wondered why they were using them now. It seemed to me that they were great for shuffling supplies around in the rear areas, but in the jungle, they were too big and too awkward, and they put too many people at risk at one time to be of much use. My personal doubts notwithstanding, the back-loading ramp was lowered, and the huge machine swallowed up our whole platoon.

The machine rose effortlessly and quickly picked up speed and elevation. Tennessee was grinning at me from the web seat across the aisle. His smile reminded me that once again, for a few minutes, if no more, we were out of harm's way. After what seemed to be an unusually long flight, the magic bus leaned into a sharply banked turn and started to lose elevation rapidly. Wondering if this was a tactical maneuver of some kind, I twisted myself around and looked out of the small window behind me. The South China Sea rolled beneath us as far as the eye could see. The sunlight reflected off the even rows of waves, creating dotted lines of flashing silver light. As the machine completed its turn, I could see that we were headed for a beach. Ski and Speed had told me about missions they'd done along the coast and how hard it was to carry a pack on the sand, but when I saw a small concession stand with a couple of surfboards leaning against it, I hoped that this was going to be a mission of a different kind.

Sure enough, it was to be in-country R & R. It was all McDouche could do to keep the platoon from going completely bananas as we exited the aircraft. He managed to corral about half of the platoon to tell us that this was going to be a three-day R & R and that anyone who got sunburned would be disciplined to the full extent of the Uniform Code of Military Justice. By the time he'd issued his stern warning, a third of the platoon had stripped on the spot and had run, screaming, into the water. I was tired and hungry and in no particular hurry to do anything. Doc Mock, Bruce, and I stashed our packs and made our way to the concession stand to check it out. We each ordered a burger and a Coke and snarfed them down. Bruce noticed a small sailboat behind the guy who was running the stand and asked if we could use it.

"Do you know how to sail?" the guy asked.

The three of us almost fell over each other in an effort to convince him which of us was the best sailor.

"Well, sure," he responded. "It's here for you guys to use, but I thought I'd better ask. Big water out there, ya know."

"Yeah, yeah, sure. We gotcha."

Doc Mock had spotted a snorkel hanging on the wall and had the concession man throw it in for good measure, and we were off like a dirty shirt, carrying our prize down to the water. After a few minutes of fiddling around, we got the sail in what looked to be the right position, and three naked sailors sailed off to the horizon. We'd been moving along nicely for about fifteen minutes with Bruce at the tiller when Dock suggested heading toward a spot up the coast.

And since no one really cared one way or another, Bruce readily agreed and gave the tiller a healthy shove. The little boat stopped altogether and floundered on the waves.

After a while, Doc asked Bruce, "Hey, I thought you were going to take us up north there?"

"I was, but the boat stopped."

After a few minutes of Three Stooges dialogue, it became clear that none of us had the slightest idea of what we were doing and that each of us had hoped that at least one of the other two did. I had an idea, however, and jumped off of the boat, swam its bow toward the direction we wanted to go in, and pulled myself back on. It worked; the wind caught the sail, and we were off again. But now that we'd "learned how to sail," Bruce grew quickly bored.

"Ya know what would be really nice right now?" he mused aloud. "Some dope. Wouldn't that be far out?"

Doc grabbed Bruce by the shoulder, looked him right in the eye, and said, "Ask and you shall receive, brother Bruce. Seek and ye shall find. Knock and it shall be opened unto you. If you have an intent heart to look, it will be there." And at that, Doc held up a bag in front of Bruce's face, and hanging on to one end, let it unroll in front of him.

Bruce recoiled in surprise and laughed with abandon. While we'd been setting things up and getting ready to set sail, Doc had stashed a pipe, two ounces of pot, and three books of matches aboard without either of us catching on.

As Doc crouched over his stash and started to fill the pipe Bruce nervously watched him and finally burst in excitement, saying, "Don't get it wet, Doc. For God's sake, don't get it wet!"

"No problem."

When the pipe was cooking, Doc reached down in the small foot-well in the bottom of the boat, held up the snorkel, and asked, "Hey, Bruce, wanna try it?"

Bruce looked puzzled for a second, and then a lightbulb went on over his head. Smiling, he fitted the mouthpiece of the snorkel between his teeth and lips and leaned so that the open end of the tube pointed toward Doc. Doc put the mouthpiece of the pipe in the snorkel's tube, sealed the leak, and blew through the bowl. Bruce's eyes bugged out like a stomped-on frog. He spat out the mouthpiece and reeled backward, coughing, gagging, and laughing all at once. I thought we were going to have a man-overboard drill for a while, but Bruce grabbed the mast and lay on the deck, giggling.

"Damn, you sure have a set of lungs for such a little fucker," he said to Doc. "Here, Baby-san, you try it."

I readied the snorkel, and Doc wound up for another shot. Halfway through the blast, I thought I was going to pass out. I wanted some slack but couldn't talk with the snorkel clamped between my teeth. Doc had given me a tremendous hit, and when I finally settled down, my entire being had entered another dimension. It seemed as if we had sailed into a sea of tranquility; the sun, the waves, the sky, and the rocking of the boat filled me completely with joy and contentment. Bruce and I made sure that Doc had a taste of his own medicine, and now, if there had been anyone there to see, I'm sure he would have wondered about a little boat carrying three naked sailors with Mona Lisa smiles. For a long time we just sat there as the boat slid quietly over the water. The boat itself had a course, a direction, and a destination, but its occupants were home—at home in each moment as it passed. There was no need to talk; we knew that we were experiencing the same thing. We had survived. We were alive. Any attempt to conceptualize or explain it would have come off as a rude attempt to gild the lily.

There were practical considerations, however, the most pressing of which was that we needed something to drink. I dove overboard and pointed the boat back toward shore. It wouldn't go exactly in the direction we wanted it to, but it was close enough. When we finally beached it, it took us a while to wade along the beach, pulling the boat back to the concession stand. We returned the boat, got some food and drink, and found a shady spot to eat, lounge, listen to music, and have a siesta. Relaxation at last. I felt like a cat on a sunny windowsill, soaking up the warmth and a gentle breeze.

Most of the day had slid by us, and even of that, we hadn't a care. We watched as one of our platoon approached the concession stand, mask, fins, and snorkel in hand. It was Tex.

He smiled in passing and hollered, "Hey, Doc, I see you guys have already used the snorkel."

We returned his smile, waved, and shot him a peace sign. Having Tex as a squad leader wasn't the worst thing that could have happened.

He took his position of responsibility pretty seriously, but he was willing, usually, to accept advice from people of lower rank but greater experience. I had the feeling that he, like Cowan, had had a strong religious element in his upbringing, because in many ways, he was innocent to the ways of the world. I could tell that he was even more shocked than I was to be in Vietnam, and he seemed to view most of the people in the platoon as strange and bizarre characters with whom he had little or no experience or connection. Yet, in spite of the weird situation we were in, he maintained his own personal integrity and values, and for this, he was appreciated and well liked.

The remaining thirty-six hours of our R & R slipped away almost as if they hadn't existed. Time, which had for months made minutes — even seconds — seem like eternities, had accelerated beyond belief. It slowed again as the sound of choppers grew louder. We were taken back to Uplift, resupplied, and shipped out again the following morning. Our platoon now had a mission of its own, and although most of us were glad to get away from our bungling CO, we were still subject to the tyranny of Second Lieutenant McDouche. Out of the frying pan, into the fire.

Our platoon of sixteen was well short of its stateside definition, but I had confidence in our ability to function. It seemed that when we were separated from the lumbering brute strength of the company, everybody made a greater effort to travel more quietly and scan the terrain more intently. We had been told there were company-sized units of NVA in the area, and we could ill afford to be both outnumbered; outfoxed. Our experience in the field paled in comparison to that of the North Vietnamese, who, on average, had years more experience than even our old-timers. We were babes in the woods whose only hope of survival was to learn as much as we could as fast as we could. Excess weight, whether frivolous items in one's pack or dysfunctional aspects of one's personality, had to go. No old prejudices could be tolerated. The aspects of one's identity that were rooted in race, color, or socioeconomic class were immediately cast aside. Deeper, more subtle sources of self-deception and separation would also eventually be laid bare and rooted out.

In our platoon, the learning was taking place at an incredible pace. In my own experience, walls had been torn down and channels of subliminal communication had opened up. The initial, sporadic trickle of unspoken information was becoming a stream, and I was beginning to realize why I had felt so vulnerable and exposed only five months ago. Creeper, for one, had seen through me, not with his eyes, but with a sixth sense of intuitive knowing that no behavioral smoke screen could deceive. The old-timers in the platoon had seen not only my weaknesses and egotism but also something else. Whatever it was, it existed beyond the bullshit of my being. It was still hidden from me, but I knew that there was something deep down in there that they liked, nurtured, and were hoping would grow.

Along with an increased sense of connection with the platoon, I was beginning to notice that there were times when I felt that we were being watched. Although I hadn't talked with anyone about it, this feeling was happening more frequently and accurately. There would be times when we were exposed while crossing an open valley, and I "knew" someone was watching us. Other times, in equally exposed positions, I would try to feel for eyes, but there would be nothing. In observing some of the old-timers, it seemed that they were getting the same feeling. I noticed that they seemed to tighten up a bit when I had felt something and ease up a bit when, evidently, there was nothing to detect.

The platoon had been on the move for several days when, while moving up a ridgeline, Tennessee turned, held a finger to his lips for me to keep quiet, and motioned with his head for me to look in the valley below us. I quickly scanned the valley and saw three dinks in black pajamas. I nodded to Tennessee to let him know that I'd spotted the VC, and we both turned to keep up with the platoon. I knew that Tennessee had adopted the belief that if we didn't mess with the VC, they, in turn, would cut us some slack whenever possible. Whether this was true seemed questionable to me, but along with most of the platoon, I certainly had no reason to want to kill anyone.

The line stopped. Damn.

I looked up the trail and saw McDouche looking at the valley with his binoculars. Sarge was beside him holding a map, trying to figure coordinates. Dismayed that McDouche had discovered the VC, we settled in to watch the show. We listened over my radio as McDouche called in a set of coordinates and requested willy-peter—white phosphorous—marking rounds. The first two rounds were wildly off target, and at the first explosion, the dinks dashed for the tree line and disappeared. A couple more rounds followed, each "walking" toward the original place where the VC had been spotted, but by now, it was a guessing game. A few hundred dollars' worth of the taxpayers' ammunition peppered the valley before McDouche realized the futility of all and called in a cease-fire. Now, not only were we embarrassed by a futile attempt to kill three VC with a half-dozen rounds of artillery, but also our presence was surely known. If the VC hadn't spotted the reflection from McDouche's binoculars and discovered our exact location, they certainly knew that we were somewhere on the high ground in the area.

Somehow, I expected swift retaliation for McDouche's artillery barrage, but as days passed, it became certain that there would be none. My thinking was still Americanized to the degree that I expected them to respond as we probably would have. I kept forgetting that Charles did not fight the war emotionally and would wait till he had the upper hand.

Our patrol continued for two weeks without a sign of the enemy. I was beginning to get a sense of the variety of terrain in the Central Highlands. Although, for the most part, it was covered with thick, three-level canopy, we had moved through swampy areas and places where trees seemed to stop growing at twenty or thirty feet. Within each of these general types, there were smaller, unusual areas with unique plant and animal life. One place seemed to be the home of fire ants, which would shower all over anyone who was unlucky enough to bump an overhanging branch of a tree that they had claimed as theirs. Their stings were painful enough to cause even the most hard-core GI to strip on the spot in an effort to get them out of his shirt. Another place was a niche that seemed to be the land of the giant centipedes.

During a break, one of the guys on point spotted one of them, drowned it in insect repellant, and left it beside the trail for the rest of us to see. It was six inches long, black on top and orange underneath, with a huge set of pincers protruding from its head. A man from our platoon woke us up one night, screaming, when one of these grabbed hold of his cheek just below his eye and refused to let go. He was dusted off, and we never saw him again.

Now, however, we were traveling through a rain forest with relatively light vegetation at ground level. The place gave me the creeps. The traveling was easy, but I felt that we could easily be spotted and were prone to ambush. Tennessee was cutting point, with Creeper pulling slack, and through the luck of the draw, I was behind Creeper. Although a less-experienced point man probably would have been seduced into trying to make good time, I noticed that Tennessee was as cautious and alert as a cat on the prowl. He moved slowly, scanning everything with extra care and would occasionally stop and listen. Creeper, too, was tight as a frog's ass, not only scanning intently, but also keeping his M16 pointed in the direction of his gaze. Feeling that they had things under control at eye level, I spent extra time checking the treetops for snipers and lookouts.

The trail had long stretches of relatively level ground, but just before we came over a small rise, my peripheral vision caught unusual movement ahead, in the trees to our right. Tennessee and Creeper stopped and squatted in unison. Tennessee turned and signaled me to get down, and I passed the command to the man behind me. Lying on my stomach in the middle of the trail, I watched Tennessee intently, flicked the safety off on my M16, and unbuttoned my shirt pockets for quick access to the fragmentation grenades I carried there. Five seconds passed. Sure that the platoon had taken cover, Tennessee slowly raised his head over the rise. He continued to rise very slowly, very smoothly, leaned his cheek on the stock of his rifle, and took aim. One second, one shot later, he ducked down again, turned, and for an instant looked me right in the eye. An icy-cold chill ran through my body.

Seconds — or was it minutes? years? — passed, and Tennessee again peeked over the rise.

"They're headin' off to the left — through the bush," he said.

McCoy had already worked his way up to point and ordered, "Get on line, we're going to make a sweep."

"Okay, move out."

The platoon moved slowly, at first, down the steep embankment on our left. In training, we would have kept sight of the fellow soldiers to our left and right, but in the jungle, even as light as it was, I quickly lost sight of everyone. I slowed to make sure that I wasn't getting ahead of them and, after a few seconds of near panic, heard someone holler that we were to regroup on the trail.

When I got back to the trail, McCoy was already debriefing Tennessee.

"There was a squad of them — NVA, for sure. They had uniforms and the whole bit. I had to shoot. We were going to run right into them."

Tennessee paused for a bit, but he continued when he saw McCoy's probing stare. He knew what he was going to ask.

"I got the first one for sure. I saw his shirt puff out when I hit him. Other than that, I don't know. They split so fast, I didn't have time to get off more shots."

I strongly suspected that Tennessee could have wasted at least three other NVA in the column. There would have been an instant of bewilderment as their point man collapsed, leaving the next in line vulnerable to Tennessee's old-country-boy sharpshooting, but he held his fire. One shot was sufficient; one dead man was enough to get us out of a bind.

McCoy put his hand on Tennessee's shoulder. It seemed to be a gesture that combined congratulations and sympathy. He nodded slowly for a second, looked around, and said, "All right, saddle up. We're movin' out."

He turned to move back to his place in line, took a step, and stopped. He bent over and picked up two grenades that had fallen out of my shirt pockets.

"These yours?"

I nodded.

"You'd better get your shit together, Ulander. These here moth-erfuckers coulda easy been down the trail somewhere with a trip wire on 'em."

I nodded again to acknowledge that I'd heard him, but I felt too foolish to answer. He was justifiably pissed, but in control. Seeing that the matter didn't need any further discussion, he turned and walked back to his position in the center of the platoon.

Under other circumstances, a mistake of that magnitude would have sent me into a spiral of depression and self-doubt, but here, there was no time for regrets. Ten minutes on the trail, and what would have been a debilitating emotional storm was displaced by the constant and urgent need to be in the present. It allowed me to get some emotional distance from the events of the day and to recharge energetically before reviewing them.

When we were setting up that night, Tennessee was quick to pick up on my distress and reassured me that it was no big deal. He told me that I should just tighten up a tad. "Keep on truckin'," he said. While we were talking, I noticed that he would sometimes lapse — seemingly involuntarily — into what was referred to as the "thousand-yard stare." He'd say a few words, then shift his eyes slightly away from me. If his body hadn't remained there, I could have sworn that he had left. In those long moments, it seemed that, for the most part, he was oblivious to his surroundings, and I doubted that he could see or hear anything. I also noticed that when he "left," the warm, nurturing energy that was usually so evident in his presence disappeared. During one of his lapses, I looked into his eyes and had the disturbing feeling that I was falling into a bottomless pit. My first reflex was to shake him, to try to bring him back somehow, but a thought bubbled up from inside me that said, *Don't; he's okay; this needs to happen.* Responding to the strangely intrusive thought, I waited patiently for his return and, while waiting, had the feeling that Tennessee was healing in some way. To me, the whole pro-cess was awe-inspiring, deep, and far beyond anything I could relate to, yet I trusted it and felt that Tennessee, too, had faith in it.

Later, while on guard, I reran the mental movie of the moment when Tennessee had caught my eye after firing up the NVA's point man. The images came clearly to mind, and I realized that what I had seen in his eyes was fear. I had a strong feeling that his fear wasn't for his life, in the sense that he was afraid of being killed in a firefight, but rather something in him feared the consequences of his act. Surely, all the cultural conditioning told us that in war, killing was necessary, totally justifiable, or even honorable, but it seemed that in that instant, something deep in Tennessee's being knew that this wasn't true. His eyes had revealed the shock and horror of a person who suddenly realized the depth of his dilemma — kill or be killed, with neither offering a viable way out. Yet, I knew that Tennessee would never give up his job at point. He knew that the platoon's survival depended on his skill, and he would rather sacrifice himself and his personal future than give the impossible task to someone else.

After three more days in the field, we were extracted and returned to Uplift. Once again, we made a beeline to Linda's. I could now see why there had been such a warm welcome and sense of reunion when we were there before. Our future, she knew, wasn't that certain. She offered the ritual smoke, and in minutes, I was again a mute witness to the mellow, strangely domestic scene. Katy came in after a while, followed by two wide-eyed baby-sans, and Linda, who was always clearly in charge, allowed the little ones to be there, provided they would be on their best behavior. For kids of four and six, they were remarkably well behaved, by American standards; only occasionally did they talk quietly to each other. Slowly they made their way across the room and, softly, like a couple cats, they climbed up on my lap. They seemed quite content to sit quietly, and after just a gentle pat or two to tell them it was okay, they leaned against my chest as if I were a long-lost uncle. Drifting along on the smoke's euphoria, I mused about how I'd always really liked kids and how — somehow — kids always knew it. Culture, race, and language, evidently, were no barriers to this type of communication.

Leaning against the mud wall of Linda's house, I mused at what a sanctuary it had become for us. Amid the war, it was a place of peace.

The very atmosphere of the place hummed with a deep and tranquil vibe, deeper even than the jungle at night. The source of this energy was truly mysterious, yet watching Linda and her silent sister, Katy, it became apparent that they resonated it with ease. Linda was the more active of the two, but there was clarity to her thoughts and crispness in her demeanor that I knew (from watching Speed and Doc Mock) had its roots in stillness. She pounced on signs of arrogance and unkindness like a tiger on a goat. We weren't the only troops from Uplift who visited Linda's, and it was clear that she had considerable experience with the rather pathetic and shallow American value system. Newbies fresh from the States were occasionally shocked when, while bragging about having a Corvette at home or about kicking someone's ass in a barroom brawl, she'd blast them without mercy, saying, "How you gonna act, dude? How you gonna be? You in Linda's house now, you in Vietnam. You betta get your shit together."

After such a severe reprimand, the offender would usually sit for a moment looking dazed and confused, then look to Speed or Doc for support. Receiving none—zero, zip—they'd sit stunned and humiliated for the rest of the visit and either avoid Linda in the future or grant her the respect she deserved. During these or any other goings-on at Linda's, Katy would stand at one end of the room with her hands folded over her midriff, watching with unruffled serenity, neither offended nor surprised. Though Linda dealt with disruptive influences with much less slack than we granted each other, she was amazingly adept at interacting with people, such as me, who were shy and gentle. By allowing the kids to sit in my lap, I had no doubt she approved of this less-than-macho behavior.

The following morning, we were told to report to the bleachers to be briefed for our next mission. Our colonel had gathered the whole company and explained yet another harebrained adventure that we were about to take part in. According to him, there was a large valley in our territory that was crawling with NVA, and we were going to join forces with the air force in order to wipe them out. Three platoons from our company were going to be positioned at one end of the valley in order to prevent escape from that direction, and our platoon was going to cover the narrow bottleneck at the other end. A precisely synchronized orchestration between the army and air force would start with Phantom jets, which would pepper the wide end of the valley with cluster bombs of CS gas that was intended to confuse and disorient the NVA. The three platoons at that end would then sweep through the valley, wiping out most of the enemy and forcing the rest to fall right into the trap, which was our platoon at the other end. I had to admit, it sounded great on paper, if you thought that the NVA went around with their heads in their asses.

We were herded to supply and issued the army's new and improved compact gas mask, the M17A1, which none of us had seen before. From there we were marched, reluctantly, to the chopper pads. We waited for the rest of the company to be flown into position, boarded a sortie of Hueys, and were off. A surprisingly short flight brought us in sight of the valley, which appeared exactly as shown on the map. Our chopper was the last to land, and as we were just about to touch down, a choking cloud of CS gas filled the helicopter, causing our noses to run, our skin to burn, and our to eyes water. Our pilot, who didn't even have a gas mask, must have flown out by memory. By the time I got my gas mask on, I could barely see. Although I could now breathe freely, a little flap inside the mask that was supposed to separate the eyes from the nose-and-mouth section of the mask had twisted itself up, causing my goggles to fog with each breath. We moved out at once, and I strained to follow the blurry green blob in front of me.

Either the air force had been early or we were late. Regardless, we were off to a bungling start. We moved several hundred yards from the hilltop where we had landed into a saddle, where, any time now, crazed NVA were supposed to come running wildly up the ridge to meet us. We stopped for a few minutes, and one of the guys tested the air and found that the area was free of gas. At last, I could take off my mask and see again. I heard a pair of Cobras, but couldn't see them through the high trees. Suddenly they opened up with their miniguns, blasting the shit out of the area just ahead of us.

They were way too close for comfort and drifting behind us.

McDouche looked at me in panic and hollered, "Pop smoke!"

I grabbed a smoke grenade from my belt, pulled the pin, and flipped it onto the ground. The smoke seemed to cling to the ground.

"Won't work. They'll never see it," McDouche hollered again. "You're going to have to climb a tree."

I threw off my pack, stuck a purple smoke grenade in my shirt pocket, and got a boost up the biggest tree in the area. The climbing was easy, and as I got close to the top I saw the Cobras just overhead and slightly behind us. They let loose with another long burst from their miniguns as I struggled to wedge the grenade between two branches. I looked at the little cloth patch on the bottom of the grenade, trying desperately to remember which end blew out. Normally you weren't this close to a grenade when it went off—you just pulled the pin and tossed it. Suddenly the roar from the miniguns convinced me that it didn't matter. The Cobra was so close overhead that I would see the sparkling waterfall of spent brass pouring from their guns. I pulled the pin and let it fly. The grenade blew the square patch off the bottom and scorched my face. I bounced from branch to branch and landed on the ground with a thud. Luckily, I wasn't hurt except for a purple face, a singed forehead, and a few paint chips in my eyes. While Doc was checking me out, I heard over the radio that the Cobras had spotted the smoke and agreed to back off.

I couldn't help but chuckle at myself as we moved down the ridge to the valley. From the looks of my shirt, I must have been quite a sight till Doc cleaned up my face. We set up in a line across our end of the valley and waited. No sign of the NVA. In the morning, we packed up and moved farther into the valley, met up with the rest of the company, and set up again. I was almost certain that we would see neither hide nor hair of Charles, and I was equally certain that it was June 11, the day I was to be extracted for R & R.

It was pouring rain, and while sitting under a poncho, I was surprised to find myself really bummed for the first time since I'd been in country. It wasn't that I hadn't been sad from time to time, but until now, the emotion had only been passing. Now it was as if the flood-gates had been opened, and months of grief poured in. McDouche had refused to call for my extraction because of the rain, and I wondered when and how I was ever going to get out.

My indulgence in self-pity had dangerously limited my perception of my surroundings. I hadn't even noticed that Wilbur and Tennessee had quietly moved in on my log and were sitting on either side of me. Although I hadn't said a thing, they picked up on my feelings as clearly as if I'd screamed out loud. They were doing a great job of cheering me up. I had seen people help each other out of sticky emotional places many times since I'd been in Vietnam, but this was my first time on the receiving end. I was amazed how a little sympathy, a few kind words, and a little humor transformed my sadness into gratitude in a matter of minutes. Surely these were the finest friends I'd ever had.

I heard the platoon leader from one of the other platoons request a new M16 for one of his men, whose rifle had been damaged on the mission.

Immediately Tennessee started plotting. "When that chopper brings out a new 16, dash over there and jump on."

"But shit, Tennessee," I said. "McDouche still hasn't authorized me to leave."

"What the fuck? It's your R & R, ain't it? By the time he figures out what happened, you'll be gone. The pilots don't care; they won't even know what's happenin'. No sweat."

The more he talked, the better it sounded, and by the time we heard a Huey approaching, I was convinced. It started to come in about forty yards from our position, and even before it touched down, I was almost there. A man from the other platoon met it and exchanged rifles with the crew chief, and as planned, I jumped on. No one batted an eye, and I settled back for the ride, not exactly sure where it would land.

Luck was with me; it landed at Uplift. After processing through headquarters, I was given a pass, got on a jeep to Phu Cat Air Force Base, and caught a plane to Cam Ranh Bay. The army offered several R

& R destinations, including Thailand, Hong Kong, Hawaii, and Japan, but I chose Australia, because of its reputation for being the home of pretty and friendly women. In less than twenty-four hours, I was there. I could have sworn that my five days of R & R had been less than two when I found myself boarding a plane for the return flight. Sydney and its women had lived up to their reputation, but the whirlwind trip had given new meaning to the old adage about time flying.

As the jeep bounced its way back to Uplift, I tried to account for the five days. One had been spent wandering around the city, trying to get oriented, and two had been at a small airport out of town, where I'd managed to do a little civilian-style parachuting. The first three nights were spent in clubs downtown, which seemed to weigh anchor after my fourth drink and head out to the rolling swells of the open sea. These nights were filled with blurry, swirling images of faces, rock-and-roll bands, and car rides to other clubs with newfound Aussie friends, but somehow, before dawn, the tide had always washed me back to my hotel. I also remembered a pretty girl with large eyes and curly brown hair, who had appeared across the table from me in one of the night-clubs. Ah yes, the last two days, when this sweet, gentle lady convinced me that I didn't really need to stay in a hotel — that she had plenty of room at her place. I'd felt like an orphan who had found a home at last. But then the clock ran out, and it was time for my coach to turn back into a pumpkin. My olive-drab, four-wheel-drive coach made a sharp turn, and I was back at Uplift.

As we drove down "Main Street," I was surprised to see a couple of the guys from the platoon. Tennessee and Bruce were trying to talk to Tex, who, at first glance, appeared to be sick. He was sitting on the steps of one of the hootches with his head on his knees, and as I approached, I could see that he was shaking. When he lifted his head, I could see that he was totally distraught. His face was red as a beet, his nose was running, and tears were streaming down his face.

"Why did he have to die? I told him not to die, didn't I, Tennessee? And he died anyway." His face contorted in anguish, and he took a deep breath before he could ask Tennessee the inevitable, impossible question. "What are we doin' here, Tennessee? Why'd we have to come all the way over here just to get fucked up?"

I watched for a moment as Tennessee tended the grief-stricken man. It looked like Tennessee was familiar with this kind of duty. When Tex was overcome with a wave of anger and grief, Tennessee would back off a bit and let him roar away. But after the wave had passed, he'd move in again and try to offer sympathy and support. Bruce seemed to sense that the situation was being handled as well as possible, so he got up and led me away by the arm.

"What's happenin', man? Good to see you're back."

I was glad for the welcome but wanted to know what had happened.

"We got hit a couple days after you left. We got ambushed in a little valley, and it turned into a real nasty little firefight. They kept peckin' away at us till Heidigger ... 'member Heidigger?"

I nodded, remembering a tall blond kid who had been with us for about a month.

"He opened up with the 60. He was really smokin', but one of their snipers picked him off, got him right square in the head. They don't like that 60, ya know, but when Sam took over, they backed off. I looked next to me when the shit started to lighten up, and I saw Tex rolling Cowan over. He was breathing for a while, but he was shot up pretty bad. And he just slipped away right in Tex's arms. He's takin' this all real hard — Tex is — being squad leader and all. I think he feels responsible, but, shit, you know there wasn't anything he could do."

"How's the rest of the guys?" I asked. "Is everybody else all right?"

"Nah." Bruce had a wild-eyed look as he remembered the hellish afternoon. "Gomez got hit in the shoulder. Doc said there were some shattered bones in there but thought he'd probably make it."

Bruce and I kept on walking aimlessly toward the perimeter, and as we passed another hootch, I caught sight of a few other guys from the platoon. There too, some of the guys had buckled and were obviously grieving, but no one was called a pussy; no one was told to buck up. The one law agreed on by the men in the platoon was in full effect: everyone was allowed to be. The integrity and honesty of who you were and how you responded were honored. If you cried, fine. If you didn't, fine. Neither response made you less of a man.

According to Bruce's unfolding tale, the guys really functioned at the junction—no fuckups, no foul-ups. But ambushes happen. No one expected anyone to spot camouflaged gooks four hundred yards away, and when you're drawing fire, it's going to take time to respond. In the meantime, men are hit, and some die. We kept walking. The physical movement seemed to parallel our emotional movement. Feel the rage— keep walking. Feel the grief—keep walking. Now as we approached the perimeter, I felt a calm detachment starting to settle in.

We went to the nearest bunker and leaned against the sandbags in the shade. The lifers had said that we weren't supposed to leave the company area and that we weren't supposed to be out on the bunkers during the day, but neither Bruce nor I had a moment's hesitation. He pulled a bomber from his shirt pocket and handed it to me with a smile. A few tokes later, we were back into the mildly euphoric present-centeredness we'd trained ourselves to associate with the weed and were grateful for the relief, the company, and to be alive. The after-noon slid by as Bruce informed me about the details of the week I'd missed, and I told him about my R & R. We headed back to the company area to get evening chow and were met by Captain Speed and a black dude named Larry from Charlie Company.

Larry was a short-timer who had only twenty days left in coun-try, and as was often the case, they'd found a place for him to work in the rear. It had become an unofficial policy to pull short-timers from the field, because troops who had otherwise been excellent in the field would get increasingly nervous as the end of their tour neared. Larry had found himself doing clerical work for Bravo Company's CO, and up till now, he had been content and satisfied with the job.

Speed herded us into the nearest hootch, turned to Larry, and said, "Tell these guys what ya told me."

Larry looked around to make sure he wasn't being watched and said, "When you guys lost that gunner in your last firefight, I heard what happened, but check this out. That ain't the way the ol' man tells the story. He made me write a report that said that Heidigger was wounded in the firefight and was groggy as he tried to make his way to the medevac chopper, and that he stumbled and fell into the tail rotor. Dig it. Here your boy was shot in the head tryin' to keep Charlie off your asses, and they're gonna send a report back to the world that says he died a fuckup."

To me, it didn't make sense, so I asked Speed, "What difference does it make to the army? Why would it be to anyone's advantage to file a bogus report?"

"You guys don't know how the game works, do ya?" Speed replied. "Let me clue you in. The last time I was home, they were making a big deal about the kill ratio, and it sounded jive to me. They said we were killin' a hell of a lot more of their guys than they were of us. Follow me?"

"So far," I responded, "but if that's so, it isn't happening here."

"Exactly. It has to do with money, support, and whether or not they'll ever pull out of here. If the lifers can snow the people back home into believing we're winning this thing, it'll go on forever. If the report went back tellin' the truth about Heidigger, he would be a KIA, but with a little imagination, he's only been wounded in action—statistically, a different picture altogether."

As the significance of what he said took hold, I felt a powerful rage well up from deep inside. McDouche was looking for rank over our dead bodies, our first sergeant was selling our rations on the black market for big bucks, and now the old man was willing to lie about how we died to keep the whole damned thing going. I doubted that the old man was acting independently—he had no reason to, as an individual—which left the likelihood that he was acting on the orders from somebody higher up.

Bruce was about to lose it. "What can we do, Speed?"

"These motherfuckers forget that everybody here has an M16, and I'm gonna write a letter and put it on the ol' man's desk. I'm gonna tell him that if his report goes out, he's one dead motherfucker."

That action of some sort was necessary was beyond doubt, but what bothered me about Speed's plan was that he was not the sort of man to make idle threats. His training as a Green Beret and his personal cunning would have allowed him to do away with the CO without detection, but I sincerely hoped that things would never go that far.

That night on bunker guard, I heard that Speed had, indeed, left a note on the CO's desk, and I was greatly relieved when Larry showed up at our bunker first thing in the morning. He told us that the CO had had him change the report and even had him take it to the mail room at once. Although I understood Speed's motivation and frustration, I was glad that the matter had been settled peacefully. We had trouble enough with the VC and NVA without turning on each other.

The company, once again, gathered behind the hootches to prepare for a new mission. Evidently it was time for our old CO to be cycled to the rear for the rest of his tour, because we were introduced to our new CO, Captain Quick. One glance at him, and I knew we were in for some changes. He was tall and muscular, without being bulky, and looked extremely alert and confident. He watched us like a hawk as we stuffed our packs, obviously gauging the quality of the men he was to command. While he surveyed our platoon, I wasn't the least surprised to see a Green Beret patch on his sleeve. I knew from talking to Speed that Green Berets were given a great deal more training in guerilla warfare than most officers and enlisted men were. I figured that even though our new CO was probably more gung ho, at least there was a good chance that with his training, he would also be more competent.

Once again our platoon boarded a sortie of Hueys and headed to parts unknown. We landed on a hilltop, moved quickly into a saddle, and started climbing a long ridge. For hours we climbed steadily uphill, and from the information I overheard on the radio, it was clear that our new CO was in precise command. Although we had been traveling through fairly dense jungle, I heard him call McDouche on the radio and order the fourth and fifth men in our platoon to shake hands. They did, and he responded that he had visual contact. I was simultaneously unnerved and impressed. I recalled how, months before, Speed had told me with confidence that the NVA usually knew where we were. I was beginning to see how they'd been able to do what, to me, had initially seemed impossible. With lookouts posted on the high ground throughout the highlands, they could easily monitor the movement of our helicopters, and patient waiting and observation would tell them the rest.

Our long day was about to end as we neared the top of the highest mountain in the area. An explosion punctuated the otherwise silent day, and moments later, I overheard radio messages that confirmed its source. Speed had discovered a booby trap waiting at our destination and, with permission, had blown it in place. I wondered how many people might have been killed if some of the guys in our platoon hadn't opted for a second tour. Booby traps were almost impossible to spot before it was too late, and I doubted that anyone besides Speed or Tennessee could have done it. Speed had again lived up to his reputation, and it was becoming more and more clear why the lifers had refused to take his last stripe, which would have required him to be extracted from the field and forced to spend the rest of his tour in the rear.

We were ordered to stay on the hilltop the following day, which was great, as we needed to party, but we were on the move again the morning after. For the next few days, it seemed that our platoon was moving farther and farther away from the company. No one but McDouche knew where we were going, and as usual, he was in one hell of a hurry to get there. He was back to his old tricks: "We haven't got time to set up; we'll just have to make do." In the middle of one particularly soggy, rainy night (it's hard to stay dry when you aren't even given enough time to make a lean-to out of your poncho), I heard a muffled thump in the distance and recognized it as the sound of our howitzers. The whistling round that followed had an unusual ring to it, and seconds later, I realized why. The damned thing landed a few hundred yards from our position with a deafening roar. Three more thumps and three more whistling rounds, and I was nearly paralyzed by fear. They exploded progressively closer, and amid some shouting and profanities, I heard McDouche on the radio. He called the rear; they denied doing any shelling. There were three more thumps and three more explosions that sounded like they were trying to zero in on us. The rear called McDouche and said that they had located the source of the artillery and that it was the ARVNs. The guys within earshot of my radio were grumbling "those sorry motherfuckers," but at last the shelling stopped.

As my nervous system struggled to return to normal, I wondered what had happened. There were only two plausible explanations: either McDouche had us in the wrong grid square again, or the ARVNs didn't know what they were doing. It was a toss-up. Exhaustion took over, and I fell asleep.

In the morning, we were back on the trail, and for several more days, we slid through miles of jungle. In time for resupply, we broke into a clearing on the edge of a village. Opposite us, three VC disappeared into the tree line. McDouche ordered our squad to do an on-line sweep across the clearing and into the trees, and as we approached the opposite side, I saw that, for me, the VC were only part of the problem. When we had organized our line, I had wound up on the line's extreme left, and as we crossed the clearing, my position was putting me on a collision course with a huge water buffalo. Water buffalo were usually docile, but like many domesticated animals, they recognized their owners, knew their territory, and could identify outsiders. The closer we got, the clearer it was that, to this beast, I was definitely an outsider. Furthermore, the village was occupied, which put me in a double bind. On the one hand, it would have been major trouble to be responsible for shooting one of their livestock, but on the other, I wasn't all that fond of being gored or trampled to death. When I got within about thirty yards of him, he lowered his horns and started pawing the ground, and in desperation, I hollered to our interpreter, who was Vietnamese and hopefully more familiar with these animals.

"What do I do if he charges?"

Our interpreter laughed as if I'd asked the most ignorant question he'd ever heard and replied, "Shoot it."

My M16, which at other times had seemed like such a formidable weapon, felt about as worthless as a toy gun loaded with suction-cup-tipped darts. It was deadly against humans, but I doubted that it was much of a big game rifle.

I pressed on, and the beast continued his menacing display, wagging his head and stomping, until it finally gave way and moved away from me. After the sweep had been completed, we were allowed to rejoin the platoon, who had watched my dilemma with great amusement. They were all laughing and giving me a hard time. Only later did they tell me that Sgt. Sam had me covered all the way with his M60. At the beast's first threatening move, he had it in his sights, and he had kept it there until the buffalo finally turned tail and strolled off.

Our resupply arrived as scheduled, complete with a surprise from the "spoons," who served chow in the rear. They had sent us some gristly Swiss steak and their famous twice-boiled mixed vegetables. When we opened the steaming thermal box of watered-down tomato sauce in the blazing afternoon heat, the chow line evaporated into thin air. Bruce came up with a great idea, however, and suggested to McCoy that our interpreter rouse the villagers and offer them our unwanted meal. A few brave and probably very hungry kids appeared at first, and soon most of the people in the village joined in. They smiled and bowed to express their gratitude, ate, and disappeared into their houses.

# THE VALLEY OF THE SHADOW

WE WERE ABOUT TO HEAD OUT WHEN A SMALL BOY RAN UP TO MCCOY with a bag containing several unexploded M79 rounds. Others followed, each with a small cache that he or she had hidden away. We were happy to see the growing pile of munitions, including grenades, rifle rounds, and two dud 81mm mortar rounds. To us, the stuff was worthless, but the NVA were adept at transforming it into deadly and effective booby traps. The pile represented several lives and many lost limbs. While McCoy was on the radio calling for assistance in disposing of it, two old papa-sans trotted up with a 105mm howitzer round suspended from a bamboo carrying pole. This alone could have wiped out half of our platoon.

While stuffing my pack, I overheard McCoy getting his ass chewed out by some lifer in the rear. He was reminded in no uncertain terms that we had not been authorized to give our food away to the villagers. The lifer also groused about the logistical problem of removing the ammunition, as well as the time delay this would cause, which would screw up the execution of our next mission. It was outrageous that the man could complain about having to dispose of the cache, which was as deadly as anything we could have captured from the NVA. When I looked across the perimeter to see how McCoy was taking it, I saw that he was holding the handset of the radio at arm's length, laughing, and shaking his head in disbelief. His years of experience had taught him to see the humor in the ignorance, gall, and absurd behavior of our superiors in the rear.

I was surprised at the effectiveness of our accidental exchange. Our initial presence in the village had been met with closed doors and shuttered windows, but the simple act of sharing our food had eased their fears and opened a line of communication. Their response to our openness and trust had been greater than anything we might have been able to solicit through intimidation, arm-twisting, or political rhetoric. The war had placed the villagers in an impossible, no-win situation. First the VC would arrive and steal their crops and anything else of value, and then GIs would storm their homes looking for VC. Being unarmed, their survival depended on their ability to placate the current bully on the block, and I realized that their display of preference required real courage.

A chopper flew in to haul the munitions back to the rear, and once again we disappeared into the jungle. I continued with most of the disciplines that I'd developed early on. Usually, at the start of a new mission, I would have to force myself to repeat the mechanical motions—look down the trail, left, and right; scan the trees for snipers. After a time, I noticed that when my attention was completely focused in the present, the pain in my body from carrying a gargantuan pack would seem to fade away. This phenomenon alone was enough to reinforce my behavior, yet I seemed to be developing other sensitivities that I felt would increase my chances for survival. For increasingly long periods of time, my thoughts would fade to the degree that sensory information would flow through my mind without requiring the usual internal reflection and commentary. I was beginning to realize that while my thoughts were on hold, my ability to process sensory data was smoother, clearer, and more continuous, and it was also during these periods that a door to intuitive impressions would, at times, open. Slowly, the feel of a place or situation was taking priority over my thoughts or analysis.

My habit of imagining what it would be like without a body was another strange, admittedly morbid, ritual that I continued to practice before going to sleep every night. Lying on my back, I'd try to imagine what it would be like without eyes to see, ears to hear, or a body to feel. At first, I found the practice was relaxing and refreshing, but as time went on, images would appear out of the darkness. Toys and scenes from my childhood would float by, and geometric forms would change and grow. On one occasion, I saw a clear image of myself as a five-year-old, wearing a cheesy cowboy vest and hat and brandishing twin cap guns. None of it struck me as being particularly meaningful, but it was entertaining enough to encourage me to continue.

As we pushed on, I noticed that my attitude toward the jungle itself had changed. What once had been an alien and hostile environment was now wondrous and gentle. At first, it had appeared to be a confusing conglomeration of individual plants, animals, and insects, all competing to survive, but gradually I began to see it as a single, huge living entity whose parts came into being, grew, and died willingly to support and perpetuate the whole. A tree provided the shade that allowed other layers of vegetation to grow, and it was the home of birds and insects and the trellis on which vines could climb to reach the light, and later, in death, that tree supported the growth of moss and fungi and became food for termites until, inevitably, its rotting mass produced nourishment for other plants and, perhaps, for saplings that had grown from its own seeds. In the jungle, the death of an individual part was a necessary and functional occurrence that maintained the prolific life of the whole. And then there was the war. It seemed that within the beautiful and subtle harmony of this being was a disease; a blight; a sour, dissonant note in the great vibrant chord.

We were out only a week when we came across another village. Word was out that we were on a MEDCAP, which meant that we were to provide medical help to the villagers. After some haggling with local officials, we were told to set up in the schoolhouse. McDouche ordered our squad to set up a listening post along the road at one end of the small village while McDouche, the lieutenant, and their RTO set up in one room of the now-vacant two-room schoolhouse. I gathered that we would be there several days, a welcome rest after days of humping the boonies. Tennessee, Bruce, Orville, Sgt. Sam, and I found a shady place about fifty yards off the road and prepared for an afternoon of lounging and getting stoned. We strung hammocks between trees and were digging for munchies in our bags when a twelve-year-old boy, dressed only in a pair of gym shorts, approached us cautiously from the road. I had some reservations about him, but he seemed harmless enough.

"Hi, GIs," he said as he walked up to us. "What you doing here?"

"We're on a MEDCAP," Bruce replied, trusting him instantly. "Do you know what that is?"

"You bet. Where's *bác sĩ* [the doctor]?" he asked.

By this time, he was sitting down with us, eyeing our stash and the pipe that was lying on the poncho liner. I was amazed at how well he spoke English and how knowledgeable he seemed about GIs. He said his name was Tom. He hung around for half an hour before asking where our lifers were.

"Oh, they're up at the school," Bruce said.

"You give me one can of Cs, and I'll do lifer check," Tom suggested.

"What do you mean by 'lifer check'?"

"You give me a can of Cs, and I'll sit up by the road there and let you know if any lifers are comin'."

Bruce was laughing as he dug in his pack. Tom definitely had us pegged. Finding a can, he threw it to Tom, who stationed himself strategically by the road. We relaxed even more, freed of the threat of being surprised by McDouche, and got out a radio and a deck of cards. The village had a creepy feel to it, as none of the villagers had been around to check us out, though somehow we felt secure. It was great to have a chance to rest and compare notes after weeks in the field, which allowed only limited conversation. Time was sliding by peacefully, and every time I looked to see if Tom was keeping watch, I'd see him leaning against a coconut tree, fully aware of anyone who was on the road.

Three hours had passed before Tom came running to our position, waving his arms and shouting, "Somebody coming! Somebody coming! Maybe a lifer—better check it out."

Sam got up to take a look, and when he got to the road, we could tell that it was cool. Soon, he and Tom were heading back to our position, with Sam playfully mussing up Tom's hair. It looked like we had a new friend.

When they arrived, Bruce thought to quiz Tom about the situation in the village.

"Before, *beaucoup* VC here," Tom replied. "But when GIs come, VC *đi đi* [leave]."

This confirmed the creepy feeling I had about the place, and Bruce continued his line of questioning.

"VC come back?"

"Yeah," Tom replied, "but no sweat. When GI come, they *đi đi*, when you leave, they come back. They don't want to mess with GIs. No need."

I saw Sam nodding, followed the logic in the tactics of the VC and concluded that we would be okay. The path of least resistance for them would be to put the squeeze on the village when we were gone and to simply leave when we arrived. They had no desire to start a fight with a well-equipped platoon of GIs, and they couldn't booby-trap the place without endangering the villagers. It seemed that we were home free — for a while.

The following morning, Tom arrived bright and early. Knowing that we were going to be in the village for a while, he clued us in on the local mama-san, who ran a small shop.

"If you want buy something from Mama-san, give me money. I buy for you. Mama-san number one rip-off," he said, openly angry at Mama-san's behavior. "She always get *beaucoup* money from GIs and give *tí tí* [a little]."

Of all the problems we might have had, we weren't about to haggle for a few pennies with Mama-san, but Tom was adamant, so we took up a collection and sent him shopping. He returned with several packages of noodles, a few Cokes, a couple sweatbands, cigarettes, and rolling papers that he'd purchased for us at truly bargain-basement prices. Sam broke out the squad's stash of weed, and I started rolling it up.

Seeing what was going on, Tom asked, "You roll one for me, okay, Baby-san?"

I looked up from my work to see what sort of reaction the squad had to his request, and seeing that they thought that it would be all right, I handed Tom a number.

"Thanks for the jay, Baby-san," he said. "Can I use this?"

He was in my pack, unsnapping the pouch that contained the "long whip" antenna for my radio. The antenna was made up of several hollow sections that fit together, like the pieces of a fishing pole. He took out one of the larger sections and, with permission, stuck his joint in the tube. He asked Sgt. Sam for a light and then strutted around our card game looking like a cross between Toulouse-Lautrec and Patton.

Bruce, who had been eyeing the coconuts that were ripening in the village, asked Tom if he could buy us some.

"No sweat," Tom replied. "I get some for you."

He found some tall grass, grabbed a handful, and twisted it into a crude piece of rope. Standing at the base of a forty-foot coconut tree, he wound the "rope" in a figure eight around his ankles and knotted the loose end. Tied in this way, his feet could move no farther than twelve inches apart.

"Hey, GI, you tell nobody, okay? Or Papa-san will beat my ass." He quickly inchwormed his way up the tree. Sitting in the crown of the tree, he twisted off several choice coconuts and then shinnied down in a flash. He seemed to know that we were already in another fix: how to get the nut out of the larger, tough husk. We would have managed, eventually, but he saved us the trouble by grabbing Sam's machete and with a deft whack, buried the knife into the nut's husk. He squatted, with his feet on the handle and flat side of the machete to pin it to the ground and rolled the nut toward himself, peeling off a section of the husk in the process. Once he'd removed the husk, he tapped the nut all over with the back of the machete to loosen the meat, and split it in half. We were all impressed by our new little buddy's skill and agility. If it had been possible, we would have brought him with us in the boonies, but luckily for him, he was too young to be in either army.

A call on the radio ended what I'd hoped would be a day of R & R. McDouche requested that Bruce and I report to the schoolhouse. I brought my radio, as ordered, and we headed out, wondering what was to be the nature of our duty. Approaching the school, we ran into Doc, who was waltzing around with a five-year-old village kid on his shoulders. The little boy, who had a huge red flower stuck behind each ear, seemed to be thoroughly enjoying Doc's clowning. As we got closer, we could hear that Doc was singing as well to the lyrics of the Beatles' "Love is All You Need." I doubted that the kid understood the lyrics to the song, but he seemed to feel their meaning nevertheless.

Our irrepressible medic followed Bruce and me right up to the steps of the school and continued to sing until McDouche shot him a disapproving look and started giving us orders. Doc Mock knew that his position as the platoon's medic offered him some protection from harsh treatment from the lifers, and he constantly used his leverage to try to pry McDouche from his rigid and humorless ways.

We were ordered to make the rounds through the village and let it be known that medical help was available, if somewhat limited. In spite of what Tom had told us about the VC, the shuttered doors and windows of most of the houses in the village created an atmosphere of mutual fear and suspicion, and so, before leaving the schoolhouse, I chambered a round in my M16. Bruce and I were both pretty edgy at the start, but after the first few houses, we took a cue from Doc's fearless innocence and relaxed enough to be able to cautiously enjoy our job. Doc was serious when it came to patching people up, but in meeting the villagers, he maintained a lighthearted sense of humor. Some of them sternly grumbled *"điên cái đầu"* (crazy) in response to Doc's attempts at levity, but most at least smiled and seemed to appreciate his effort. None of the people Bruce and I visited claimed to be in need of medical help, but word spread throughout the village, and by the time we got back to the school, several people were already waiting for

Doc. An old man with a nasty cut on his leg waited patiently while Doc tended to several children with bad cases of jungle rot, which, without antibiotics, became large, consuming scabs that would continue to grow larger instead of healing. Later, probably as an indication of their increased trust in our medic, mama-sans brought in babies who needed attention.

The stay in the village allowed us to rest, relax, and—for once—feel like we were doing something of value. Chasing away the VC and protecting Doc while he helped the villagers was much more in line with the collective desire of the platoon than our vague and seemingly futile efforts in the field. Because we had lacked the courage and conviction needed to opt out, feign insanity, or go to jail, we had ended up here in Vietnam with M16s in our hands. Now we could only hope that we'd be lucky and that our time would run out before we were in a position of having to kill or be killed.

As we left the village and entered the jungle, I knew that, once more, I would have to leave my thoughts and doubts behind in order to survive. Only the present moment could exist if there was to be any hope of surviving this trial by fire. My intuitive perception in the field was steadily growing clearer and more certain. For long stretches of time, my thought processes would remain suspended, allowing only the flow of visual images, smells, and sounds to pass through. These were noted, analyzed, and discarded, without mental reflection, from one split second to the next. While my concentration was focused in this way, I was no longer aware of physical pain or time. I was also beginning to learn that even reflecting on this wondrous new discovery threw a wrench in the works. If my focus was disrupted in any way—even to notice how my focus affected my sense of time—it felt as if I had been thrown down a steep hill into a muddy bog. Thoughts, emotions, and my body's pain would regain center stage of my perceptual reality, and only renewed discipline and perseverance would, eventually, give them the hook.

Early in the morning of our fourth day out, an urgent call from the rear ordered us to stop immediately and cut a landing zone. Machetes and hatchets flew, and we created a small clear circle on the ridge we'd been climbing, and even though it seemed too small for the rotor blades of a Huey, McDouche ordered me to pop smoke. Amid a cloud of blowing leaves and branches, a chopper slowly nestled itself in the clearing, picked up a squad, and eased slowly out before lifting its tail and roaring off. Three more Hueys repeated the tricky maneuver, and in less than an hour from the call, we were flying above the jungle as fast as a Huey can. It seemed that we'd only been in the air for a few minutes when I spotted a wispy cloud of purple smoke on the edge of a field of rice paddies. The chopper dove for the smoke, and when it hesitated for a second above a tiny patch of solid ground, we jumped out. One of the choppers actually touched down, and as I made a dash for the tree line, I turned to see why. Five men wearing black-and-green face paint and dressed in camouflage fatigues passed within twenty yards of me and ran for the impatiently stationary Huey. One of them looked familiar, and with a second glance, I recognized him. Calendar.

My mind flashed back to scenes from jungle school where I'd met him—ages ago, it seemed—when we were both new in country. I remembered a kinship of sorts. He was a fellow college dropout who, like me, had spent more time partying than studying or keeping abreast of current events and had likewise been pinched by the draft. My memory brought up images of an amiable man who had seemed determined to "party on" in spite of the draft—or even Vietnam— and as my mind compared those images to what I had just seen, I felt a chill. It was Calendar, without a doubt; it was the same unmistakable baby face, even under the blotches of green and black. But his eyes—damn. As he was dashing for the chopper, our eyes had met for an instant. Long enough for me to recognize the cold, deep well of the thousand-yard stare. The fun-loving spirit of the man I'd met in jungle school was gone, and his eyes, which had once twinkled with mischief, were now the doorway to an unfathomably deep abyss. He carried a sniper's rifle, and I knew at once that he had used it.

I felt as if I'd been carried away by the flood of memories, and now, with a jolt, I returned to the here and now. The sound of helicopters faded as I tried to orient myself. The platoon had made a defensive position, and we were waiting for an attack. Seconds passed. Minutes passed. Nothing. Silence. I caught a flash of movement to my right and saw Creeper waving for me to follow him. I fell in place with the single-file line of men that was making its way down a trail on the edge of the tree line, heading for a grove of coconut trees. Near the trees was an open area that was strewn with bodies, North Vietnamese regulars. Some appeared to have been killed instantly and collapsed in place, but a couple looked like they had died while they were trying to crawl away; one was curled in a fetal position. The body of one man was lying right next to the trail, facedown. There wasn't a mark on him—no bullet holes, no blood—except that the top quarter section of his skull was gone, leaving his intact brain exposed to the morning sun.

The platoon regrouped in the grove near a pile of several more corpses. A few of us formed another defensive position while the rest of the platoon collected weapons and grenades and searched through the packs that were scattered around or were still strapped on the backs of the dead. The grisly scene numbed my mind. The bodies, for the most part, were intact, with only a few nickel-sized bloodstains on their clothes. They looked peaceful, as if they were sleeping, and I caught myself looking at them with envy. For them, the struggle was over. No more pain, rage, or grief, just this eerie, seductive stillness.

We were to spend the night among the corpses, waiting in ambush, as it was well known that the NVA almost always tried to recover the bodies of their fallen comrades in order to give them some semblance of a proper burial. While digging in, I heard the story of what had happened. Calendar's group was an LRP (long-range reconnaissance patrol). They had set an ambush along the trail by rigging thirteen Claymores for simultaneous detonation. The five of them sat tight and waited, expecting that maybe a squad or possibly a platoon would fall into their trap. In the predawn darkness, Calendar, who had a starlight scope (a night-vision device) on his sniper rifle, saw them coming down the trail. It was neither a squad nor a platoon. A whole company of NVA moved right into their trap. They waited until the center of the column, which is where the company commander usually travels, was centered in the kill zone, and then they blew the bush, cutting the company in half. Fearing that they might be able to regroup, Calendar opened up with his sniper rifle on anything that moved. The NVA, not knowing the size of the unit they were up against, scattered.

We spent a long and nearly sleepless night waiting for them to return, but luckily, they never showed. In the morning, we packed up and left, moving only a few miles to a road, where we were picked up by two deuce-and-a-half trucks that drove us to a nearby Military Assistance Command, Vietnam (MAC V) compound. MAC V was a rear-echelon bunch whose function, other than shuffling supplies around, I never really understood. They were quartered in a building that had been left by the French, and I suspected that we had been moved there to back them up in case of a retaliatory strike by the NVA. It was clear, even at first glance, that the CO who ran the place was running some sort of major scam, something that would have made even Sgt. Bilko blush. He greeted McDouche in a pair of silk pajamas, and while they were talking, Tennessee and I slipped into the building to check it out.

The place was deluxe even by air force standards. The guy had a television, a large kitchen, and several bedrooms upstairs, and a large rec room/movie theater on the ground floor with a fully loaded wet bar. We ran across several Vietnamese maids — *or whatever* — on our tour of the building and slipped out just in time to hear McDouche ask the man if he could put us up inside for the night. The CO responded that he would have liked to but that he really didn't have the room.

We were able to set up poncho hootches in the area surrounding the building before the afternoon rains set in, which, for us, was luxury enough. Although the platoon had grown accustomed to sleeping with only the barest of necessities, considering that we were there to defend the compound, it would have been a nice gesture for the CO to invite us inside for a rare, truly dry night. Evidently, the man who had created this Shangri-la felt that it might be spoiled by harboring a bunch of funky grunts with mud on their boots.

After two days of his gracious hospitality, we were loaded on trucks again and shuffled back to Uplift for three days of stand-down. The rear was quite cozy after our last stretch in the field. It wasn't pretty, but it felt safe. In less than an hour, Tennessee, Speed, Orville, Bruce, Doc Mock, Creeper, and I were on another truck heading for Linda's. Each time we visited, I trusted her a little more, but there was always a nagging doubt in the back of my mind. What if she was VC? What if she was only pretending to appreciate our efforts in order to get us stoned and hope for a tidbit or two of useful information about our activities in the field? Speed and the other old-timers trusted her implicitly, and though she was slowly earning my trust, I always kept track of my M16 during our visits, just in case.

I knew that she sensed my mistrust, and although she was cordial, I could tell that she was making a conscious effort not to push herself on me. She kept her distance, and I thought she felt that, in time, my fears would fade and I would become comfortable there. I wasn't so sure, but I appreciated the way she was handling the situation.

We were well into the usual ritual. The little kids had found my lap, and I was beyond my troublesome reflections, when the sound of laughter came from an adjacent room. Speed chambered a round in his M16 and demanded an explanation from Linda. He was across the room in a flash, standing by the curtain that divided the rooms. Linda was making a desperate plea for him to calm down.

"No sweat, Speed. Be cool," she pleaded. "It's only ARVNs. They buy *cần sa* [pot] from Linda."

Heedless to her appeal, he flung the curtain aside, revealing three sinister-looking Vietnamese men in ARVN uniforms, who—sure of Linda's protection—sneered at Speed.

Speed was only marginally relieved to see the ARVN uniforms. He, like most of the old-timers, had been burned by ARVNs during supposedly cooperative missions and considered them cowardly at best, treacherous at worst. He demanded that Linda throw them out.

She pulled Speed back across the room and convinced him to sit down.

"How you gonna act, Speed?" she asked, trying her best to cool him down. "They ARVNs, not VC."

Speed cooled a bit but was not impressed by her argument. To him, the distinction was questionable. He finally conceded that she could have dealings with them if she wanted, but that while we were there, he didn't want them around.

In the meantime the ARVNs had been pointing at me and laughing.

"Mama-san" they taunted, referring to the kids on my lap.

Their remark only heightened the tension in the room. Creeper and Bruce glared at them, telling Linda that if she didn't throw them out, they were going to have to kick ass. Fearing that things were about to get out of control, Linda asked us to wait, went into the room with the ARVNs, and closed the curtain.

She returned in a few minutes with assurances that they were gone and that she would concede to Speed's demand in the future. When the matter was resolved, she turned toward me and spoke sharply in Vietnamese to the kids on my lap. Reluctantly, they slid off and were herded out of the room. I was dumbfounded but didn't want to interfere with her disciplining of the kids.

We'd had enough hassle for one day and decided to return to Uplift. Speed, as usual, was buying a supply of weed for our next trip to the boonies. While stuffing a kilo of weed and several packs of bombers into a brown bag, Linda cautioned him about the new battalion commander at Uplift. He had installed a new bunker at the entrance and had it manned, during the day, by MPs who checked everyone entering the compound. She said that a grunt from Delta Company had been smoking a bomber on the way into Uplift, and the MPs had tried to bust him. Before they could grab the joint for evidence, the guy ate it, and the infuriated MPs punched him several times in the stomach in a futile effort to make him vomit it up.

Forewarned, Speed and Creeper plotted how to avoid getting caught by the MPs on the return trip. They decided to throw the package into the weeds along the road before we were stopped by the MPs (the dreaded Military Police) and to crawl through the concertina wire later that night to retrieve it. As the truck approached the perimeter of our base camp, Speed smoothly executed the first part of the plan without detection. We were stopped by the MPs at the gate and were checked thoroughly before being allowed in. Phase two was going to be the difficult and dangerous part. According to the plan, before Speed snuck through the concertina wire, he would inform the guys manning the nearby bunkers of his mission, so—in theory—he'd be able to get in and out safely. But there was always a chance that the base would be attacked while he was outside the perimeter, leaving him in no-man's-land.

At dusk, Tennessee, Creeper, Bruce, and I were kicking back in lawn chairs on our assigned bunker. Under the old battalion commander, I'd felt comfortable that there had been almost tacit approval of our partying on guard. He had, seemingly, made a distinction in the behavior expected of his people. He required the clerks and supply sergeants in the rear to be all spit and polish, but he basically left the grunts alone. It seemed fair enough. After all, we were the ones who were doing the dirty work and getting shot at; nearly everyone felt that we deserved the slack. Now our new colonel, fresh from the States and fighting the war by pushing colored pins in a map, was going to try to change all that. I could understand why he would try, but what bugged me was that he obviously didn't know the nature of the men he was fucking with. To say that we were outraged would be putting it mildly, and considering that some of us were near the breaking point already, I wondered which straw would be the last. I shared my fears with Tennessee.

"Shit, man, don't sweat it," he replied. "It's out of our control. Even if you and I agreed with his policy, which we don't, it wouldn't make any difference. He's fuckin' with four hundred men here, and sometime, somewhere, he'll learn he's fuckin' up. The guys in Delta Company already threw a frag in his shitter, and if the motherfucker can sit on the throne every day, count the shrapnel holes in the door, and not get a hint, it isn't like we didn't try."

Tennessee laughed and patted me on the back. Surely it was an absurd situation, and it eased my mind to realize that, for the most part, he was right. It was beyond the control of any individual.

Speed climbed on our bunker and gave us each a bomber with a grin. I was glad to see that he'd retrieved the stash without any problems.

"Hey, Baby-san, you got a stick of C-4, don't ya?" he asked.

I nodded. At the last resupply, I'd grabbed a stick of the Play Doh–like plastic explosive for personal use. Technically, we carried it to detonate booby traps in place, but it had a number of other applications. The stuff was very stable unless matched to the proper heat and concussion rate of a detonator, and it would burn with a quiet yellow flame when lit with a match. A marble-sized piece would do a nice job heating a can of Cs or would dry your shirt if you sat down and stretched your shirt over your knees above its flame.

"Well, let me have it, will ya?" Speed asked.

Without thinking, I fished around in my pack and found it.

"Thanks," he said as he slid off the roof of our bunker. "I'm taking up a collection."

I was worried again, but the party continued. I saw two men coming down the road behind our bunker and elbowed Tennessee. He crouched down low to get a silhouette and in a few seconds recognized them.

"Don't worry. It's Tommy Hendricks and Big Ernie," he said. "You haven't met them yet but don't freak out when you do. You might think that Big Ernie is a lifer at first, 'cause he has shiny boots and wears starched fatigues with all the right shit sewn on 'em, but he's cool. He works in headquarters and keeps us informed about what the lifers are planning. Tommy's a clerk and does typing for our first sergeant. Every now and then they can sneak out on the bunkers and cop a buzz."

As they approached, I saw that Big Ernie surely lived up to his name; he was six feet four, at least. And true to Tennessee's description, I could see the toes of his boots shining in the moonlight. Tommy was much shorter and wore round granny glasses, like Doc. They were accompanied by a yellow dog, the first I'd seen in country.

They were both grinning as they climbed onto the bunker, and Tennessee wasted no time in breaking out our stash of bombers. After we were introduced, Big Ernie clued Tennessee in about the details and habits of our new battalion commander while Tommy told me about the dog, Sesame.

"He'll do a great lifer check for ya. Great dog. Watch him."

After collecting pets from the crew on the bunker, Sesame perched himself on the roadside edge of the bunker and stood guard vigilantly.

"If there's a lifer within fifty yards, he starts doin' this low growl," Tommy continued. "Hasn't missed yet."

"How does he know that they're lifers?" I asked, amazed that a dog could sense one's career plans.

"Don't know for sure, but I think it has something to do with vibes. It must be that lifers have different vibes. All I know for sure is that he can spot 'em a mile away."

I looked again at Sesame and saw that he was vigilant as ever, but something that Big Ernie was telling Tennessee caught my attention.

"But that's not the half of it," he said with a nod acknowledging that I was listening. "He's got the officers in the rear doin' checks on the bunker line. Last week a lieutenant that he sent out slipped up behind a grunt from Delta Company while he was on guard and cocked a .45 behind his head. He thought the guy was sleeping, but he wasn't. At the first click, the grunt spun around and leveled his M16 in the lieutenant's gut and damn near blew him away.

"We have a system now, though, so if you hear anyone say 'Lima Charles' on the radio, it means lifer check. If I'm in headquarters when they're getting ready to go out, I'll let ya know."

Their conversation drifted to distant mumbling as I contemplated the possible outcomes of Big Ernie's info. Ostensibly, there was no problem. If the lifers thought for a moment that they could infiltrate the tight-knit brotherhood of us grunts, they were gravely mistaken— nevah hoppen, as Linda would say. Already they had underestimated us more than they had underestimated the North Vietnamese, but one thing bothered me. For months I'd heard guys say things like, "Hand grenades don't leave no fingerprints" and "Don't worry, man, we're in Vietnam. Everybody's got an M16." For the most part, these had been idle threats used to blow off steam when the lifers got petty or outrageous, but now there was a new and dangerous factor to the equation. Heroin.

I'd seen a few guys use it at Linda's and didn't like what I had seen. The guys who were shooting up would arrive at Linda's with a mad, hungry craving in their eyes. After some messing about with needles, candles, and such, they'd tie their arms with some surgical tubing, find a vein, and be gone, unconscious, in some dark netherworld. Five, ten, sometimes fifteen, heart-stopping minutes would pass while some outfit's medic was taking their pulse and wiping the sweat from their bodies before they'd return, weak and ghostlike. The whole trip was completely antithetical to smoking pot or even opium. With heroin, there was no ritual sharing, camaraderie, laughter, and opening of doors. It was a selfish, solo dance with death. So far, our platoon had resisted this siren on the rocks, but her seductive wail echoed loudly in times of confusion and despair. As my musings came full circle, I realized why Ernie's seemingly innocuous information had made me feel so queasy. I felt sure that a dash of heroin in the cauldron of our discontent would surely, inevitably, make for a very nasty brew.

Then there was Speed, prowling the base camp with the quarter-pound stick of plastic explosive I'd given him without question. I'd seen him stash it in a sack along with a dozen others, some det cord, blasting caps, and fuse, and I was only now wondering what he was going to do.

*Baroom!* An earthshaking explosion rattled sand loose from the roof of our bunker. The sound echoed off the mountains that surrounded our base camp and was followed by a spontaneous cheer from those close enough to realize what had happened. Speed had demolished the MP's new bunker at the base entrance. Even in the twilight of a nearly pitch-black night, I could see that he had done a masterful job. All the main timbers had been blown, leaving a useless heap of rubble. It would take weeks to get the materials to build another one.

"Them fuckin' Ps will think twice before fuckin' with us again," laughed Creeper. "Now they're gonna be standin' in the rain, and if they got the brains God gave a goose, they'll know it was jus' a friendly warning. Speed don't fuck around."

Instantly, intuitively, I knew Speed was right—precisely right—in giving the MPs a "subtle" hint before things got entirely out of hand. But as was my nature, my mind flipped through its memories, as through a Rolodex, for scenes that would fill in the blanks and confirm the precision and efficiency of Speed's actions. I remembered walking slack for Speed while he was walking point on our last mission. No longer mystified by the cat like grace of his movements, I knew that he was just in the groove, as I referred to it—that state in which your muscles relax, and you go from trudge to glide, from struggle to float. But it was only on this last mission that I was able to pick up on some of the finer points of Speed's skill. We had come to the edge of a clearing when I realized how he had survived all those months at point. He stood stock-still for an instant, and I felt him slide into a place of deep calm. He wasn't looking, listening, or smelling the area consciously. He let go, and trusting that he would be aware of any relevant sensory information, opened himself to the vibes, the energy of the place. He relaxed. And I relaxed. We both knew that in spite of signs of recently cut vegetation and the remnants of a cooking fire, there was no one around. I felt him shift again. We were no longer in sync. He had attuned himself to a finer, more subtle level of perception, yet I knew what he was doing. He was feeling for finer energies. Traces of feelings left when people handle things: watches, rings—booby traps. He relaxed again. It was cool; there weren't any grenades with trip wires or feces-covered pongee stakes in the area. As we crossed the clearing, I knew that he knew, but I couldn't help straining to see if there weren't any impossibly fine lines or suspicious-looking vines that could get us blown away.

My Rolodex fell open to another card, a scene from seven months earlier, the first night I met Speed. He had handed me a bomber on my first, scared-shitless night of guard duty in the field and was telling me a story. The scene replayed itself with amazing clarity, but without dialogue. Silently, with twenty-twenty hindsight, I could perceive the more ethereal layers of significance in our first encounter. I remembered being in a bit of a panic as the powerful Vietnamese reefer took effect. I felt as if all that I had considered to be me was slowly being stunned. I was finding it nearly impossible to maintain a coherent train of thought and grew increasingly frightened that without them, I would dissolve into oblivion. Speed watched me struggle for a while and began to talk. The tone of his voice was calm and reassuring. It tethered me to the wet mud beneath my butt. He spoke in a hypnotic cadence that eased my fear. It was his apparently absurd story about my magic poncho liner. My memory didn't repeat the story, but it allowed me to understand its intent. Speed was well aware that there was a dogged determination in me to maintain a steady stream of thoughts, and to this dog he had thrown a bone. My mind grabbed the story the way a drowning man would grab a life buoy and drifted with it into uncharted seas, completely content to unravel its multilayered meanings. Understanding Speed's story about being invulnerable while wrapped in a poncho liner was like getting the punch line of a joke. What had been mysterious was suddenly hilarious, and at that instant, I realized I was naked in the void. There was an almost palpable pop—or perhaps it was applause—when my incessant thoughts took a bow and left the scene. I knew what I had feared. Death. Somehow I had believed that without my precious thoughts, there would be no me. Yet they were gone now, and I was still alive! Now there was only a profound calm, a stillness both ancient and timeless. I reached out to feel Speed, but he was transparent now, allowing me to explore on my own. It was as if I'd been introduced to an old, old friend, and though there were no words, she said:

> *Listen,*
> *You can hear the jungle for the first time now.*
> *Its sounds have forever been thus:*
> *Rich, lush, and beautiful.*

*Look around you and wonder at the pale blue light filtering through*
*the trees.*
*The forms around you are perfection.*
*Feel the damp air caress your skin.*
*Smell rotting wood and fragrant plants.*
*The air not only smells of life, it* is
*Life.*

This was what the ritual of communion alluded to. I remembered slowly being aware of Speed again. When I looked at him, he was smiling. When I looked at him, I realized I was smiling.

My memory scan complete, I felt relieved of my temporary confusion about the explosion that had torn the MP's bunker to shreds. I knew that, whether it was nursing a newbie, finding a booby trap, or blowing up a bunker, it was from this stillness that Speed functioned. And as I gazed across the top of our bunker, I could see Tennessee, Tommy, Big Ernie, and Creeper sitting in silence. They were taking communion. Sesame sat with his back to them, facing the road, ever vigilant to his duty of lifer check.

In the morning, after chow, we were herded to the company area, where stacks of Cs, ammunition, and supplies informed us of our fate. We were going to the boonies again. Though we were used to the routine, a hush settled over the company as we stuffed our packs. At this point, only two things were clear. We knew that the lifers had already been briefed and that we wouldn't know the strategy or intent of our mission until it became obvious in the field. I could almost hear the thoughts swirling around the somber assembly. Would military intelligence be right for once, would we really be landing in a hot LZ or near an NVA base camp? Or, more likely, were they intending to drop us in a "safe" place that would be loaded with booby traps and set up for an ambush? Had the general tenor of the war changed from hide-and-seek to an out-and-out battle somewhere? As I snapped a fresh clip of rounds in my M16 and buttoned a grenade in my shirt pocket, I knew one thing for sure: we'd soon find out.

From the start, it was an unusual mission. The company was loaded on deuce-and-a-half trucks rather than Hueys and driven north along the coastal highway. After an hour on the road, the convoy entered a small village, where it stopped to drop us off. We quickly regrouped into squads and platoons and headed east through the village on a footpath that I knew, inevitably, would lead us to the mountains. The surly villagers acknowledged our passing with icy stares, and it seemed that they had even positioned three teenage boys to give us a parting shot of their scorn as we left the area. The boys were sitting on a fence that separated the villagers' territory from the no-man's-land known to us as a free-fire zone — a zone in which we were authorized to shoot anyone on sight. They laughed at us as we strained under the weight of freshly loaded packs and were quick to point out, for their added amusement, anyone who was unusually tall, short, or black or, most hilarious of all, had red hair. Evidently, they were oblivious to the purpose of our mission, which was to protect their village from the NVA, who — our intelligence sources contended — were waiting for them to finish harvesting their rice so they could raid the village and steal it.

Two miles from the village, we joined forces with a company of tracked vehicles (lightly armored boxlike vehicles that rode on tracks, like tanks) that had formed a defensive perimeter and was awaiting our arrival. Their company comprised a dozen armored personnel carriers (APCs), each with a top-mounted M60 machine gun, and two tanks. Since the army had discovered that anyone riding inside an APC was likely to be killed by the concussion if it happened to hit a land mine, we were ordered to ride on top, one squad per track, with the tanks picking up the slack by providing space for the remaining infantrymen. Tennessee, Creeper, and I climbed on the back deck of a tank that was in the middle of the single-file column, which was already moving down the center of the wide valley.

It was the first time we'd worked with an armored unit, and while I had to admit that riding was surely easier than grunting under a heavy pack, the high-profile nature of their operation seemed out of place in a guerilla war. They had plenty of firepower at their disposal, but I doubted that this alone could compensate for their awkwardness and lack of maneuverability. Surely, any NVA within twenty miles already knew exactly where we were and where we were headed, since for a company of tracked vehicles in this area, there weren't many options.

The valley narrowed until there was only one possible avenue that would allow us entrance into an elongated box canyon, which was our destination. As the options for the tracks grew slimmer, they were forced to pass through bottlenecks that were dotted with large, flat boulders. Having one track on stone and the other churning up soft earth in the narrowest part of the valley had caused the track on another of the APCs to be wrenched off the sprocketed drive wheels. We had passed two that had stalled in this manner. Their crews, aware of their sudden vulnerability, were working frantically with huge steel pry bars to lever the heavy track back on the drive wheels.

We were about to encounter yet another deadly snafu as our tank entered the narrowest passage in the valley. I was only mildly relieved to discover that the sensitivity that I had developed during months of silent stalking in the jungle still functioned well, even amid the cacophony of the diesel engines. I knew beyond a doubt that we were being watched and that those who watched us were more contemplative than afraid.

A deafening explosion confirmed my perception. A command-detonated mine had been blown by the NVA, who had been waiting for our tank to enter the kill zone of their ambush site. Their timing, slightly off, harmlessly sprayed the area between our tank and the APC ahead of us with shrapnel. Instantly, the turret on our tank swung to the left and fired its main gun. The recoil caused the tank to squat and jerk backward, throwing Tennessee, Creeper, and me into the air like fleas on a horse's back. We crash-landed onto the steel deck and immediately jumped alee of the tank for cover. A squad was dispatched to scout the hill from which we'd been ambushed, and Capt. Quick snagged Tennessee, Creeper, and me for a recon patrol of our right flank. He had our *Chiêu Hồi* scout (a North Vietnamese soldier who had surrendered or been captured and had agreed to work with us) take point, with me behind him in the slack position. In keeping with the style of his command, Capt. Quick came along behind me, with Tennessee and Creeper covering our rear.

We traveled a wide loop to the right of the tracks, and although I'd been in country long enough that I wasn't pee-your-pants scared, the NVA scout was an unnerving distraction. He was extremely young—couldn't have been older than seventeen. The other thing that bothered me about him was that he seemed to be scared and green in the field. Bringing him along was one of Capt. Quick's recent innovations, and I couldn't bring myself to trust him. I couldn't help thinking that at any instant, he might turn, spray us with automatic fire, and disappear into the jungle. To make things worse, I knew that when our patrol broke into clear areas, we were being watched. The NVA were tracking our movements and could, from the high ridge that overlooked the valley, open fire at their discretion. As we approached our own perimeter, I remembered that, although they probably could have wiped out our patrol, the NVA preferred more calculated moves. They would rather wait for an opportunity to employ a clearly defined strategy than reveal their precise location by acting on impulse. An expert chess player doesn't capture every available piece, and thus we were left on the board, I was sure, because it suited the NVA's larger game plan.

We'd barely had time to get settled on the tank again before it lurched forward and blasted its way through the few remaining obstacles that, minutes before, had caused it to move at such a measured and cautious pace. The tank plunged into the canyon amid a spray of flying mud, executed a sudden and amazingly agile right turn, and wheeled into position in the already partially formed perimeter. Even over the roar of our mechanical monster, I heard the terrifying sound of explosions at five-second intervals. The NVA had, indeed, anticipated our destination, and they were lobbing in mortar rounds as fast as they could stuff them in the tube.

"Medic, medic!" The shout came from across the perimeter. "I've been hit, Doc! I've been hit!"

McDouche's voice faded in the din of Hueys that touched down near our tank. The chopper crews quickly off-loaded a dozen wooden crates, along with a German shepherd tracker dog and its handler. The gunner on our tank motioned for Tennessee, Creeper, and me to retrieve the crates, and we instantly complied with his command. While dashing across the open grass toward the stack of crates, I could hear from the sound of the incoming rounds and knew that the NVA were "walking" them toward the pile. I frantically tore open a crate and saw what I knew must have been a round of ammunition for the tank's main gun but was surprised to find that instead of the brass canister at the base end, this thing had only a rubber boot. Like almost all army munitions, from the M16 to heavy artillery, there was a projectile fitted atop a brass canister filled with powder to propel it, but this strange thing had only a projectile in front of a rubber sleeve. Under the sleeve was a white cylinder that looked and felt like baked clay. Cradling the thing in my arms, I ran back to the tank and handed it to the driver. His eyes nearly fell out.

He shook his head and yelled, "Don't take off the sleeve, this shit'll go off with a match!"

I'd never been schooled about tank munitions, but I immediately realized that in modern ammunition for the tank's main gun, the army had done away with the brass cylinder full of powder and replaced it with compressed explosives. In relieving the tank's crew from having to deal with the hot brass of a spent round, they'd lost the security of the old ammunition, particularly if some hapless grunt tears off their only line of defense—the rubber sleeve. In the middle of a mortar attack, the tank's driver was staring at thirty pounds of raw explosives.

I nodded, turned to get another one, and was greatly relieved to see that the pile had disappeared.

Savoring a moment to catch our breath, Tennessee, Creeper, and I huddled near the tank for cover. Creeper elbowed me and pointed across the perimeter, where Capt. Quick, Speed, the dog, and its handler were disappearing into the bush. They were heading toward the most likely placement of the NVA's mortar tube.

"There's two bad motherfuckers," Creeper said, in reference to Quick and Speed. "If I didn't know better, I'd swear they liked this shit."

I had to agree. Since Capt. Quick had taken command of our company, he and Speed had grown inseparable. Fellow Green Berets, they were the only two among us who had been adequately trained to fight in a guerilla war. For the rest of us, with only eight weeks of infantry school after basic training, it was really an OTJ—on the job—affair, and our focus was more on how to survive rather than on how to win this weird and unjustifiable war. Although we greatly appreciated Speed's competence and willingness to serve the company as our best point man, both he and Capt. Quick had an enthusiasm about the war that boggled our minds. Often, when we traveled as a company, the two would patrol outside our perimeter for hours, as if they were hunting pheasants in Kansas. The two of them—Quick with his .45 and Speed with an M16—could move swiftly and with such stealth that it was far more likely that they would surprise any of the NVA who were usually prowling about, keeping tabs on our company's movement. We could only guess what they were doing now, in this valley, but whatever it was, it had been effective. The mortar fire suddenly ceased.

Our attention was drawn to one of the army's miniature Loach helicopters, which had been circling the ridge, but now was zipping about like a hummingbird. At treetop level, it darted back and forth until we could hear that it was drawing fire. Heavy fire. *Chunka, chunka, chunka.*

"Goddamn!" Tennessee shouted. "They've got a .51 caliber up there in the hills. Thank God they didn't use it on us." He pointed to the gun's location.

I'd never heard of the NVA being in possession of a bona fide anti-aircraft gun, and knowing the havoc they could wreak with the rifles and rocket-propelled grenades that were their mainstay, I shuddered to think of what they could do with it. The Loach slid down the hillside and floated into position a hundred yards to the right and slightly above the gun's location. From there, it gathered speed for one last passing spray at the placement. Red tracers poured from it, but we could hear the .51 returning fire so, wisely, the little Loach retreated. Two heavily armed Cobra gunships arrived minutes later to take up where the Loach had left off. Those of us who watched helplessly from the valley thought that the Cobras would make short work of one anti-aircraft gun. Flying in a large circle, 180 degrees apart, the Cobras set themselves up to keep a steady barrage of fire on the placement. Taking turns, they blasted the location with everything they had, but the NVA were not to be intimidated. Their return fire had, evidently, either made some hits or come too close. The Cobras also retreated.

With the Cobras' retreat, a cold shadow seemed to pass over the valley. We all knew that, man for man, the NVA could kick ass. This display of the impotence of our technology only served to remind us of what we already knew—they'd been fighting this war with equipment that was barely out of the Stone Age, and they were winning. None of us needed to be reminded about the strategic disadvantage of our position on the valley floor; yet, it seemed to be the army's way of fighting. We'd been set up as bait for the NVA in order to entice them into capitalizing on our vulnerability and revealing their presence by blowing us to kingdom come, in trade for a few casualties of their own. Then, with a little juggling of statistics by the lifers in the rear, the folks back home could be deluded into thinking that we were actually winning this goddamned futile war. And thus the lifers could keep it going for a few more months.

Speed slipped up behind us with a sort of good news/bad news joke about our situation. The good news was that he and Capt. Quick had found an indentation in a log that had served as a base plate for the NVA's mortar tube. The dog had led them directly to it, but it appeared that the NVA running it had already been alerted by observers on the ridge, who had surmised Capt. Quick's intentions. The mortar tube had been silenced by the pressing need to relocate it; it hadn't been destroyed. Also, somewhat questionably in the good news category was the news that when Doc checked McDouche for his alleged wounds, he couldn't find a mark on him. Feeling the concussion of one of the mortar rounds, he had imagined that he'd taken hits of shrapnel. Evidently, McDouche, who had always been so willing to lay someone else's ass on the line, had buckled under the strain of being under fire himself.

Then there was the bad news. Speed had overhead Capt. Quick talking to the rear on the radio. Our intelligence had intercepted NVA radio communications regarding their strategy in the valley. They had been given orders from their higher-ups that, at all costs, they were to keep us trapped in the valley until reinforcements arrived that would allow them to wipe us out completely. Grim news, to say the least.

During his report, Speed had reached into the thigh pocket of his fatigues and handed me his stash of weed. I tamped it carefully into the bowl of my ivory pipe, thinking, *With news like that, what the hell.* I fired up the pipe and passed it around for hits. Tennessee and Creeper each took a long draw, and after copping a toke for himself, Speed handed the pipe to the tank's driver. Several minutes later, the driver returned my pipe to Speed, hot and empty. I leaned against the tank and stared at the ridge, thinking that surely the NVA were polishing their prized weapon in preparation for their next move. The waiting was getting on my nerves, and my emotions vacillated between anger, worry, and resignation.

Tennessee must have noted my dark mood, because he interrupted the downward spiral of my thoughts. "Hey, man, I've got some peaches in my pack. I'll split 'em with ya," he said with a grin.

I was almost irritated that he could read me so easily, but I couldn't help but smile and feel grateful for his help. He dug in his pack and pulled out the can, and for an instant, he almost looked like old St. Nick himself, eyes twinkling. He'd been helping me out every chance he could during the eight months I'd been in country, which had seemed like eight years. Like the other old-timers, he liked to pounce on you in times of greatest distress and slip in a lesson or two. We could almost read each other's minds by now, and I had a pretty good idea what he was thinking. It would go something like this: "All these months, you thought I was making these great sacrifices on your behalf, but now maybe you get the picture. We could have been blown away any minute. If anything I did made you feel good, it made me feel good. I haven't sacrificed a thing. All I've been doing is sharing my joy. Joy is worthless to have alone."

He opened the can of peaches, which were widely considered to be the crème de la crème of C-ration fare, and handed them to me along with a plastic spoon. He watched me carefully and giggled like a child. He knew that I had understood his wordless communication and his sympathy with my dilemma. There had been times in the last few months when I had experienced a measure of the clarity, humor, and joy that seemed to be such innate qualities of his personality and that had been able to be of service to the less experienced members of the platoon. Yet, for me, these were fragile and all-too-temporary states, easily disrupted by environmental circumstance or the gravity of my habitual thought processes. I felt that he saw the humor in my present state the way a father might find his child's first attempts at walking rather comical. I had taken a few wobbly steps, beamed a self-satisfied smile, lost concentration, teetered a bit, panicked, and fallen on my rump. His twinkling eyes and giggly laugh had lifted me out of my serious, self-critical sense of failure to a higher and more forgiving perception of my condition.

A pair of Phantom jets made a pass over the valley. We knew their routine and watched eagerly as they jockeyed into position. As expected, they fell into formation across from each other, on the circumference of a wide, imaginary circle in the sky. Next, they would each make a practice run at the machine-gun placement, and then, well organized and oriented, they would commence bombing it to dust. They would alternate dropping HE and napalm bombs until there was only a bald spot left where the placement had been or until our CO called them off, whichever came first. All eyes were on the first jet as it screamed in low, just over our heads. It maintained its altitude until it neared the ridge, where it raised its nose to keep its course parallel to the terrain. From our perspective, it looked as if it was performing yet another demonstration of precision flying, but to our shock and horror, it crashed into the top of the ridge, shot out of the sky by the fearless NVA and their .51 antiaircraft gun. A huge, yellow-orange ball of fire erupted from the site. Seconds later, the other Phantom — the remaining member of what had once been a team—screamed in, firing its cannons at the gun placement and, in the same pass, dropped a pair of HE bombs on his partner's crash site, in an attempt to completely demolish the wreckage and render it unsalvageable to the NVA. After its pass, the second jet kept climbing until it was out of range of the .51. With a wide arc, it set a course for the air base.

An eerie hush settled over the valley. Stunned by the apparent ease with which the NVA had destroyed one of our most sophisticated war machines, the emotional atmosphere now had the quiet, contemplative, slightly guilty feel of a church on Sunday morning. I'm sure that more than a few prayers were said for the welfare of the spirits of the men who had perished before our eyes.

The sound of a lone Huey shattered the silence. It snaked its way through the valley and landed near our tank. We could see Capt. Quick and Speed calmly making last-minute equipment checks before making a dash to board the anxiously waiting chopper. During the brief moments before takeoff, I noticed a confident look of grim determination in Quick's face, while Speed appeared to be jovial and excited. The Huey lifted its skids a few feet off the grass, spun around in place, and zigzagged through the narrow entrance of the canyon.

What those two were up to was anyone's guess, but for us, it was nearly the end of another long and stressful day. The clouds above the ridge were turning pink, and since Doc Mock and Bruce had managed to slip over to our location—fuck it, it was time to party. Tennessee unstrapped the ammo can from Speed's pack, opened it, and reeled out 150 rounds of belted M60 ammunition to reveal a neatly organized stash that was hidden at the bottom. He pulled out a pack of bombers and carefully repacked the can. After passing the pack around to us, he traded what was left for the use of the tank crew's radio. Although it was the only English-speaking radio station in Vietnam, the military-run AFV network played all the popular music of the time. Their disc jockey Sgt. Pepper seemed to have a knack for timing his music to our situation. Nestled against my pack, in a tranquil, opiated womb of euphoria, I watched Doc engaging Creeper in an animated discussion about

God-knows-what—with Doc, it didn't matter. Just to watch him move and smile was to share in his lighthearted joy.

While observing a living example of what it was to be free, I realized that Doc, even more than Tennessee, had always mystified me with the consistency of his positivity. If cowboys died with their boots on, I was sure that Doc, should his number come up, would die with his grin on. He seemed to be in possession of a rare and fine source of well-being, one that I hoped, one day, to discover myself.

Two hours into our party, Speed slipped in to tell us of his adventure with Capt. Quick. He was amused to hear that we had thought that they, for some reason or another, had gone to the rear. It was exactly what they wanted the NVA to think, when actually their Huey had circled and dropped them off behind the ridge. They had managed to sneak over the ridge and surprise the crew that was running the .51 from behind. Drenched with sweat and wired from the dangerous operation, he told of how they nearly ran out of ammunition (in their weapons, at least) before finishing the job. Having caught the NVA totally unaware, they had had a chance to plan their move before they attacked. Using hand signals, they had decided that Capt. Quick would take the two men on the right with his .45, leaving the other three for Speed with his M16 on automatic. They executed the plan with lightning speed and precision, but there was a hitch.

"The officer that ran the crew was one tough son of a bitch," Speed said. "I'd hit him with three rounds on the first spray, but he just wouldn't die. I knew I'd hit him—I could see the holes across his gut, but when I turned to collect their weapons, he leaned up on one elbow and tried to shoot me with his 9mm handgun. Capt. Quick saw him move out of the corner of his eye and laid him back with a blast from his .45 but—*dig this*—it stopped him for only a few seconds. He leaned up again! His face was so bloody he could barely see, but he leaned up again and was waving his pistol at us, trying to aim it. I had to empty the clip in my M16 to get him to die. You should have seen it. It was too much."

I was glad I hadn't. As with 90 percent of the company, I couldn't rejoice over anyone's death. The only thing easier to take about the death of the "enemy" was that I didn't know them personally. Most of us felt that they were as much the victims of circumstance and political propaganda as we were. And given the chance, they—like us—would probably rather have gone home and forgotten about the war. There had been times when we were on a hilltop and had seen them in a valley, but we never told. One of the guys from second squad, known as Wimpy, was alive only because they had done the same for him. He had gone down to a stream to fill canteens for his squad, thinking that it would take him just fifteen minutes and that he could do without his rifle. At the stream, he looked up to see a lone NVA soldier with an AK-47 over his shoulder, who, seeing that he was unarmed, just turned and walked away.

I woke in the morning to the sound of a Chinook and was able to see it head for the rear with the .51 caliber gun dangling below on a steel cable. An hour later, a Huey arrived to pick up the tracker dog and its handler, drop off our new platoon leader, whose name was Anderson, and pick up McDouche. Although I was greatly relieved to know that McDouche's tyrannical command had come to an end, I couldn't help but pity our new lieutenant, who had to join us under such dire conditions. Even from a distance, he looked wide-eyed and scared, and I could tell that he was as freaked out to meet the men he was to command as he was to find himself in combat. Watching his reaction brought to mind my own first day on the job, shyly meeting the weather-beaten, hollow-eyed members of the platoon in my brand new fatigues and shiny boots. I could only imagine that he was even more shocked than I had been to see that the whole platoon was officially out of uniform—wearing gold peace-sign necklaces and strings of beads, sweatbands, and every color and every style of sunglasses except the ones that were army issue. It would only be a matter of time before he would learn that the FTA emblazoned on most of our helmets in Magic Marker stood for *Fuck the Army.*

Shortly after his arrival, Capt. Quick introduced us to Lt. Anderson and outlined our mission. We were to join forces with a platoon of five APCs and attempt to leave the valley through the treacherous series of bottlenecks that we had struggled through on the way in. No matter what sort of strategy Capt. Quick had in mind, the one thing for certain was that we were in for a tough time. If our intelligence reports were right, there was no way we could leave the valley without a fight.

Tennessee, Creeper, Speed, and I climbed on the nearest APC, which took its place in the center of the single-file formation. All the bells and lights of my internal sensors were working overtime, trying to alert me to the danger of our predicament, but when the track shifted into drive, there was no turning back. I knew that the NVA had been watching us for two days and could feel that they were watching us even now, but somehow I wasn't nearly as scared as I had been before, during equally hairy operations. As we entered the narrow passage, I wondered if my nervous system and adrenals hadn't burned out, leaving me with only a fraction of their usual response, but this was no time for such idle musing. I shifted into the mind state that experience had taught me was appropriate for the situation. My thoughts were put on hold; for now, they would be dangerously distracting and a waste of energy. Sensory input was brought into crystal-clear, present-centered focus, and with this shift of perception, my ability to access an intuitive-level feel of the environment was greatly enhanced. Now I knew beyond a doubt that the NVA watching us were feeling both anger and fear.

The lead track veered slightly to the right and detoured around the base of a small ridge that extended into the valley from the mountain to our left. Following the contour of the ridge, it curved back to the left and disappeared into the bush. Suddenly, I flew off the track, executed a graceful half twist, and landed on my feet about a yard behind the APC. In a split-second reflection, I remembered that only a moment before, I had been sitting on the roof of the track, completely extending my legs in front of me across the open hatch in the track's roof. My right hand had been gripping the stock of my M16, and my left had been gripping the rifle's handguard around the barrel. From that position, it was not humanly possible for me to have jumped off the track, let alone land upright behind it. Equally strange was the fact that, at that instant, there was no reason for having done so.

I took a step and heard the crackle of gunfire—M16. Another step, semiautomatic *gotcha, gotcha, gotcha*—AK-47. With the third step, I entered into a profound tranquility, accompanied by an awesome feeling of clarity and power. Without fear, my movements became smooth and spontaneous. My pocket Bible and sunglasses had fallen out during the jump and were lying on the ground at my feet. I picked up my sunglasses and stood up to see Lt. Anderson directly in front of me. His face appeared to have been greatly magnified, and I gazed for a moment directly into his eyes. From a place of utter calm, I felt ever so slightly bewildered at his expression. His eyes and mouth were wide open, and his head was shaking as if he was being electrocuted by high voltage.

"Get on the line," McCoy's voice called over the din. "We're going to sweep the hill."

The platoon formed a line at the base of the hill and moved in unison, like a giant comb, up the ridge. It was our predictably futile response to being ambushed. Ten minutes into the sweep, a pair of gunships took position just ahead of us and finished our job by pelting the ridge with minigun fire. We regrouped by the waiting tracks and boarded them for the return trip to the company's perimeter. As I settled into position on my assigned APC, something shiny caught my eye. It was a reflection from the lid of an ammo can that had been strapped on top of the track just twelve inches to my left. The shine was coming from a fresh, elongated dent in the top of the can, and it told the tale, at least in part, of what had happened. Our track had been momentarily stalled in the center of the kill zone of the NVA's ambush, and the machine gunner to my left had been their prime target. AK-47 fire from the top of the ridge had been aimed at him. Had I been sitting on the track a second longer, the round that dented the can would have—with absolute certainty— torn through my left lung and quite possibly found my heart. I tapped the gunner on the arm and pointed to the dent in the can. He stared at it for a moment and responded with a slow, sober nod.

When we regrouped with the company after our short-lived recon to the mouth of the valley, they quietly celebrated our safe return. Only then did I hear the details of what had happened. We had driven straight into the jaws of an NVA ambush. McCarthy, one of the new guys in our platoon, was sitting on the front of the lead track, and when it rounded the curve to the left, he spotted an NVA soldier about forty yards dead ahead, hiding in the bush, taking aim with his rocket launcher. The NVA had intended to demolish the first track, stalling us indefinitely in the kill zone, but their man hesitated a split second too long, allowing McCarthy to spray him with his M16. Had things gone according to the NVA's plan, the snipers on the ridge would have devastated us with sustained fire. But, knowing things had gone awry, they managed only a few parting shots.

Much of the deep calm and clarity that had so unexpectedly come over me during the ambush was still with me as I observed the platoon's celebration. Tennessee and Doc Mock had both noted the change and gave me a subtle smile or a slight, timely nod. They knew what had happened to me, and although they acknowledged it, I could tell that this wasn't the sort of thing that was talked about. They knew that something in me had snapped during the ambush that had displaced terror with an incredible, crystal-clear calm. I could only guess at their reason for their reluctance to talk about it, but I trusted their judgment and kept still.

One of the army's huge Skycrane helicopters settled down in the center of the valley and left us with the bottom half (the tracks and frame) of a bulldozer. Capt. Quick's bold and decisive strategy was now clear to everyone, especially the NVA. Having cleared our escape route of its apparently inevitable ambush with our patrol, he was preparing to smooth a path for the tracks before the NVA could set another trap. The flying crane returned with the engine half of the bulldozer, and in less than an hour, mechanics from the armored company had it bolted together and ready to roll. With a tank and a squad of grunts for cover, an APC driver mounted the machine and headed for the bottleneck that had caused us so much trouble on our way into the canyon.

The mood in the valley was hopeful. At worst, we would have to survive only one more ambush before leaving the place for good. I doubted that the NVA, being that they were a superstitious lot, would try even that. After losing their precious antiaircraft gun and blowing what should have been a surefire ambush, I felt sure that they would now suppose that the fates were against them. Most likely, they would wait for us to do something stupid again (which probably wouldn't take too long) and then strike us with the vengeance of a wounded bear.

In the rear, the lifers could crow that they had only lost two pawns and taken six. I could picture the despicable bastards toasting their success and voraciously relocating the colored pins in their wall maps, which, to us in the field, were far more than markers on a game board. They represented human lives — our flesh and blood.

Half a dozen deuce-and-a-half trucks roared through the narrow entrance into the canyon, circled inside our perimeter, and formed a single-file formation heading out. Nervous drivers revved their engines as they anxiously waited for us to scramble on board. Obviously, they were as intent as the rest of us to get the hell out of this godforsaken place. The tracks pulled away from their positions around the perimeter and led the way for our convoy. Tennessee, Creeper, Doc, Speed, and I had jumped on the truck that would be the last to leave the valley. When it finally lurched into gear, we saw a small boy in red gym trunks closing in behind us. The little guy had run for all he was worth — half the length of the valley — to reach us.

"Wait, GI!" he hollered above the roar of diesel engines. "Wait! Wait!"

Tennessee finally recognized him. It was Tom, the jungle boy.

Speed slapped frantically on the truck cab's canvas roof, which, at other times, would have brought the truck to a screeching halt, but here it had no effect at all. The driver was in no mood to be separated from the convoy. As we pulled away from the tiny figure, we could see him slow, then stop altogether. His shoulders went limp, and his head hung low. I knew he was crying.

As we wound our way out of the valley, the big deuce-and-a-half trucks started picking up as much speed as the terrain allowed, and when they hit the highway, it was pedal to the metal. I got the distinct impression that the drivers wanted to get as much distance as possible between themselves and that god-awful place. We wheeled into Uplift in a cloud of dust after only fifteen minutes on the road, disrupting the softball game that was being played in the company area. It seemed odd to me that only one day's hump away, we had been battling it out with what was probably at least a company of NVA, yet here it was Sunday in the park. We wandered to supply for some clean fatigues and hit the showers.

In the morning, Speed, Tennessee, Creeper, Bruce, Doc, Orville, and I headed for the road and flagged down a truck that was headed toward Linda's village. As usual, none of us had passes, and even though there was supposed to have been some sort of crackdown, we wheeled right by the checkpoint where the MPs had been posted to curb such unauthorized escapes. After the events of the past week, none of us was in the mood for being fucked with, and the MPs, standing by the wreckage of their bunker, didn't appear in the mood either. Our ride screeched to a halt in the middle of the village, and once again, we bounded over fences and streams to the sanctuary of Linda's house. She greeted us, as always, with her personal welcome, somewhat formal, but quite cordial. Once we were seated and settled, Katy, her sister, made the rounds with a two-handed offering of Bong Son bombers.

The atmosphere of Linda's was almost always one of politeness, calm, and security, and clearly it was Linda who was in charge there. Linda's sisters—Katy, who was probably in her very early teens, and a couple others, who were even younger—treated us as honored guests, constantly making the rounds and doing minor housekeeping while we were there but never talking unless pressed to do so. We barely had time to finish our first bomber when Katy brought around a white porcelain bowl containing neatly folded, ice-cold damp washcloths. After this soothing ablution for our brows and necks, she quietly collected the soiled washcloths and retired to the kitchen to fetch a round of

Cokes. Between rounds, she'd stand in the doorway to another room and serenely survey the goings-on with her soft doe eyes. She often reminded me — particularly after I'd drifted away in a cloud of euphoria from the first bomber — of one of those bodhisattvas standing on a cloud in Asian paintings.

While visits to Linda's were usually a welcome respite from the intensity of our normal routine, today was not one of those days. I was doing my best to get comfortably laid back, but I could hear Linda talking to Speed in an uncharacteristically excited and agitated tone. They usually spoke in an infuriatingly hard-to-understand combination of Vietnamese, French, and English, which I didn't even attempt to follow, but today Linda was using more English, so I listened in. She moved toward the wall and took a veil from a picture hanging there. It was a photograph of a GI, and from the looks of it, he was a medic.

"This dude in Delta Company, Speed. He a new guy. He come here, I treat him like anybody, but he a foul dude, Speed. He a CID (Criminal Investigation Department officer)! Already he get four guys in Delta Company busted. Number ten dude for sure. You kill him for Linda, okay?" The term *number ten* was shorthand for "the worst." It was part of an agreed-upon scale of values — with *number one* being "excellent" — that helped to overcome the language barrier between us.

At this point, I heard Orville moan. "Oh, goddamn, if that don't beat all. Must be that fuckin' new colonel. I ain't believin' it. Here they tell us to kill anything that moves in a fuckin' free-fire zone, and we're criminals for smokin' dope."

I was shocked that Linda had asked Speed to kill the guy. If Speed were to waste anyone, he'd do it of his own accord. I was surprised at Linda too, but evidently that "hell hath no fury" thing applied cross-culturally. When Speed quizzed Linda as to the villain's whereabouts, she could only say that the guys from Delta Company had told her that he had disappeared. This eased my mind. The lifers had tried to infiltrate Linda's, with only moderate success, and now it could be considered a one-shot deal. From now on, new guys would be scrutinized with the same intensity as a potential ambush site. Nevertheless, the lifers' persistence was worrisome, and any illusions on my part that the situation would ease were immediately dispelled.

*Bam, bam, bam!* A pounding at the door stilled the quiet mumbling of rage.

"Open up! MPs."

We stared at each other, shocked and dumbfounded. Here we were, supposedly hardened and cunning guerilla fighters, trapped like rats in Linda's mud-walled house. Katy flew into action and locked the wooden shutters on the windows while Linda checked the bolt on the door.

*Bam, bam, bam, bam!*

Katy, a model of calm efficiency, rolled up a straw mat that covered the floor, lifted a trap door, and motioned for us to jump in. In seconds, the trap door was quietly eased shut, leaving us whispering in the earthy, inky blackness.

"Go 'way, fuckin' MP," Linda shouted through her door. "This Linda house. No fuckin' MP gonna come in here."

Linda's defiance was as admirable as her knowledge of military law. The MPs, unless they could confront us directly outside of private property, had no jurisdiction to search her house. The point would be moot, of course, if a waiting game were to follow. It was possible that they would simply rotate guard on the house until circumstances forced us to leave. Dark images of us being paraded through the village with our hands over our heads like POWs filled my mind. I'd heard enough about Long Binh Jail to shudder at the prospect of spending the rest of my tour sweating in a steel box.

Linda persisted in feigning innocence and outrage, eventually threatening to call the village magistrate to settle the matter. Evidently, this last ploy must have intimidated the MPs, who were probably also questioning the legality of their move. They retreated. After a long and increasingly tense silence, Katy opened the door of our tomb.

"Boy-san say MPs leave. Boy-san say truck coming. Go! Now! Leave! Hurry!"

Grabbing our M16s, we blasted out of our earthen hideaway and flew out the door, squinting in the bright light. The residual adrenaline in my system gave me the distinct feeling of flying as I followed Creeper, leaping over fences and the stream with gobs of room to spare. When we hit the road, Speed had us set up a defensive perimeter as if we'd been attacked by the NVA. Panting and peeping through the grass along the ditch near the road, I could see that half the village had rallied in our defense. Mama-sans and children had formed a wider perimeter around us and were on the lookout for MPs. The truck arrived in seconds, and as we clambered on, I noticed that Speed had not been unnerved enough to relinquish the prize of our foray into the village. He smiled as the truck roared off and held aloft the rumpled brown grocery bag that contained our supply of smoke for our next mission.

As we approached Uplift, Speed pitched the package into the weeds along the road. He would retrieve it later that night, crawling again under the concertina wire in a risky half-hour mission. Tension rose again as the truck slowed for the MP's checkpoint. We all awaited that heart-stopping moment when the MPs would either stop the truck, as they were instructed to do, or wave us through. It was at that moment—and in full sight of the MPs—when Speed, Bruce, and Creeper chambered rounds in their M16s. They were pissed, really pissed, that any REMF would have the unmitigated gall to hassle us boony rats. They spent their tours sleeping on cots and working eight-hour days in relative luxury while we were pounding the boonies and sleeping in the mud. What's more, we were the ones who would be sent out to protect their perimeter if there was any hint of VC activity around Uplift. I understood the contempt and outrage that my buddies felt for the MPs. But at the same time, I knew that it wasn't really the MP's fault. They had their obscene, absurd job to do, and we had ours. Neither was commendable. We rolled through the checkpoint unopposed.

I was actually relieved to be looking at the jungle under the toes of my boots as we were flown out on our next mission. The rear, which had once afforded us an opportunity to shift down a couple of notches from the electric intensity and immediacy of attention required in the field, had become a nerve-wracking, potentially dangerous game of cat and mouse. I remembered overhearing a conversation months before about the question "Who would you kill, given the choice?" At that time, it seemed to be a toss-up among the men between the ARVNs, who would split at the first shot in a firefight (sometimes before), leaving the GIs holding the bag, and our lifers, some of whom would crawl over our bodies to advance their own careers. Lately, our lifers, particularly our new colonel, were on the top of everyone's list. I remembered being surprised at the time that the North Vietnamese regulars weren't even up for discussion, but now I knew why.

The NVA were simply experts at the game. Renowned for their cunning and patience, they fought with conviction, bravery, and consummate skill. They knew our tactics and thoroughly understood our mind-set and weaknesses. To play the game with them was to be confronted with our own ignorance. To survive, one had to assimilate as much of their subtlety and finesse as possible in an incredibly short span of time and reevaluate one's erroneous assumptions about these "ignorant, third-world savages." Yet for all the respect we had for them, we knew that they were as much the victims of circumstance as we were. We'd had scouts from time to time, ex-NVA regulars, who told us that they hated the war every bit as much as we did. Clearly, their societies and their politicians had sold them a bogus bill of goods, just as ours had, and now they, like us, were sent to die for it. One scout who worked for us, who called himself Tracy, had been with the NVA but had *Chiêu Hồi-ed* (surrendered). His personal story closely paralleled our own.

Tracy had fought the war for years, first with conviction, then with growing disenchantment. His breaking point came when a new, somewhat overzealous commander was sent to lead his company. His new CO, he said, was not content to follow the carefully planned strategies formulated by his superior officers, and at every chance, he initiated firefights with GIs, hoping to kill as many as possible, regardless of his superiors' overall strategy. Although they'd been somewhat successful in this endeavor, his company was taking more than their usual losses as a result of their CO's ambition. Finally, the night before they were supposed to spring an ambush on an unsuspecting platoon of GIs, Tracy could take it no more. He loosened the pin on a grenade, tied it to his sleeping CO's bootlace, ran away in the night, and surrendered to the GIs. I remembered that when Tracy told us this story one night on bunker guard, it was met with immediate recognition. Speed, Tennessee, Creeper — all of us — started laughing and patting him on the back. Irrespective of his former alliance, he was recognized as one of us.

As our chopper settled in the bush, I allowed myself the luxury of one thought. Given our recent experience in the rear, I thought, *It's hard to fight an enemy we've learned to respect.*

Even after we'd formed a perimeter and the last helicopter had thumpa-thumped its way over the ridge, I found it dangerously difficult to clear my mind and focus on the job at hand. Throughout the first mile or so on the trail, the heebie-jeebies from our stay in the rear clung to me like my uncle Henry's cigar smoke — stale, foul, and bitter. Eventually, however, the weight of my pack brought me back to the here and now. My collarbones screamed and my thighs burned, letting me know that if I didn't find that clear, calm, empty space, it was going to be a long day. We were making our way up the side of a steep mountain when I remembered to coordinate my breathing with my steps. Inhale, lift, step, exhale. Inhale, lift, step, exhale. Two hours later, as we started to follow a ridgeline, it happened. I was back. Colors brightened and my pack disappeared. My body dissolved, and once again, I was a pair of eyes and ears floating through the jungle. My vibes-detector was working again, too. There weren't any NVA around, not now, at least.

Relieved as I was to be back, I knew it wasn't something one could assume would always be there. What had once been a tightrope walk was now a narrow path; there was some slack, but not much. One thought could lead to another and another and another, and then I'd be back in hell, feeling the full torment of my body. Or worse still, I could start feeling sorry for myself and become completely exhausted.

Our new lieutenant had us loggered-in with plenty of time to heat our Cs and even brew a cup of instant coffee. I stole a few moments with Tennessee to get his impressions of our new CO, Quick.

"Oh, he's tight, alright," Tennessee whispered as we watched twilight envelope the valley below. "He sure won't be havin' us do the kinda stupid stuff our ol' CO did."

"Yeah, that's for sure," I said. "But he seems to know where the gooks are and how they act or somethin', doesn't he?"

"He knows better than most, but he's still goin' off of army intelligence."

We both laughed.

"Know what you're gettin' at, though, man," Tennessee confided. "You're worried 'cause you think he's gonna run us into more shit than the other dude. Who knows? I don't know, and if I did — well, you know ya can't be sweatin' the small stuff."

Tennessee lit a bomber and passed it to me for a toke.

"Oh, yeah, that reminds me," I said. "Do ya think Quick is gonna get all gung ho and try and bust us for smokin' dope in the field?"

Tennessee pushed hard on my shoulder, almost knocking me over.

"What's the matter with you tonight?" he asked with a grin. "Here, ya better smoke some more of this; you're all kinds of worried. Do I think Quick's gonna bust us for smokin' dope?" Tennessee giggled for a while, as if I'd asked the dumbest question on earth. "Let me put it this way," he said, reveling in the fact he had a chance to mess with me. "Who does Quick pick when he goes on those two-man huntin' trips when we're in the field?"

"Captain Speed," I said, already feeling pretty stupid.

"That's right!" Tennessee said with a giggle, patting me on the back. "Come on, man, give Quick a little credit. If he doesn't know Speed smokes dope, nobody does. Shit, it's in his records. He's been busted three times. So, you tell me. But really, man, I know what's happenin' with you. If you can't bring yourself to worry about the big stuff, ya start worrying about little stuff. But hey, man, ya can't worry about none of that stuff, 'cause fuck it. Jus' fuck it. It don't mean nothin'. But really, there's one thing that worries me."

"What's that?" I asked, honored that Tennessee would confide his worries in me.

"You're bogartin' the joint, man. Look at ya! You're bogartin' the joint!"

Tennessee grabbed the joint from my hand and took a toke. A seed exploded and blew sparks all over his shirt. He started to say something, but when he realized I already knew what he was going to say, we both started laughing. We said it together, "Pop! There goes another problem!"

For the next few days in the field, my system grew increasingly more adjusted to the routine. I had noticed when we flew out that we landed not all that far from the site of our last mission — the valley we went into on APCs and tanks. Perhaps we were circling around behind it; it was hard to tell exactly, but I knew we were somewhere around there. I had the distinct feeling that the NVA knew we were there and that they were choosing to avoid contact. Also, it was unaccountably clear to me that they felt that after our last go-round, we had the mojo going for us and were best left alone. I was beginning to get a feel for them. They were like that, kind of superstitious, kind of psychic. Sure, they'd shot down a jet, but they'd also blown two ambushes on the grunts — perfect setups. There were no dust-offs coming out of that valley.

As the days passed, I felt myself more and more completely immersed in the groove. There was an unmistakable way it felt. I trusted it and went with it, even though, sometimes, my silent, solitary wanderings led to some strange spaces. Lately I was obsessed with the thought that at any time, a sniper could shoot me right in the center of the forehead, right between and above the eyes. For hours, my attention would be drawn to that spot, and I would rub it when we took a break and before I went to sleep. Normally, I wouldn't allow myself to indulge in such constantly negative thinking, but this, whatever it was, was so persistent, so seemingly natural, that I let it ride. Surprisingly enough, the thought did not invoke a great deal of fear. Rather, it made each moment of my existence in this reality seem a priceless gift. I'd realize I wasn't dead, and I'd look around. How fantastic! How wonderful! That last step could have been your last, but you're still here.

Another thing that was happening was that before I went to sleep, I'd fold my arms over my chest, the way corpses are posed for burial, and I'd imagine that I was in my casket, the lid was shut, and now dirt was being shoveled over the top. *You're dead*, I would think. *Now, what's left*. I felt I had to know. I'd relax my muscles to minimize my awareness of them, slow my breathing, and still my thoughts. *What's left? What's left?* For a time, it would seem that all that would survive was a dot or point that knew of its own existence. Night after night, I felt totally compelled to do this exercise. It was part of the groove, and I would not fight it.

Three weeks later, the platoon followed a well-worn trail down a ridgeline and set up on a small hilltop overlooking a field of rice paddies. Across the field, palm trees and a few thatched roofs revealed the presence of a village. The rice in the paddies was half-grown and evidently not in need of much care, as none of the villagers were to be seen. We were told to dig in and to do an extra good job of it, complete with overhead cover and firing lanes — the whole bit. For the platoon, it was a sign that we were going to be there for a while. Speed made the rounds, making sure each squad had a supply of smoke. I set up my recently acquired hammock, and we were ready to party. Our new lieutenant seemed to be unusually forthcoming as to our purpose and told us that Captain Quick and the rest of the company were sweeping the area. Our function was to sit tight and keep a lookout for any NVA that might be traveling through in an attempt to avoid Quick's sweep. Evidently he suspected that they might infiltrate the village and use the civilians for cover. It sounded good, in theory.

In the morning, Bruce and Canary, one of the newbies, asked the lieutenant if they could slip into the village and refill the platoon's canteens from the well. Bruce was careful to explain that while we could fill our canteens with rice-paddy water, it was hard to filter out everything, excepting the larger chunks of water buffalo shit, and that

Doc required us to dose that water with extra halazone tablets to make it potable, if unpalatable. I could see our new lieutenant getting a little green as Bruce described the condition of the rice-paddy water — justifiably, to be sure — but he was working on him so shamelessly I was glad I had my boots on. The water buffalo doo-doo was getting pretty deep. I saw a nodded approval for the plan, and Bruce and Canary wasted no time emptying their packs and collecting empty canteens. When they left, I felt a little anxious, thinking that they should have had an armed escort, but they returned in short order, resupplied us, and were ready to party.

Creeper, Bruce, Tennessee, and Doc started a card game near my hammock. I was feeling somewhat distant and withdrawn at the time. It might have had to do with my macabre preoccupation with death during our last hump, but whatever. I was content to swing in my hammock and observe, and they were content to let me be.

In the days that followed, there was a progressive disintegration in the integrity of our ambush site. It started the next morning, with the arrival of two Coke girls — as girls selling Cokes were called — from the village. No harm, it seemed; we hadn't had an ice-cold anything for almost a month. That afternoon, a couple of boy-sans tentatively approached us with ripe coconuts to sell. Two days later, it was a veritable caravan from the village to our position. Boy-sans, Coke girls, mama-sans with their trays — like those cigarette girls who plied the nightclubs in the 1930s and 1940s — selling sunglasses, sweatbands, cigarettes, and candy. They all congregated around the platoon like bees on honey. But what topped it all was the two crazed boy-san pimps who drove their Honda 90s deftly across the rice-paddy dikes to our position with their girls sitting sidesaddle on the back. It wasn't much of an ambush, but hey, we were winning the hearts and minds of the Vietnamese people. It was our job.

Things were going swimmingly even into the next day. The lieutenant had lost the exasperated look on his face and was actually starting to have a good time. Our new platoon sergeant, the Bastard Rat, as he called himself, might otherwise have been a wet blanket, to say the least, if one mama-san hadn't given him such a good deal on a couple of bottles of cheap whiskey. The old fart was happy as a clam, staggering around and harassing us troops. Good old mama-san. I had to hand it to her; she really knew how to grease the wheels of the free-enterprise system. The place was really starting to have some atmosphere—kind of a combination flea market, garden party, and outdoor whorehouse. It was great. Given time, I suppose we would have strung some Chinese lanterns in the trees and hired a band, but this was not to be. Late in the afternoon, we had an uninvited guest.

I just happened to catch it out of the corner of my eye. Our new lieutenant was standing at attention, face red as a beet, while some other guy dressed in camouflage fatigues, with his back to me, paced back and forth in front of him. He needed no introduction. It was Captain Quick. He had slipped up on us with the party going full tilt boogie. I could tell from the captain's movements that he was doing all he could not to lose it altogether. He showed no appreciation whatsoever for our attempt at winning hearts and minds and was chewing the lieutenant's ass out without mercy. I felt sorry for our new platoon leader but figured it might be all for the best. I knew from the first time I met him that, regardless of his rank, his heart wasn't in this war. He might be getting his ass chewed out, but still, he was better off being soft and cared for by his men than being a hard-ass like McDouche and hated. I was getting short, but Speed and Tennessee had plenty of time left in their second tours to keep him out of trouble, and I knew they'd try.

Word of our visitor passed quickly and quietly through the platoon. We did our best to pick up scattered equipment and get things shipshape before the shit hit the fan. The lieutenant was still getting reamed when the Bastard Rat descended on our squad. He did his best at acting pissed off, but it was thoroughly unconvincing. He was an old soldier from the boys-will-be-boys school of thought, and we all knew he was just going through the motions, reprimanding us only for appearance's sake. Though he obviously had a great deal of affection for the men in his command, he was enigmatically distant when approached on a personal level. From time to time, various members of the platoon had approached him outside the context of his official capacity and offered friendship, but they were always decisively rebuffed. Living up to the namesake moniker scrawled on his helmet, he'd act like a cornered rat on those occasions, snarling, baring his teeth, and even going on the offensive. I'd seen it happen, and it was frightening. He had all the earmarks of someone who'd lost too many buddies in battle and believed that his friendship was the kiss of death. Tennessee had some of the same symptoms, but he could talk about it and, in doing so, was gradually coming out of his shell. But the Bastard Rat had built a defensive perimeter around his heart so formidable that none but the daring or foolhardy would hazard an approach. Except for the times when he was drunk enough to forget himself, he seemed destined to die from a case of terminal loneliness.

# 6 INTO THE LIGHT

WORD CAME DOWN TO SADDLE UP, AN UNUSUAL ORDER THIS LATE IN the day, but considering that we'd stolen a few days of fun, none of us was going to beef about it. From where we were in the valley, any path led up. But luck was with us, and we took a gently rising trail, following a ridgeline that led to higher elevations. I was happy to be in the bush again. Playful interludes like the one we'd just had would, for me, bring about a sense of uneasiness, dissipation, and eventually a kind of panic. Thoughts and emotions, long held at bay while humping the boonies, would reassert themselves and disrupt my sense of clarity and calm. I'd sense a slight, but noticeable, drop in my energy level and confidence, resulting in the fear that they might be lost for good. If I could catch these emotions in time, I'd revitalize myself by swinging in my hammock and staring at the clouds or stars, but more often than not, I'd get carried away by the "school's out" attitude and the pleasant, if unwholesome, distractions at hand.

In spite of the physical demands and danger, I felt that when we were on the move, I was going somewhere, not just physically but also in a nebulous, internal sense. Keeping my attention fixed in the present—from one microsecond to the next—had, I thought, allowed me to find a state of mind in which the weight of my pack seemed to disappear. I knew it had something to do with my increasing sensitivity to emotional energies or vibes, be they those of an NVA soldier or a friend, and I was positive it had something to do with the exhilarating sense of well-being I'd feel at the end of the day. Yet without the discipline enforced by the skills of our opponents—the knowledge that a lapse in concentration could cost a leg or one's life—I felt set adrift, vulnerable, and lost. I was sure that this had something to do with why Captain Speed, Tennessee, and Sgt. Ski had opted for a second tour, particularly after seeing Ski come back from a thirty-day leave in the States. The man was a wreck—depressed, untrusting, and confused. It took him the better part of our first mission to recover, laugh again, and get some spring back in his step. Something strange and incredibly ironic that had happened to him, but I couldn't for the life of me understand what it was.

At any rate, I was glad to be back in the groove again. The groove wasn't a static thing; it changed, evolved, and expanded, leading to new strange and exotic lands. Lately it was taking me on a tour of Morbidland, where death was behind every bush and around every corner. The groove allowed me to take the tour with calm detachment rather than stark terror. Although I was absolutely certain there weren't any NVA around and my position in the middle of our squad protected me from booby traps, Death, *my* death, leered at me from behind trees and taunted me in the calls of jungle birds. He constantly reminded me that a sniper's round to the center of my forehead could deliver me to him at any instant, and he drew so close to me at night that I could feel his chill. Never before had I been on such intimate terms with this inevitable aspect of my personal reality, yet the groove had led me there, and I knew not to fight it. That same groove that had led me to dizzying heights and uncontrollable laughter had revealed the exquisite beauty of the jungle. It now required a nodding acquaintance with my own mortality—who was I to resist? I felt that it was being gentle with me, easing me into acknowledging death's inescapable embrace, yet I sensed that there would come a time when the groove would fix my gaze and demand a face-to-face confrontation with the reality of the complete obliteration of my physical being.

We had gained enough elevation to free ourselves from the densest jungle, and at the first grassy patch large enough to accommodate a Huey, we stopped for resupply. We formed a perimeter, and when the chopper pilot requested identification, I popped a purple smoke grenade and tossed it into the center of the clearing. Hearing his approach, I stood at the end of the clearing that would allow him best clearance for his machine and raised my M16 overhead with both hands. He settled neatly in the clearing just long enough for his crew to kick off a few cases of Cs, bundles of clean fatigues, and a bag of mail. I dragged the mailbag to the lieutenant for distribution and found a place next to Doc Mock to wait while Bruce and Creeper doled out our rations and fatigues.

Doc's aid bag was open and ready before the first of several ailing boony rats found his way to his location. The usual cases of jungle rot, blistered feet, and insect bites were dispatched with Doc's expected efficiency, but when Creeper rolled up his pant leg, Doc's levity turned to serious concern. Creeper's machete had glanced off of a particularly hard branch a couple of days earlier and struck him in the shin. The cut was deep, and Doc surmised that the machete had possibly nicked the bone, though it was hard for him to tell exactly what was beneath the golf-ball-sized lump that festered on Creeper's leg.

"This is bad," Doc announced to the already annoyed Bastard Rat. "The whole thing's infected, and if it's gone to the bone, there's nothing I can do for him here. He's gotta be dusted off."

Noting the Bastard Rat's look of total exasperation, Doc was quick to add that our resupply chopper was yet to circle back and pick up our dirty fatigues and that since there was nothing he could do for Creeper there, that chopper would suffice. A nod of approval and some hurried goodbyes were the extent of Creeper's send-off party. They were all that was possible under the conditions, and in fifteen minutes, Creeper was gone, close enough to the end of his tour for us to know that he'd never return. We'd miss him, of course, and perhaps would have liked a chance to express our gratitude for his services and friendship more completely, but all in all, we were glad to see him go. He was home free, without even having to deal with the usual short-timer's paranoia about getting fucked up in his last few days in the bush. He'd made it, and we were happy for him.

I tightened the last strap on my now fully loaded pack, leaned it against a tree, and kicked back to savor yet another soggy Camel. Mail was brought around. Nothing for me this time, but I noted that Doc had gotten a huge care package from his folks in Kansas. This fact hadn't gone unnoticed by the Bastard Rat either, who was lustfully eyeing Doc's goodies as he stuffed them in his pack.

"Doc!" he growled. "Gimme a pudding."

Though Doc had heard him, he hesitated for a second and fiddled with his pack.

"Doc!" he growled even louder. "Gimme a pudding!"

Doc fiddled a little longer, just to get the Bastard Rat a little more irritated, and pulled an aluminum can of pudding out of his pack. He held it up, zeroed in on Sarge—eyes sparkling with impish humor and delight—and said, "Ask and ye shall receive, Big Sarge. Seek and ye shall find. If you have an intent heart to look, it shall be there!"

Big Sarge looked as if he were ready to explode. "Don't want any of your shit, Doc. Don't gimme none of that shit. Just hand it over."

Doc flipped him the can and shook his head in mock astonishment at the Rat's bad temper. Even though everyone in Vietnam knew that nobody but nobody fucked with the medics—not wanting to be on the bottom of the list were triage ever necessary—Doc pushed Sarge for all his position was worth. I wondered why Doc actually went out of his way to mess with Sarge; most of the rest of us were convinced that he would never come out of his shell. My wondering ceased when I realized that Doc simply responded to things in an entirely different way than me. While I might consider someone's character and likely response, Doc just acted, spontaneously and without judgment, and was free. He seemed to be able to enter any situation, act, and leave without a trace of sticky emotional residue or any sense of lingering, unfinished business about it. Like Captain Speed, he functioned with confidence from a place that had nothing to do with mental evaluation or consideration of results, yet his behavior showed unmistakable signs of clarity, compassion, magical precision, and completely effective timing. But these qualities were apparent only in retrospect.

Soon enough, I heard the call of the Bastard Rat signaling that it was time to hit the trail. The call was as persistent as that of any jungle lizard, though not nearly as melodious. "Doc, get your shit on, we're headin' out. Doc! Get your shit on. Damn it, Doc, stuff that shit in your bag, or we're leavin' without ya!"

They'd been playing this game for weeks, and it was getting to the point that anyone in the area would have to turn away to hide his snickering. Doc would be sitting there, calm and unruffled, intent on handing out one more handful of antibiotics or treating one more cut until Sarge got to the breaking point. He'd stall Sarge to the limits of his patience, then act as if he were frantically trying to get his shit together.

Once again, I felt the straps of a fully loaded pack dig into my shoulders as we slipped into the jungle, and for yet another time, each of us entered his own deeply personal inner realm. During the seemingly endless hours of silent stalking, we each stood before a mirror that uncompromisingly reflected our innermost thoughts and attitudes. In the field, on the trail, the self-created suffering resulting from anger, worry, and self-pity was never slow in coming. One slip, one minor indulgence in any form of negativity, and one was cast headlong into the region of hell specific to the offense.

At times, I'd feel myself transformed into a wild-eyed demon raging against the army, the ignorance, and my fate, ranting to no avail. The jungle's heat would become unbearable, my stomach would knot, and my mind would feel like it was stewing inside my steel pot. Then, sweating, sick, and with passion spent, I'd catch myself and thank God that my tantrum hadn't caused me to miss a booby trap or sniper. At other times, I'd load sandbags of self-pity into my pack till my legs would burn, then chill, making me feel cold and weak from nausea. These were admittedly useless endeavors—but hey, ya never know until you try. Once I knew the consequences, I learned not to try them too often. Over the months, I'd learned to assign an internal monitor that would warn me of these dangers, and from time to time, he'd break my train of thought, like Barney Fife: "Here it comes — Andy — here it comes. Ya gotta nip it, nip it in the bud!"

I realized why the old-timers had so often repeated their repertoire of stock phrases in response to newbies' grousing and complaints, real or imaginary. The dialogue would go like this:

NEWBIE: *God. Ya know what I could go for right now? A Big Mac with cheese, a shake, and a large order of fries.*

OLD-TIMER: *Wish in one hand, man, and shit in the other, and see which one fills up first.*

Or:

NEWBIE: *Gee, this pack is really heavy, and my boots don't fit very good.*

OLD-TIMER: *Sounds like a personal problem, man. Tell it to the chaplain.*

Or:

NEWBIE: *The water in my canteen tastes like plastic.*

OLD-TIMER: *Fuck it, man. It don't mean nothin'.*

Or:

*To a newbie who was pining over a letter from his sweetheart at mail call.*

OLD-TIMER: *If the army would have wanted you to have a girlfriend, they would have issued you one.*

I'd been stung by the old-timers' rebuffs countless times during my early weeks in the field and was only now fully able to appreciate their intent. They seemed brutal at the time, but rather than offer some half-hearted sympathy, they'd made it clear that I was the one responsible for my own attitudes and their emotional consequences. For the first time in my life, it was clear to me that my well-being was a matter of choice. I was free to rage, fret, or go on a bummer—that was entirely my own business—but if it was painful, they didn't want to hear about it. I'd be left to bear the full weight of my choices, and they theirs. At that time, the nature of their choices was a mystery to me, but the results were clear. They were calm, generally of good humor, and had an infuriatingly consistent sense of gratitude.

As we moved along the trail, I realized that the jungle was not at all the frightening place it once had been. I slipped deftly past some tangled vines of thought and, in doing so, missed getting snagged by some thorny emotions. The jungle required constant vigilance, but I gave it its due, knowing the trail led to a sunlit clearing with a spring of cool, clean water. We climbed a small hill, and while going down the slope that followed, I could see the front half of the platoon: Tennessee, Bruce, Doc, and Speed. Their movements—our movements—harmonized like a school of fish or the branches of a tree in a breeze. We were no longer separate selves, but one being, gliding through the jungle, looking for a clearing in the sun.

Though there was no sense of time in this, days passed. My radio crackled, "Hotel Fox, Hotel Fox, this is Hotel Alpha, request Lima Zulu." We stopped on the rise of a small hill. There were no large trees in the area, and the platoon took to the hilltop, machetes flashing, like cane cutters in a field, and soon cleared a circle big enough for a Huey. Our location had been compromised by the racket, so we carefully guarded the perimeter while a sortie of Hueys scouted for our location. With the sound of choppers still quite distant, I popped a green smoke in the center of the clearing. Not long after, the pale wisp of mint-green smoke drifted above the brush, I heard a pilot on the radio. "Have green smoke. Do you copy? Have green smoke."

"That's a Roger on the copy and a Roger on the smoke," I confirmed, letting the pilot verify our location. It was his job to verify the color of smoke, so that the NVA, listening in on our radio communications, couldn't try to lure him in with smoke of their own. Soon we were stung with flying brush as the first of the sortie eased in and momentarily touched down. With the efficiency of a diving hawk snagging a rabbit, it plucked up a squad of men and flew off. The remaining choppers swooped down in rapid succession to scoop up the rest of us, and in minutes, we were flying in formation at altitude.

As we floated over the sea of mountains, I allowed myself the luxury of entertaining a few thoughts about our destination and the nature of our next mission. We hadn't been told to prepare to land in a hot LZ, which, though mildly reassuring, left a multitude of options. Too many, I finally concluded, to bother myself with needless speculation. Finding myself becoming increasingly irked at the lifers' need for secrecy about such things, I shut down the thinking part of my mind and refocused in the present. We floated over miles of steep mountains before the terrain eased into rolling hills. As the chopper carved a wide arc in the sky, I could feel that we were losing altitude. Instinctively, my mind cleared and my body tensed. Preparing for the worst, I scanned the area, trying to pinpoint the most likely LZ. Below my boots and billowing pant legs were palms, indicating an unseen river, along with thatched roofs and flooded rice paddies. We skimmed in low over the paddies. Suddenly the chopper lifted its nose and dropped its tail, like a bird coming in to roost. It settled gently on a hilltop, in the middle of a circle of a dozen well-fortified bunkers; it looked like we were in for a boony rat's dream vacation—bunker guard on a minibase.

It was truly the best of all possible worlds for a platoon of grunts. No humping, no lifers (except for the Bastard Rat and Lieutenant Anderson), and no booby traps. It was defendable enough that only a major suicide mission on the part of the NVA could overrun it, yet it had obviously been established long enough that they weren't going to stumble across it by accident. As it was on a hilltop, every "room" had a view and was outfitted with genuine army-issue cots—no more of that waking up in the mud in water-logged fatigues for us. There was only one catch, and as Lieutenant Anderson briefed us about our mission, I heard the groans as he revealed it.

"A platoon of ARVNs is going to join us every night just before sun-down, and they're going to man every other bunker."

His news that they'd return to their village after two hours was met with sighs of relief. The ARVNs were generally considered to be a first-class pain in the ass. They'd steal your rifle or personal effects in the blink of an eye and hide behind the language barrier if you tried to get anything back. "*Noooo biết, noooo biết*" (I don't understand) would be their plaintive cry under such circumstances, but if there was some-thing they wanted, they could always produce someone who could speak enough to ask for it. If the shit hit the fan, they'd vanish into thin air, sometimes before the first shot was fired. My only consolation was that I spoke just enough French Vietnamese to say, "*Tí tí* time. GI *fini* Vietnam" (In a short time, the GIs are pulling out of Vietnam). To which they'd invariably reply, "*beaucoup xạo, beaucoup xạo*" (Big lie). It was outrageous to us that while we were fighting and dying for their country, their only concern was how much money they could make on their thievery and the black market.

ARVNs notwithstanding, I was happy to be out of the boonies for a while and was determined to make the best of it. Tennessee, Bruce, Captain Speed, Orville, and I were assigned a bunker on the village side of the perimeter, which afforded a tremendous view of the valley below. It looked like a scene from hundreds, quite possibly thousands, of years ago. A lone farmer in the distance waded in the paddies behind a water buffalo and wooden plow. Timeless palms shaded the bamboo, mud, and thatch houses of the village, while the eternally self-renewing jungle crowded the paddy fields on three sides. The serene scene spoke volumes about life, continuity, simplicity, and harmony with nature. I had little doubt that this bit of land could have sustained the village for yet another thousand years of tranquil acceptance of the laws of nature had not the ugliness of war invaded this peaceful place.

Late in the day, in the steaming, sweltering heat of the after-noon sun, the ARVNs came trudging up the trail that connected the village to the minibase. For the most part, they acted like unmanage-able preadolescent boys, pushing, shoving, and tripping each other and marching in a bouncy exaggeration of military style. Until they entered our perimeter, that is. There they suddenly changed their demeanor to that of a frightened child. They gathered together at one of the two bunkers in the center of the perimeter for assignments and looked at us sullenly, though they were not frightened enough to dispense with one of their favorite pastimes: pointing at one of us, yammering to each other in Vietnamese, and laughing. I knew that there was much about them I didn't understand and tried my best to make allowances for their behavior, but they didn't make it easy.

We retreated to the cool of our earthen bunker for the remainder of the afternoon. I lounged in a hammock strung from the beams, listening to the radio. It was luxurious. Noticing the lengthening shadows, I left my comrades and positioned myself on the bunker's roof, facing west, for my sunset-gazing ritual. Given the chance, I found myself doing this at every opportunity, whether in the field or back at our base camp. There was something about evening that I'd long ago realized had a wonderful effect on me. It evened and balanced the competing aspects of my inner self that were constantly vying for attention. Along with the setting sun, thoughts from my overactive mind would ebb enough for my emotions to make their presence known. Acknowledging the emotion of the moment, be it melancholy, anger, or fear, seemed sufficient to allow it to retreat for another day. At twilight, my system was usually quiet enough for me to send out my intuitive feelers for a read on the environment. I could feel the reassuring confidence of the trees or the carefree caress of a breeze as it slipped over the hilltop.

Lately, it seemed that the sun itself had found a pinprick in my personal armor. As I sat, silently immersed in the beauty of yet another sunset, its light wormed its way in and shone on my heart. I could feel in my chest the wan smile of my heart's reply—feeling, yet unbelieving, that anyone or anything would care to nurture it. It tricked me into no-time time, for when I once again became aware of my surroundings, night had fallen, and I'd been enveloped by the cool, black air. The glow in my heart remained for quite a while, making me smile unknowingly. Its light gradually waned, the way the glowing embers of a campfire shine brightly at first but eventually fade into darkness, leaving me feeling calm, loved, and reassured. Had I the desire to think at the time, I would have noted that something strange and mysterious was going on.

Except for Orville, who pulled the morning watch, we slept in till midmorning. I dug in my pack for some Cs, made a stove out of a cracker can, and was heating some water for instant coffee when Speed handed me a bomber for hits. A couple of tokes, and I was grinning like the Cheshire cat as I added a package of hot chocolate mix to the nasty C-rat coffee. Sgt. Pepper, our army DJ, was into a marathon from the new Crosby, Stills, Nash & Young album when Doc Mock dropped in for a visit. Army regulations had it that Doc was supposed to travel and camp with the lifers — in this case, the Bastard Rat and Lieutenant Anderson — which, though somewhat confining for Doc, offered us access to the somewhat confidential nature of our mission.

"Looks like we're going to be here for a while," Doc confided. "They don't know for sure, but it looks like at least a week."

"Out fucking standing," Bruce shouted, as he broke into spasmodic stoned giggling. He jumped off his cot and made the rounds of the squad for a series of uninhibited high fives. He wanted to make sure everyone shared his enthusiasm at our unexpected good fortune. We did.

Orville was suddenly suspicious. "But what's the deal? Are they gonna send us out on five-man patrols during the day, or what?"

"Nah, man, don't sweat it," Doc responded. "That was totally McDouche's doing. No one from the rear requested that shit."

"Yeah," Speed interjected. "Remember that ranger handbook McDouche used to carry in his shirt pocket? That's where he got those fucking bright ideas. He was just doin' that shit to cover his own ass. He didn't care if we were out there stompin' on booby traps or runnin' into shit so long as he could be sure no one was sneakin' up on *him*. Likely fuckin' story anyway, but Anderson's cool. I been scopin' him out. He ain't up to that kinda shit."

"But what if somebody tells him what McDouche used to do?" asked Orville.

At that, Tennessee and Bruce pounced on Orville in a playful mock fight. Tennessee held his hand over Orville's mouth so he couldn't ask any more worried questions while Bruce rapped his knuckles on his head. Doc jumped in and started tickling him till it looked like poor Orville was going to explode. They held him down while Speed shot-gunned him by blowing backward through a pipe filled with dope. Then they suddenly let him go.

"You fuckers better stay offa me," Orville said, trying to act serious. But he was grinning, and though a little skittish about another attack of tickling, he was no longer worried about our stay at the minibase.

Feeling a little claustrophobic in the bunker, I decided to scout the hilltop and see what was going on. Squinting into the blazing light of day, I felt instantly seared by the heat. Most of the guys stayed inside to avoid the heat, but I found Sgt. Sam, our 60 gunner, sitting in the shade of his bunker, polishing his machine gun. It was like meeting a long-lost friend; our reconnaissance missions in the field offered little opportunity to talk with the guys in other squads. I'd always liked Sam. He had a great sense of humor, as did most of the guys in their second tour, and could always be counted on in a pinch to bring smoke with his 60. He had Nordic good looks and nearly white, sun-bleached hair, but he could do a great impression of Stan Laurel when he sensed the need for a laugh. He carefully leaned the barrel of his 60 against the bunker, stood, and offered me a hooked-thumb handshake.

"How goes it with Baby-san?" he asked, with a knowing grin. He could tell that I was a little buzzed.

"It's cool," I responded. "No fucking sweat, GI. If we can hang out on this hilltop for another couple of months, I'll have it made."

In the conversation that followed, Sam clued me in on one of the new guys in his squad who had been added to the platoon during the last resupply. The guy's name was Cory, Doc Cory—he was a medic. Sam viewed him with uncharacteristic suspicion.

"He's way out there," Sam confided. "Sometimes he seems okay, but at other times, he's kind of gone. He's a transfer from Delta Company, and you know they don't do that very often. Says he's been in the field for six months, but he seems pretty flaky to me. Worst of all, he acts like he's hiding something. I don't remember anybody who's been in the field that long acting like there's something to hide. It's weird. I don't like it, but I haven't figured him out yet. Maybe he's doin' smack or something. I just don't know. There he is! Check him out."

I saw a short, blondish guy with a round face messing with his pack by the next bunker and wandered casually over to the area to get a feel for the newest member of our platoon. As I approached, he waved me over. Without hesitation or checking me out at all, he opened his aid bag and assembled a makeshift water pipe out of an IV bottle, a syringe, and some surgical tubing. Before I could even comment, he filled the syringe with some loose grass, fired it up, and offered me a toke. He had done all this within direct sight of the door to Lieutenant Anderson's bunker. One trip to the latrine by the lieutenant, and he would have been busted on the spot. I looked over my shoulder at the vacant doorway to Anderson's bunker, took a toke, nodded thanks, and headed back to Sam's bunker. Walking back, I could see Sam shaking his head in disbelief. Though the lifers knew we smoked, we were careful not to flaunt it, allowing them plausible deniability if we were ever confronted by anyone outside the platoon. It was an unspoken agreement that seemed to keep everyone happy, but this new dude was sure to throw a wrench in the works.

"See what I mean?" Sam asked when I was within earshot. "I just talked to him yesterday and told him to be cool, but look at that."

I looked back at the bunker to see Cory toking on his pipe in full view of anyone who had happened to venture out into the sun. It was upsetting, but I hoped that, all in all, it would be a minor snag. I knew that the rest of the platoon had enough cohesiveness and competence to compensate for one off-the-wall character, but I didn't exactly relish the thought of Doc Cory working on me if the shit hit the fan.

That evening I settled in for another sunset. Gazing to the west, the colors of the sky had returned and offered me solace. The blazing light had already softened. Splashes of neon orange appeared before my unfocused eyes, filling me with wonder and gratitude. The tension in my body fell away as I glided into no-time time. Gentle purple and rose mists infused me with their light. Warm waves rippled from my heart, filling me with peace. A quiet joy made me smile. Hours-long moments lingered as the colors slowly faded. At twilight, it seemed as if the light had fused with the air for a moment, giving it life and power. Breathing deeply of the sun's last light, I felt myself dissolve into the growing shadows — almost, almost gone.

The crunching of boots on gravel told me someone was approaching, yet I sat still and unperturbed. Tennessee slipped up beside me, his eyes throwing sparks of mischief like a pinwheel on the Fourth of July. He reached in his shirt pocket and handed me a bomber, then lit it with his Zippo. One toke, and I was expanding beyond my body, electrified and euphoric.

"Thanks, dude," I said. "That's real nice."

"Aw, fuck, man, it ain't nothin', and you know it," he said, shoving me on the shoulder and laughing at my body's rubbery response.

"Ya know," he continued, "I was just thinking you're getting short, aren't ya?"

"I don't know," I managed, already having a hard time thinking.

"Ya gotta be. You got here right after I started my second tour, and I'm gettin' pretty short myself."

I started feeling giddy and amused. It all seemed so serious and real to Tennessee, but to me, it didn't seem to matter. As I strained to figure things out, I realized that I had absolutely no idea what month it was. The last frame of reference I had was R & R in June; anything past that was a complete mystery.

Tennessee giggled at my confusion. "Well, when did ya get in country then?"

"I left Seattle December 11."

"Okay, good enough," he pulled a dog-eared calendar card out of his wallet, squinted at it for a minute, then flicked open his Zippo for better light.

"Here it is," he said excitedly. "Here we are. Today's October 7. Wow, man! You've been a two-digit midget for better than a month and didn't even know it. Hey, man, we gotta celebrate." A two-digit midget was someone with ninety-nine days or less left in his tour.

Sparks were still flying off of his eyes as he dug in the side pocket of his fatigues. He pulled out a can of Cs and handed me an opener.

"Here, have some peaches."

My tongue seemed to grow fat and dry as I wrestled the little opener around the can's lid. The stoned munchies had already set in, in a big way. When the can was open at last, I sipped some of the juice so as to not spill its sugary ecstasy. Nearly overwhelmed by the shock of sweet, I dove in with my spoon and carefully guided a piece of fruit into my mouth. I felt like one big taste bud as peachness filled my mind. Still chewing, I handed the can to Tennessee. He refused. I tried again to no avail.

"Nah, go ahead, man, really! You're so short everybody's gonna think you're standin' in a hole. We gotta celebrate!"

I wasn't about to argue. The peaches were delicious—everyone's favorite C-rat treat. In seconds, the small can was empty.

"Wow, man, that was great, but hey, you didn't have to do that."

"I didn't," Tennessee replied with a mischievous grin. He was twitching with barely controlled laughter. "Those weren't peaches."

At that, we both burst into uncontrolled laughter. A couple of times Tennessee tried to say the punch line we both knew all too well, but he was laughing too hard to talk. When he finally got himself under control, he blurted out, "They were apricots." At which we both exploded in sidesplitting convulsions of laughter.

It was the oldest trick in the book, a Vietnam chestnut. Get a guy stoned and suggestible and pass off a can of rubbery, furry apricots for peaches. We loved to pull it on the newbies, and in fact, Tennessee had hit me with this one at least twice before, but he had spaced them out just long enough for me to forget. And this time, with the elaborate prelude of the calendar and all . . .

*Brrrrrap! Pop! Pop! Brrrrrap!*

Rifle fire! An electric jolt went up my spine. A flash of stark terror. Then nothing. Calm. Clear. The tinkle of brass empties told me the source of the firing was behind and above us. I grabbed my M16 and chambered a round. Tennessee was already on his feet and hollering in Vietnamese, "Get out of here, motherfucker. Get out! Get out!" He was pointing his rifle at something I couldn't see on top of our bunker. I heard the banter of Vietnamese and then nothing.

The Bastard Rat must have been roused from his bunker, as I heard him growl. "What the fuck is going on over there?"

"Nothin', Sarge," Tennessee hollered back across the compound. "Just the fucking ARVNs. They think we're under attack."

"Well, tell them to shut up. Slap 'em. Tell 'em I'm not putting up with any of their bullshit," he bellowed.

While Tennessee translated the Bastard Rat's message to the ARVNs, I loosened the clip on my M16 and flipped the chambered round into the dirt. I was polishing the round on my shirt when Tennessee slipped back around to the front of the bunker and sat down beside me. He seemed to have cooled off, as he was giggling again, but suddenly he got real serious and said, "Don't trust those fuckin' ARVNs for a second, Baby-san. I know ya got the scope on 'em, but you've never had to fight with 'em. They'll do anything to save their own asses, and as you just saw, they're squirrelly as hell. If we get hit while they're on the hill with us, get back to our bunker and get on your radio. Keep tabs on the rest of the platoon and watch your backside. I'm tellin' ya, if the shit hits the fan, it'll be hard to tell which side they're on."

At that, we returned to our bunker. While Tennessee filled the squad in on our misadventure, I felt suddenly fatigued. Perhaps it was my first case of short-timer's nerves, but I was sure glad to find an empty cot. It seemed that my mind had taken off without me, running at full speed, thinking about things I hadn't thought about in months—like time. It was so strange to try to comprehend something like sixty days when, for months, my attention had been focused almost entirely in the present. Even when they told us we were going to man a fire base for two or three weeks, it didn't really register. Things changed, there was nothing we could count on, and we knew better than to try. But this sixty-day thing weighed on me. It was an impossible burden, and it colored my view of the present like a pair of dark glasses. I wished Tennessee hadn't mentioned it, but I knew that I would have discovered it anyway. Mercifully, my mind shorted out, and I fell asleep.

As the days slid by, I could sense a growing tension in the platoon. We all knew that, in spite of the ARVNs, we were fairly safe on the hilltop and that manning the base was a hell of a lot easier physically than humping the boonies. No one mentioned it, but there was a growing sense that we would soon be out on another mission. For me, Mr. Short Time, another mission was a particularly ominous concept. Everyone knew that when your number was up, it was up, but after it's been in the hat for a while, it's hard to fight the feeling that your number might float to the top. Until now, I hadn't understood why guys who were short would dig deep trenches for themselves in the bush or sleep with their helmets on. Now, with time a part of my own reality, I realized how difficult it was not to review the struggle and the suffering, the close calls and the lucky breaks. Like everyone else who had neared the end of his tour, I wanted to make it to the light at the end of my personal tunnel, and I wondered if my luck would hold.

A raucous commotion shattered my worrisome contemplation and zapped me back to the here and now. I looked up to see the small yellow puppy that had become the platoon's mascot snarling and running in circles while Lt. Anderson tried to draw a bead on it with his M16. Foaming at the mouth, the dog was obviously rabid, but Doc wanted to be sure and implored the lieutenant to not shoot it in the head, which would be needed for analysis. One quick pop, and the little puppy was dead. Its body was placed in a plastic bag, and within an hour, a chopper arrived and carried it away. It was a sad, grisly scene that had dire implications for the whole platoon.

Late that afternoon, Lt. Anderson called the platoon together for a meeting. He asked anyone who had handled the puppy to step forward. This elicited a confused response. Did it mean that we had to have fed it? What if it had licked us? If it licked us, did we have to have a cut to get rabies?

"Fuck it," growled the Bastard Rat, ending any further discussion. "We're all going in for rabies shots—the whole fucking platoon."

When we got to the rear, word had it that the colonel, our gung ho new battalion commander, was absolutely livid about our platoon being deactivated for twelve days for a series of rabies shots. In the rare times we'd seen him outside the triple-thick fortress of the tactical command bunker, it was easy for us to reason why. His starched fatigues with all the right shit sewn on them and his shiny boots told the tale. He was a lifer to the max and, like many of the officers, he considered his tour of duty a great opportunity to advance his career. Push a pin in the map here or there, concoct some brilliant strategy (a virtual impossibility, considering the intelligence reports he had to work with), get an impressive body count, and presto, he'd have himself a chest full of medals to wear back in the States. And, who knows, maybe even a promotion or two. It was amazing to me that someone could have been in Vietnam for three months and still be so deluded, but every time I saw him, it was déjà vu Fort Benning. He had the tight-ass walk, flat-top haircut, and crisp salute of a man who definitely didn't know where he was.

Even before our first rabies shot, I learned that the colonel was still cracking down on the dudes who smoked dope. Some of the boony rats from Delta Company had tried to drop him a subtle hint—in the form of a grenade tossed into his private shitter—that maybe the guys in the field had seen too much death and too many crippled bodies to be intimidated by his rank and the authority of military regulations. We were truly beyond reform. Yet he persisted. I couldn't imagine a man sitting in his private shitter (rank has its privileges), looking at the shrapnel holes in the door, and thinking, "Well, things take time. All I have to do is keep the pressure on, and sooner or later, they'll conform." *Nevah hoppen.*

So we lined up at the aid station for our shots. As the line moved inside, I could see my buddies lying on stretchers as a team of medics administered the shots. After the horror stories I'd heard about rabies shots, I was relieved to see that all they did was take a pinch of skin near the navel and slip in a normal-looking needle. We were told that they were going to inject us at twelve and six (above and below the navel), then three and nine, and they would fill in the remaining gaps as the days passed. I was thinking that the next twelve days were going to be a piece of cake until I left the aid station and saw that the Bastard Rat was riding herd on the guys who had left before me. The colonel, we were told, had plans for us.

We were escorted to an area behind the colonel's bunker, where a deuce and a half had just dumped a sizable pile of dirt. The shovels and bundles of empty sandbags clarified our mission. We were going to put yet another layer of sandbags on the colonel's bunker. Though fortifying bunkers was a laughably easy job, I could tell from the banter that most of the guys considered it punishment for our having exposed ourselves to rabies. It also seemed that the colonel's bunker had been chosen to remind us of our subservience. Both points were noted, but neither had the intended effect.

As soon as we finished the task, which we all knew was to be followed by eleven more days of menial labor, Doc Mock headed straight for the aid station. In the books of army regulations regarding the treatment of personnel, he found our salvation in black and white: during the administration of rabies serum, "only light duty shall be allowed during the series of injections." Doc was euphoric when he brought us the news. It seemed such a fitting touché to the man who insisted on going by the book. He said that when he first presented his find to the lifers, they tried to squirm out of their own regulations. But using his medical savvy and a measure or two of BS, he convinced them that severe reactions could set in if they persisted in using us as beasts of burden for the duration.

So we were free. Free to shop at the trailer PX, to run the gauntlet of MPs and go to Linda's for a buzz, and to catch the occasional movie shown on a piece of white painted plywood. And for me, it meant that I was down to only six weeks of possible time in the field.

That night, bunker guard was a no-holds-barred blowout. We had tunes, Cokes, bombers, and food from the EM club in abundant supply, but as we settled in to party, I noticed two things were missing: Sesame the Wonder Dog and Big Ernie. I asked about them and was told that Big Ernie had inexplicably joined a recon team. I had a vague feeling that he had always wanted to emulate us to some degree. Perhaps he thought that being in the field had put us all through some kinds of changes that he wanted to experience firsthand. He wanted to share in our camaraderie and felt he had to go into the boonies to do it. Not everyone needs to get hit in the head the way we had to value brotherhood, honesty, and loyalty. I'd always felt that Big Ernie had gotten the hang of things even without experiencing what we had, and I was somewhat saddened to think that he felt he had to prove it to himself in such a dramatic way. But that was his choice, and there was no turning back.

Sesame, nemesis of all the lifers in the rear, had been ordered destroyed soon after it was discovered our platoon had to return to the rear for rabies shots. The lifers had wanted to get rid of him for a long time and jumped at the chance. Tommy, my REMF buddy, told me that they had taken Sesame to the aid station the day before and shot him up with tranquilizers, then they unceremoniously threw his body in the dump. A truly undeserved fate for such a steadfast friend.

In spite of everything, we partied on. Captain Speed and Tennessee had command positions in their twin lawn chairs, and Bruce and Doc dug in their packs for sweets after our evening smoke. I sat contentedly with my feet hanging off the bunker's sandbag roof, watching the sky change colors with the setting sun. As the clouds began to change from neon orange to violet, on their way to dusty blue-gray, I felt secure in knowing that I'd be able to watch the entire hour-long spectacle without being interrupted. There was an unspoken code among the men in the platoon—time for solitude was respected. Unless I looked lonely or troubled, no one would intrude. After some indeterminate time in the velvet darkness of an overcast night, I slipped back toward Speed and Tennessee to listen to their conversation.

*Phaap.* We could almost hear the light as the guys on the hill switched on their 150-million-candle-power searchlight. Bruce let out a long, drawn-out "Wow" and started laughing as the light's blazing white amoeba crept around our perimeter, just outside the concertina wire. As it was almost impossible not to, we watched, transfixed, as the light tracked its usual course, but then something went terribly awry. The amoeba jerked suddenly and stopped, settling directly over bunker sixteen.

We sat stunned and helpless, knowing full well that this was the kind of fuck-up that the VC rarely let slide. Seconds dragged by. Enough time to zero in a rocket or mortar. Nothing happened. Then to our amazement, we watched as a lone figure climbed atop the bunker and faced the light, standing stock-still. Even a VC who was a lousy shot could have taken his head off with one shot at three hundred yards.

Bruce bellowed in alarm, "What the fuck is he doing?"

As he started to bob and weave, I heard Tennessee tell Captain Speed to turn up the radio. The army DJ had just started playing Steppenwolf's "Magic Carpet Ride," and suddenly it was obvious what the nameless man was doing. He was dancing, prancing, marking time, and pantomiming with such style and grace it was as if he were spirit incarnate. Fearless, weightless, precise, and light, he pierced the night, all but outshining the blazing white amoeba that enveloped him.

In the reflected glow of the light, I copped a glance at Captain Speed. He was smiling; he knew. A lot of new guys had been added to the company recently and needed to see this. They were groping for ways to survive the insanity of being in Vietnam, and they might as well let a master show them how it was done. This was no self-conscious flaunting of death, but rather an expression of full awareness. The dancer's timing was superb, spontaneous, and exact, full to the brim with unrestrained joy. When the song ended, he finished his act by getting down on one knee and spreading his arms to the light, like some ham actor in an old vaudevillian play.

The light went out. Whoops, hollers, and applause erupted across the half of the perimeter that had seen the show. In one small moment in time, the mysterious man had revealed, to newbies and old-timers alike, the essence of his presence, in the night, in the light, in Vietnam.

# 7 SHORT TIME

THERE HAD BEEN SILENCE FOR ALMOST AN HOUR WHEN I HEARD A cheer from the bunker next door. *Could be anything,* I thought, straining in the misty light to see the latest cause of celebration. For a moment, I thought I was hallucinating as I caught the barely discernable silhouette of an animal walking up the road toward our bunker. It trudged in a wobbly but determined way, and as it drew nearer, I understood the cheer. It was Sesame, returning from the dead—or the nearly dead. He'd been downed but not out. We watched in amazement as he climbed to the roof of our bunker with such resolve that we felt he would have been insulted to have been offered a hand. Once on top, he almost disappeared beneath a swarm of hugs and pets from Tennessee, Bruce, and me. But Sesame had never been one to bask in the limelight. He stood up and shook as if trying to dry himself after a swim in the stream and returned to his post at the bunker's edge.

We'd been in the rear for six days when I happened to run across Neil. He had carried a radio for Capt. Quick for a long time. I realized I hadn't seen him for months. Though we hadn't exactly been the best of friends—in fact, I always thought he had ratted on me for smoking dope when I was first in country—he seemed glad to see me, so I went along for the ride. While he chatted away, I became aware of some nebulous shift that had occurred in me during my tour. The concept of friends and enemies—or adversaries, even—seemed odd, artificial, and totally contrived. For me, it no longer applied. There were people with whom I felt no sense of separation at all, like Tennessee, Speed, Bruce, Creeper, and Doc Mock, to name a few. To call them *friends* seemed absurd and almost demeaning to the quality of our relationship. We called each other *brother,* but it was far beyond that.

As I mused over this new revelation and tried to formulate what I was feeling, a memory returned to bail me out of my quandary. The platoon had once loggered on the peak of the tallest mountain in sight, and since we'd been told that we would be there for a couple more days, we stayed up well past midnight. Invariably, when we partied, guys sat in a circle. It made it easier to pass pipes and bombers, but this was no major consideration—three guys or thirty, we were always in a circle. This particular night the circle grew to about ten of us, and then we were unexpectedly approached by a guy named Donald Lohman.

Now Donald was an unusual character; he seemed to epitomize the concept of carrying a low profile. He'd been with us for months, but no one claimed to know anything about him except that he was the platoon's master "ghoster." Rarely verbal and neither friendly nor standoffish, he'd float along with the platoon for weeks, then he'd suddenly seem to disappear. Usually we'd find out that Doc had diagnosed him with terminal athlete's foot or some other minor malady and sent him to the rear. In the rear, he'd blend in with the woodwork so well that it would be a month or more before they'd realize that he'd been long since healed up and ship him out to the boonies again. Even his normal voice was almost a whisper. He'd smoked with us from time to time, but not very often; he said it made him feel uncomfortably aware of his internal organs. No one questioned him about this or pressured him in any way. He was free to come and go as he pleased, but this night he was with us.

It was one of those nights when the cool air seemed to bring calm to your very bones. Starry and still, and the circle was quiet, with only reassuring murmurs and the occasional giggle to gently push back the silence. The soft noises waxed and waned rhythmically until suddenly there seemed to be a hole in the sound, a moment of complete silence.

"Ya know."

God, it was Lohman's voice filling the void! An electric anticipation filled the air.

"Ya know, it's like we're a flower, and each one of us is a petal."

Bruce, who was sitting just to my left, let out an altogether too loud, "Wow" and fell over backward, trying to control a case of the giggles. I heard a couple quiet voices say, "Right on" and "Right on, motherfucker, right on," and I could feel a huge, nodding grin settle over the circle.

Having filled me in on the information I had fumbled for about my past encounters with Donald Lohman, my memory switched off and dropped me back into the here and now. As I looked at Neil, his words were just beginning to register, and I realized what I was trying to articulate about all of us being more than brothers. We were all petals on the same flower. Some of us didn't know it yet, and some of us weren't sure. Neil wasn't sure, but fuck it—that didn't mean anything.

"And so they dusted me off and sent me to Cam Ranh for a while," Neil continued, as he rolled up his shirtsleeve, "but I had too much time left in country so they sent me back here. My hand is still pretty stiff, so they made me a reporter for the base paper. It's an easy detail, and I can get lots of passes to the air base 'cause they have a darkroom there for developing pictures. Hey, they've even got an air-conditioned movie theater there, a swimming pool, and a mini-putt golf course. Those air force guys really know how to live. But, anyway, I've only got a couple of weeks left, and the colonel is looking for someone to take my place. Ya want the job?"

My mind was spinning as I watched Neil working his left hand, demonstrating how well it worked. He had a nasty purple scar in the middle of his forearm, and it was obvious that the bullet he'd caught had damaged some of the tendons that controlled his fingers; he could only partially close his hand.

I knew that for Neil, working in the rear would have probably been easy. Even in the field, he used to hang out with the lifers, and since he didn't smoke dope, he had little to hide, but for me, it was a

different story. I was one of the guys the colonel had been campaign-
ing against—an unrepentant, nonconformist pothead. Questions
filled my mind. Would I be deserting the platoon and shirking my duty
helping with the platoon's newbies? Could I somehow use the position
in a subversive way? I felt swamped and confused. But then my mind
hit upon the bottom line, and the answer was clear. Could I live with
myself if I lost my legs in the last weeks of my tour after having had
the opportunity to opt out? The answer was a resounding no. I had to
consider that my presence in Vietnam had already allowed someone
else in the States to avoid the draft, and the old-timers' axiom "cover
your own ass first" seemed to be more than applicable in this instance.

I heard myself say, "Sure." I felt as if I were in a dream.

"Ya know how to work a 35mm camera, don't ya? And develop film?"

"Just vaguely," I responded, thinking that my lack of experience
might extricate me from any guilt regarding my decision.

"Well, don't worry about it. I'll get us a couple of passes for the air
base. We'll go down there tomorrow, and I'll show ya the ropes. There's
nothin' to it. All we use is black and white."

In the morning, Neil caught me right after chow, passes in hand.
He'd even borrowed the lieutenant's jeep for the day and seemed
extremely anxious to start my apprenticeship. Being still somewhat
conflicted about my decision, I could hardly share his enthusiasm but
went along for the ride.

"Here's your first assignment," he said excitedly. "Did you notice
the new flagpoles the colonel had installed in front of headquarters?
He wants a picture of them and an article."

*Jesus,* I thought to myself as Neil babbled about ASA, depth of field,
and shutter speeds. *What kind of lifer bullshit is this?* With Neil's coach-
ing, I took a few snaps of the colonel's prized flagpoles and wondered
how to tell Neil that I'd rather not be a reporter. Actually, I hadn't
even noticed them before. Usually we kept a wide berth from headquarters—liferland. On the way to the air base, the open jeep was too
windy and noisy to allow much conversation, so I spent much of the
time mulling over my dilemma. What was there to say about a pair of

flagpoles flying the American and South Vietnamese flags? The thought was revolting, but it made a light go on in my head. Neil didn't notice my mischievous grin. I'd found an out. I'd tell them what they wanted to hear and then some.

After a day-long crash course in developing film and making prints, Neil introduced me to the typewriter he was confident would soon be mine and left me to my work. Although I felt out of place amid the officers in headquarters and noticed the colonel giving me less than approving looks (probably because of my ragged fatigues, scuffed boots, and the beaded necklace I was determined to keep wearing), I kept to my plan. I wrote how appropriate it was that we had the twin flagpoles and how aptly they symbolized the cooperation between the American and ARVN forces standing side by side in our mutual effort to liberate South Vietnam. I shoveled it on so thick that the pages of my article were oozing with sarcasm and contempt. I slid the article and pictures into a manila envelope and slipped them into the colonel's in-box with a smile. Anyone who read it would think that the author was either a complete idiot or someone who was trying to make a fool out of the colonel, but I didn't care. So what if I had to spend a few extra weeks in the field. No sweat, GI.

After my short apprenticeship with Neil, I was returned to the field until it was time for him to go home. Although I'd had a few minor attacks of short-timer's nerves in the rear, once I was back in the field, it was business as usual. My concentration, clarity, and calm returned with the greatest of ease. By now, there were no conflicting inner voices vying for attention. By the slightest act of will, my thinking mind would obediently retreat into silence, allowing me to slide effortlessly into the relaxed ease of present-centered experience. For the first time, I realized that the guys who had such a hard time being short had experienced a completely different tour. Being aware that one's tour of duty was only a few weeks from its end—being *short* or *short time*, as the Vietnamese called us—opened one to a myriad of distractions if one wasn't careful, but there was only one way to get nervous about things, and that was to think about them. Evidently, some of the guys were still in that mode at the end of their tour. I couldn't imagine how they could have survived the suffering without developing the ability to either merge with or detach from the physical and emotional pain, but it happened. Surviving being short had long been recognized as one of the last obstacles confronting soldiers in Vietnam. If one thought about it too much, it added stress upon stress. They'd be easily overwhelmed with the fear that their luck would run out during their last few days in the field. Tragically, some guys did lose it—some mentally, some physically—just before they could go home.

Two weeks slipped by without a hitch. I was fully prepared to start stuffing my pack with Cs when Lt. Anderson motioned for me to come over. He had to holler over the sound of the Huey whining in the center of our LZ as supply sergeants threw off cases of rations. "You're going back on the next chopper, don't miss it."

He offered me a handshake, and I readily accepted. He was a good man. Green as all get-out, but flexible enough and good-hearted enough to survive. I knew that Speed and Tennessee would take good care of him. The Bastard Rat, however, stayed true to form and glared at me. I waved goodbye to him anyhow, and as I made a dash for Tennessee's place, I heard the lieutenant holler, "Thanks." With no time for sentimental goodbyes, I got right down to business and emptied my pack of personal effects that might make my buddies' lives a little easier. Extra shoelaces, a hammock, a dog-eared copy of *Siddhartha* that my girlfriend had sent me, and a tiny transistor radio seemed paltry gifts in return for all these guys had done for me, but it was all I had. There was time for a few extended handshakes and some back slapping and hugs, and just when I wondered where Captain Speed was, he appeared from the bush with a pipe full of pot. It was lit and cookin' to the max, and when I saw him take a deep breath and put his mouth over the bowl, I knew I was about to get my last shotgun. For a little guy, he, like Doc, had the lungs of an elephant, and not to be ungrateful, I hung in there with him till the end. I inhaled deeply and held the hit with my eyes closed. Reeling, dizzy, and grinning like the cat that ate the canary, I opened my eyes just in time. Tennessee grabbed me by my shoulders and spun me 180 toward the chopper, which was getting ready to take off. I made a dash for it on wobbly legs, while Tennessee, Bruce, Doc, and Speed laughed loudly at me from behind. No sooner had my butt hit the deck, the chopper started to rise and, with it, my heart. It had been a brief, no-nonsense send-off, but never in my life had I been showered with such genuine affection.

With exactly one month left in my tour, I fully intended to start ghosting as soon as the chopper landed at LZ Uplift, but no such luck. Neil snagged me even before I could sneak into the stand-down barracks and hide under a poncho liner.

"The colonel really liked your article about the flagpoles." He fell into step with me as I hurried to the barracks. "He wants you to start tomorrow."

He followed me right inside. My attempt to be invisible was futile. And he continued talking while I sat on a cot with my head in my hands.

"What's the matter? You sick or something?"

"Nah, I'm all right."

"You won't have to crash here anyway. You get your own room. It comes with the job. Come on, I'll show ya."

Neil's excited chatter persisted all the way to my new lodgings. As soon as we got there, however, I got a break; he had to leave on "official" business. I sat on the edge of my new cot with my head in my hands, contemplating the mess I'd gotten myself into. I secured the job of reporter, but — given that the colonel liked my article — I was to be working for probably the most deluded man in Vietnam.

He overestimated the value of the ARVNs, underestimated his own troops, and insisted on bringing petty stateside regulations to a place where they no longer applied. Not only was he a hazard to his own troops but also, ultimately, to himself as well. Miscalculations in the field, with their attendant casualties, and pettiness in the rear made him a man living on borrowed time. He was a walking dead man.

Feeling myself sinking into a blue funk, I rallied myself to action. I hung my nearly empty pack on a nail in the wall and inspected the room's furnishings. They consisted of the cot and a footlocker nailed to the wall in such a way that its lid, when opened and held level by light chains on either end, could serve as a writing table. The footlocker was empty as a tomb, so I made the trek across the base camp to the truck-trailer PX for some munchies, maybe some magazines, and an ashtray for my Spartan abode. At the PX I noticed newly arrived boxes of large candles, which reminded me that Christmas was rolling around again. Of the two choices, red or green, I chose a red one and bought it along with the munchies.

Later that evening, as twilight receded and my little room began to darken, I took the candle from my brown paper sack of goodies and used an empty C-ration can for a candle holder, dripping some melted wax into the can so the candle wouldn't fall over. Feeling somewhat oppressed by the sterile solitude of my plywood box of a room, I set the candle on my footlocker lid and gazed at it forlornly. The thought occurred to me that the thick candle, being slightly over a foot long, could be used to mark my remaining time in Vietnam. Using some rough calculations, I determined that if I watched one half inch of the candle burn each night, by the time it was melted down, it would be time for me to leave. Sitting on my cot, I settled in to watch the flickering flame. I focused on it the way I had focused on a trail in the boonies, and I was delighted to discover that the flame was not the static thing I'd been conditioned to believe. It wavered, danced, and sputtered occasionally from the moisture in its wick. In time, it seemed friendly—alive and responsive to subtle changes in my mood. I found myself smiling for no apparent reason. The little flame was bringing me a measure of joy, similar to what I felt watching sunsets, and as my gazing continued, its light became more diffuse, filling the room with a pleasant yellow glow. In spite of the day's chaos and confusion, all was well once more. Comforted and relaxed, I blew out the flame and went to sleep.

After morning formation and chow, I tried my best to look busy at my new desk so as to not draw much attention to myself. I opened one of the drawers and found a camera that Neil had told me was mine to use for the duration. Fumbling with the camera, I felt Neil's crash course in photography evaporating from my mind. Although I remembered what most of the levers and buttons did, the functions of a few of them eluded me, which worried me. As I was looking through the viewfinder at the fluorescent light above my desk, the colonel's voice jolted my nervous system.

"Come with me, Ulander," he commanded in a senatorial baritone. "You're going to take some pictures."

He marched across the street with me in tow, occasionally looking over his shoulder to see if I was keeping up. At the headquarters for Delta Company, one of the enlisted men was waiting, as per orders, for our arrival. He had been seduced into reenlisting in the army for another five years, and the colonel thought that this warranted some special attention. While they posed, awkwardly shaking hands, I stared through the viewfinder of my camera, making adjustments for lighting and focus. When everything seemed right, I pressed the shutter-release button. Nothing happened. If the thing had made the least bit of a click, I would have faked it and gone on "taking" more pictures, but the thing just sat there like a stone. The colonel was not amused. He glared at me with undisguised contempt.

Out of nowhere, Neil arrived to save the day. He looked at the camera for a moment and surmised the problem. I hadn't pressed the film-advance lever far enough, leaving the camera in limbo. He discretely fumbled with the camera, convincing the colonel that something was wrong with it, then advanced the lever and handed it back to me as if he had fixed it. Emboldened by Neil's revelation, I took several pictures in rapid succession before the colonel called it quits.

"I'm going to give you guys passes to Phu Cat," he commanded brusquely. "I want the prints of this on my desk in the morning."

In less than five minutes, Neil had cleared our passes with the first sergeant and commandeered a jeep. He drove like a madman to the air base, as if these pictures of some poor slob re-upping were of the crash of the Hindenburg or something. We made it to the darkroom in record time, but Neil's face changed to an interesting collage of white-and-red blotches when he opened my camera. It was empty—no film.

"Hey," he said in a voice wavering with panic, "you're going to have to get the hang of this! This is my last day here. I'm going home, and you're going to have to handle this by yourself."

Neil's panic diffused some of my own. When he looked up at me, I gave him my best "What are they going to do? Send me to Vietnam?" smile and shrugged my shoulders. He relaxed a bit and said that we'd best spend the day reviewing his lessons. We stayed in the chemical stink of the darkroom for hours while he explained the mysteries of stop bath and fixers, glossy and matte finish. By the end of the day, I was actually getting the hang of it and fully enjoyed watching ghost images gaining clarity in a tub of developer.

Mercifully, the colonel was inexplicably absent the next morning. I knew that I had to come up with something to justify my existence, or he'd be calling the shots and concocting stories, real or imagined, for me to cover for the rest of my tour. I knew what he wanted—patriotic stuff, gung ho stuff, we're-kicking-their-asses stuff—and knew that if I didn't come up with something on my own, he'd find something for me. As I leaned back in my padded office chair, the sound of a Huey gave me an idea. The dust-off crew! That was it. I'd write about the medevac helicopter crew. They were the only guys in Vietnam who were actually doing some good. Granted, they were picking up the pieces of failed policies and ignorant strategies, but that wasn't their fault. As a former grunt, I had every reason to express my gratitude and appreciation for the great job they did, and what could the colonel say? Diddly. They were part of the army.

I told the colonel of my intentions and made my way to the hootch near the medevac chopper's pad. I knocked on the thin wooden frame of their screen door and was greeted by a handsome blond guy in his early thirties with captain's bars on his collar. The insignia on his collar was the only indication of his rank. Almost immediately I sensed that he had nothing of the air of superiority of most of the other officers I'd known, from the lowliest butter-bar lieutenants to the colonel, Mr. Bigwig himself. I told him of my intentions and let him know that even though he'd probably rarely been thanked for doing his job (since most of the guys they picked up were either unconscious or in morphine heaven), the guys in the field really appreciated their work. I was trying to be low-key, but I couldn't help but tell him that during my entire tour, the dust-offs had always arrived when requested, come hell or high water.

"Well, that's not always true, ya know," he said modestly, in a slow Georgia drawl. "There's been times when we just couldn't make it. Y'all must have been lucky. Besides, I don't make the decisions around here; I just fly the thing. There's three of us here, and we all get an equal vote. Which reminds me. These here guys are the crew. This little guy's Angel, and this is Ghost. Angel's our medic, and Ghost's the crew chief. And me — they call me Cap'n mostly, but every now and again it's Son of a Bitch."

As they dealt me in for a game of hearts, I couldn't get over how young Angel and Ghost seemed. Not that I was ancient, at twenty-one, but Angel's round, little-boy face looked like it came straight out of a junior high school yearbook. As the game progressed, Cap'n related how they'd been shot down twice, once in the Highlands and once in Cambodia. He nonchalantly explained that even with a shot-up engine, Hueys could be autogyroed to a fairly gentle landing.

"If ya got the altitude, alls ya got to do is bring her into a steep dive. It gets that big ol' main rotor spinnin', ya see. Then all ya have to do is pull back on the stick just before ya hit the deck. It ain't the softest landin' in the world, but it works okay, don't it, guys?"

I looked up at Angel and Ghost to see them both smiling and shaking their heads, amused at their pilot's exaggerated, nonchalant description of the maneuver. In spite of Cap'n's down-home rendition of the crash-landing, I could tell from their response that it had been a horrifying experience. Having talked to other Huey pilots, I knew that the standard crash-landing technique left much to be desired. If, when the pilot realized his engine was out, he reacted immediately and if he had enough altitude and if he could find a place to set down and if they didn't draw any more fire and if the pilot made the maneuver with absolutely no hesitation or mistake, they had a chance — maybe. And these guys had done it twice. After only a moment's reflection on what I knew about Hueys, I found myself smiling and shaking my head along with Angel and Ghost. We all looked at Cap'n, who, seeing our incredulity, grinned and shrugged his shoulders like some old fisherman who'd just been caught telling a whopper. I had no doubt that they'd crash-landed twice, but I knew for sure that it hadn't been that easy.

Halfway through our game of hearts, the radio on the shelf crackled and sputtered a message. "Lima Zulu, Lima Zulu, this is Hotel Papa. Request Mike Victor at coordinates...." The crew threw their cards in the middle of the table and began a well-choreographed dance, prepping to fly.

"Get this man here a helmet and a flak jacket, will ya, Ghost?" Cap'n said as he bolted out the door. "I'll warm her up."

Cap'n had assumed that since I was writing about them, I'd be flying with them. The thought had never crossed my mind, but it was too late to argue. Ghost motioned for me to take the starboard seat, where a door-gunner would sit, if they'd had one, and he busied himself with his own preparations. Angel sat on the chopper's floor and grinned. Clearly I was in for the ride of my life. Cap'n lifted the chopper gently at first, but as soon as there was clearance, he lifted the bird's tail and poured on the heat. Its main rotor slapped viciously at the air, protesting the strain, but soon it got a hold, and we accelerated as fast as the machine would go. No sooner had we gained some airspeed than we were in a steep, banking turn. The Gs of the turn and the sudden view of blue sky almost emptied my bladder, but as we settled in on our course, the carnival ride came to an end—almost. Though he was pushing the chopper to its limits, Cap'n guided the machine with the deftness of a surgeon. By habit or instinct, he kept us low, no more than a couple hundred feet above the coastal highway. If there were any VC looking to get a shot at us, the best sight they would get would be a passing blur.

Angel must have been amused at my reaction, but he caught my attention long enough to motion with his head toward the village directly in our path. It appeared an oasis in the middle of a sea of rice paddies, a cluster of tall palms protruding from an otherwise flat expanse. I had just enough time to wonder whether we could somehow thread the needle between the palms when the chopper rose, tracing their contour like an artist's brush. For a moment, I considered Cap'n to be something of a cowboy, but considering our mission, I knew he was flying with great skill and professionalism. Speed was the utmost priority. A minute here or there could make the difference between life and death, and keeping us low not only made us a difficult target but also saved precious time. Rather than fly a sloppy, looping arc, Cap'n made a beeline to his destination.

After several minutes of flying, Cap'n veered the chopper ever so slightly west of our northward course and landed near a smoldering green smoke grenade near the edge of a small village. There, an army medic and a small contingent of ARVNs hoisted a stretcher onto the chopper's floor. Angel skillfully eased the wounded man into position while keeping a keen eye on his IV bottle and the length of plastic tubing that ran to the man's arm. I had heard enough conversation between the medic on the ground and Angel to determine that the man, an ARVN regular, had tried unsuccessfully to set a booby trap on a trail near the village. It had gone off and peppered him with shrapnel. Though the man was conscious and stable, he needed to be attended to at the aid station at Uplift for removal of the many tiny bits of steel that had riddled his body.

Fully informed about the man's condition, Cap'n flew the return trip with a tad more ease and caution than on the way up. It afforded me the time to study the crew and take a few pictures.

Through the viewfinder of my camera, I noticed that Cap'n's helmet had twin peace signs painted in gold over the earphone bulges, as well as an Egyptian ankh on the back. In the frame, I could see that he had installed a child's squeeze-bulb bicycle horn to the chopper's ceiling. Angel and Ghost each had neatly painted cartoon characters of their nicknames on their helmets, and Angel's also sported a rather self-deprecating Band-Aid in the front. Everything about them—their nicknames, the gentle way they treated each other, and their consummate skill—indicated that they both understood and accepted the danger inherent in their job. Though they'd seen more death and destruction than I ever had as a grunt, we shared an unspoken understanding. We all knew—too well, perhaps—the tenuous nature of our existence, and we all were extremely grateful to be alive.

Out of the corner of my eye, I could see Ghost trying to get my attention. He tugged on the coiled cord connected to his helmet and pointed to mine. I reeled it in to find that it had been dangling in the breeze. As soon as he saw that I'd found the plug, he gestured to a receptacle near my seat and motioned for me to plug it in. After some buzzing and a loud pop, music filled my ears. They had hooked up the chopper's intercom and radio to a tape player. Skimming over the highway with a head full of music was an orgasmic sensory overload, and their selection of tunes was right on target. It was Hendrix's "All along the Watchtower." Our heads bobbed in sync to the music, but when Jimi came to the line we were reminded not to talk falsely since the hour was getting late. Angel punctuated it with a huge grin and a thumbs-up.

For the crew of dust-off one niner, this had been a routine, even easy, mission, but I felt completely overwhelmed. I felt as if these guys had torn open my chest and revealed to me the miracle of my own heartbeat. I felt like crying.

When we landed, I thanked them for the fun and made an excuse to leave. I needed time to settle down and compose myself. Though the mission had been no big deal, really, I knew that these were the same guys who had flown in under hostile fire to save some of my friends.

I flew with them several times over the next few days. Joyriding, mostly—things were pretty quiet in the boonies. In the meantime, I'd sit in front of my old beater Underwood typewriter and stare at a piece of blank paper. Finally, disgusted with myself, I let my feelings pour like water from a broken dam onto the paper. The result, though honest, was sure to win me no friends among the lifers in headquarters. In honoring the crew and their mission, there was a palpable sense that I, among many others, resented the fact that they had to do it. After a trip to Phu Cat, where I developed and printed my pictures, I stuffed the prints and my article in a manila envelope and handed them to the colonel. Though I still had three weeks left in country, I had finished my job. I had given them the only printable comment on the war I had, and I would write no more. The hour was getting late.

For the next few days, I ghosted. I was defiantly absent at both morning and evening formations and floated around the base camp trying to be anonymous. Once in a while, I'd stop by my desk to retrieve my camera if some friends wanted me to take some pictures, and on one such occasion, the lieutenant who was second-in-command in the office caught me.

"You'd better show up tomorrow," he said. "And stop by supply on the way over and pick up a weapon. Recon has found a deserted VC base camp, and the colonel wants you to take pictures of him repelling into it."

I nodded and left, keeping my thoughts to myself. Of all the vain-glorious bullshit, I thought, this had to take the cake. The colonel was as close to the boonies as he'd ever be, and now he wanted pictures of himself repelling into an enemy base camp. I stopped myself short of guessing what sort of stories the colonel might concoct about the adventure and acquiesced to the inevitable. They'd bust me, for sure, for disobeying a direct order.

In the morning, I picked up an M16 from supply and set it and a bandolier of ammunition on my desk when reporting for duty. I waited calmly for orders to head to the chopper pad, but nothing happened. Across the room, I could see the colonel going about his business. His veneer had cracked. It was subtle, but I could see that he was looking ever so slightly sheepish and slightly nervous. Though I knew he was having second thoughts, he acted as if nothing had happened. During the sweltering afternoon in the office, I busied myself with a magazine and tried not to look too bored. At day's end, I returned the rifle to supply and headed to my hootch to rest.

In the meantime, I discovered that Bravo Company had returned from the field. Anxious to reunite with my old buddies, I hung around while they stood formation and were assigned bunkers for guard duty.

It had been a bad move on my part, because as soon as the Bastard Rat spotted me, I realized I was in for trouble. Through attrition, Bravo Company was shorthanded to man their positions, so the Bastard Rat ordered me to get on a deuce and a half with a couple of newbies to man a bunker on searchlight hill. Though I was about to protest that I was no longer assigned to Bravo Company, his mean and determined look told me he knew my thoughts and wasn't buying it.

As the beast of a truck rumbled up the steep switchbacks that led to the top of the hill, I consoled myself thinking that at least I'd have a great view of the sunset. When we reached the top, there was no one around to give orders, so I made my way to the western-most bunker and settled in for a very promising light show. It was nice, actually—a peaceful spot with a great view of the valley below. No sooner had the deuce and a half made it back to base than I noticed a water truck lumbering up the road to our position. When it arrived, a wiry, blond-haired guy dressed in Levi's shorts and a t-shirt emerged from one of the central bunkers and handed the driver what looked like a wad of bills. At the same time, another of the permanent denizens of the hill climbed atop the tank and opened the lid. He fished in the tank with one arm and eventually pulled out four young Vietnamese girls. I knew in a flash that they hadn't been imported in such a clandestine manner to do laundry.

Feeling that discretion was the better part of valor, I ignored the goings-on and contented myself with waiting for the sun to set. A few minutes later, a jeep could be seen following the same circuitous route to our position. Though I lost sight of it during the last few hundred yards of its trip, I recognized the black helmets when it pulled into the center of our perimeter—MPs. They were forty yards away, but the scene needed no dialogue to understand. From his body language, the guy in the jean shorts was confronting them directly and taking no stuff from them. The standoff lasted only a few minutes before the MPs got back in their jeep and headed back down the hill. At this point, the guy in shorts and the four other dudes who permanently manned the position made a mad dash up a ladder to the top of the tower bunker that stood on the apex of the hill. For a second, I thought we were under attack, but at the sound of the first explosion, I knew what they were doing. They escorted the MPs down the hill with a hail of M79 fire. Each shot was placed expertly — twenty-five yards behind the jeep (provided the MPs didn't slow down) — so the jeep was just barely out of the reach of shrapnel from the little grenades they were firing.

As amusing as it was to see the MPs unceremoniously escorted down the hill, for me, it was yet another indication that the colonel was intent on turning our base camp into a miniature Fort Benning. The guys on the hill had been flaky at times, but the colonel could have talked with them rather than taking the cowardly route and making the MPs do his dirty work. The colonel still hadn't a clue about the men in his command. I was sure that the guys on the hill, like most of the grunts, considered their shenanigans to be so petty as to be unworthy of any attention at all compared to the real crime, which was the war itself. The colonel's actions, as persistent as they were ill advised, were sure to make him a focal point for all the outrage and resentment that festered in our hearts. His patriotic, gung ho illusions were sure to send him to an early grave.

# 8 NO TIME

AFTER CHOW THE NEXT MORNING, I HITCHED UP WITH SPEED, BRUCE, Doc Mock, and Orville for a trip to Linda's. As we sat around her gurgling hookah, I heard even more details of the colonel's disastrous policies. He was bringing a stateside mentality to a place where it didn't belong. Usually when we returned from the field, we left our helmets and packs in a hootch and enjoyed the freedom of going without headgear. The colonel, being a stickler for regulations, noted that we were officially "out of uniform" with our lack of headgear and order the supply sergeant to issue everyone a regulation olive-drab baseball hat. He insisted that our platoon leader make sure we shaved daily and sent his lower-ranking officers on frequent, unannounced visits to the bunker line after dark. Along with setting up the bunker for MPs at the gate and sending them up on searchlight hill, these latest insults fueled the growing resentment like sparks in a powder keg of repressed rage. For the men in the field, who had suffered the loss of friends directly attributable to absurd tactics and strategies issued from the lifers in the rear, things were getting to the breaking point. Rank had its privileges, we were all reluctantly accepting of that, but when rank was abused, it seemed that symbols of privilege were the first thing to come under attack.

I leaned against the mud wall of Linda's house in a swirl of confused emotions only to find Linda herself tugging at my sleeve.

"Baby-san! Baby-san! Get up. You come here with Linda!" she commanded with authority.

She pulled me into an adjacent room and pulled the curtain for privacy. I'd never seen her do this to anyone before, ever. She demanded that I sit in the room's only chair, then sat on my lap, without the least hesitation. She looked me straight in the eye and admonished me, "Baby-san, why you don't tell me you short time."

"I did," I protested honestly. "I told you before."

She sat quietly on my lap for some time. Though not a word was spoken, it was as if we were having a conversation. I told her that it was only at this moment that I clearly realized that she was not VC. I'd suspected it for my entire tour, had kept my distance from her, and only now, in some mysterious way, knew with absolute certainty that it wasn't true. Reviewing my many visits to her house, I realized that she had known how I had felt all along and, with extreme delicacy, never stressed the issue. She had consistently treated me with hospitality and kindness and never once had asked even for trust in return. I felt her wordless forgiveness, and my heart warmed in my chest. In a matter of moments, it opened from a stingy, tightly closed bud to a flower in full bloom. My eyes welled up with tears, and I wanted to hug her till her eyes bulged, but she stood up, anticipating my move. For a moment, she looked directly into my eyes, totally unashamed that hers, too, were full of tears. We simultaneously celebrated the moment and grieved opportunities lost.

When we returned to the living room of her house, I watched her in wonder as she once again attended to her duties as hostess. Only occasionally did I catch her eye, but it was enough for me to know that she was fully aware of what she had done. I felt as if she had exorcised me of some dark demon, a demon that insisted I listen to my suspicious mind rather than my intuition and the knowing of my heart.

Back at Uplift, the colonel caught me roaming around with Speed and Orville.

"Any news?" he asked, with an ever-so-slightly sinister smile that tainted the apparently casual and friendly question.

"No, sir," I responded brightly, pretending I hadn't caught the meaning behind his smile. "Nothing is happening in the field."

There was no need for me to wonder if the colonel knew of Speed's reputation. To the lifers, Speed was a notorious criminal on the loose. Nor was there any doubt as to how I would be judged by being in Speed's company. In spite of my efforts to be as low-key as possible around the lifers, the cat was clearly out of the bag. *Hey,* I thought to myself, *What was he going to do? Send me to Vietnam?* Not exactly.

In the morning, I made a token appearance at headquarters and made something of a show of putting some paper in the typewriter, staring at the ceiling and looking frustrated, and finally crumpling the paper up and getting ready to leave. The colonel, unconvinced by my pantomime of writer's block, headed me off before I could make it to the door. He leaned against the doorjamb with one arm, as if to block a panicked exit on my part. He leered at me, clearly quite proud of himself.

"I want you to get a pack and a weapon out of supply after evening chow. Delta Company is going out on a mission tonight, and I want you to be along."

I agreed, but I glared at him with utter disgust. I was too close to home to be getting busted for slapping the shit out of him. The son of a bitch had been too cowardly to go out in the field with me, so he was sending me with Delta Company. And a night mission! I'd never heard of such a thing, at least not for regular grunts. Not only would landing at dusk put us in needless jeopardy, but humping the boonies at night would make the probability of finding booby traps go from nearly to absolutely impossible.

I was still a little steamed an hour later when I picked up my pack. But somehow the sight of the pack calmed my mind and muted my anger. I knew that if I was going to survive this senseless escapade, I'd have to find the cool necessary to get into the groove. The sound of the Huey's rotor overhead somehow did the trick. My whole system calmed, and my mind snapped into the groove. Unencumbered by thoughts, my mind focused on the feel of the terrain below, and my eyes seemed to pick up details and nuances in the bush that were impossible for an angry man to discern. When we landed, I could see on the faces of some of the Delta Company dudes that they were as bewildered as I was about starting out at twilight. But I could also feel that, in spite of the unusual nature of the mission, the guys in Delta Company were rising to the occasion. That comforted me as I watched the last Huey disappear over the ridge.

When we slipped into the bush, it was already hard to see, and in an hour, I found myself struggling to maintain visual contact with the man only two yards in front of me. In time, it grew darker still. Intuitively, we closed ranks, traveling only a yard apart. It was a clear night, but the jungle was dense enough to block out what light there was, and I only rarely caught sight of the silhouette of the man ahead of me. As the strain of trying to see increased, I found myself relying almost entirely on sound to keep myself oriented. I eventually got the hang of it, but I couldn't imagine the pucker factor of the man on point. For most of the time, he was flying blind.

As I gained confidence in my ability to keep oriented in the dark, a feeling of calm and freedom sank slowly into my bones. Without having to pay attention to the myriad of visual details one was bombarded with while traveling in daylight, I leaned into my ability to feel my way around. In the humid cool of the night air, the heat from the man ahead of me became as apparent as if he'd been a small campfire. Though I was beginning to enjoy the sensual experience of traveling at night, I couldn't shake an eerie sense of déjà vu. As we followed a contour line along the base of a ridge, I gradually realized why. Emerging from two layers of canopy, I could see well enough to determine the most salient features of the terrain. It was clearly reminiscent of the site where Calendar's long-range patrol team had blown their Claymores on a company of NVA and then shot as many survivors as they could.

We gathered on the far side of the clearing and waited for the sky to lighten in the east. Mercifully, the Delta Company CO waited until we could see before ordering a perimeter to be established that would protect us while loading on the Hueys that were due to arrive any minute. Almost as soon as I'd hooked one cheek on the floor of a Huey, my anger returned in force. Surely, the colonel had to be the worst commander the army had ever seen. He was out of touch with his men, ignorant about his enemy, cowardly and arrogant beyond belief. I raged for a while, but then an inner sense of knowing quieted my mind. If nothing changed, the colonel would surely be dead within a month.

I ghosted around the rear for a few days, neither seeking nor avoiding company. I was beginning to feel a distance from the guys in my platoon. I almost envied their position. With the specter of death still haunting them, they felt free to live each moment with gusto and complete abandon, while I was burdened with confusion, complexity, and concern. All they had to do was dodge Lt. Anderson and the Bastard Rat (who was usually on a bender when we were in the rear). I, however, was stuck playing mind games with the colonel. When I did run into them, they never hesitated in giving me support and showing their concern, but I knew I'd have to sort things out for myself.

The only thing that saved me was my Christmas candle. It was now almost halfway melted down, and it had surely been my saving grace. Even after my most intense hassles with the colonel, it comforted me. I grew to trust it, and it took me to new as well as old familiar places and brought me serenity and joy. It allowed me to sit in my hootch and access no-time time. It filled both me and the room with a soothing, healing yellow glow and made me smile. Like the sunsets in the boonies, it had become my friend — a friend I sorely needed.

After an hour or so of candle-gazing, I'd fall into a deep sleep. So deep, in fact, that it took a great deal of noise to wake me up. But tonight, the noise was so loud and persistent that I climbed out of the depths of the void to see what was going on. I heard Hueys warming up and panicked voices shouting instructions that I couldn't decipher. Still groggy, I walked out to the company area, where I found my old platoon hurriedly stuffing their packs with ammunition and grenades and trying to get at least one canteen full of water. Out of the chaos, Bruce's face appeared; it seemed to fill my entire field of vision.

"Did ya hear what happened? The dust-off crashed! I heard about it on the radio while we were on guard duty, and now we are going to secure a perimeter around the crash site."

He glanced over his shoulder to see if the platoon was leaving and then turned back to continue his story. When he started talking again, his face moved in slow motion, and his words came at a maddeningly slow pace.

"Alpha Company had a guy who had a fever of 105, and their medic thought they were going to lose him, so they called for a dust-off. Nobody — can you believe it? — nobody in Alpha Company had a strobe for bringing them in at night, so they used a trip flare. The pilot made two passes and was blinded each time by the flare. On the third shot, he tried to land, but he clipped a tree with the main rotor. They crashed and burned. Man, they're all dead, except for a major who went along with them for the ride."

Bruce might have said more, I'll never know, but when he said the word *dead*, it echoed in my mind as if it had been shouted in a huge stone cavern.

It was the last word I heard for over an hour. For a brief time, questions from my own mind filled my head. Had my article about Cap'n and Angel and Ghost made them needlessly brave? Had my attention caused them to wobble out of the groove? Could I have handled it if I had acquiesced to their many offers for the real thrill of going with them on a night mission and wound up alive amid the wreckage of their chopper and their bodies?

Inexplicably, our old company commander, the one who had tried to send home the bogus report of Heidigger's death, came from out of nowhere and wanted to shake my hand. Momentarily full of anger, I glared at him with fury. He withered before me like spinach in hot grease. Then nothing. I went numb — a nearly terminal case of the thousand-yard stare.

Though some considerable time must have passed, I had no sense of it. When I again became aware of my surroundings, I found myself standing alone in the middle of the company area, in the void. I could hear nothing except for the patter of the rain and the buzzing of the light that weakly illuminated the company area. I floated like a ghost back to my hootch, mustered the energy to say a prayer for the medevac pilot and crew, and fell into a deep sleep.

Bruce and Doc Mock were in my hootch late the following morning, waiting for me to wake up. Though their presence was initially something of a mystery to me, I understood their intentions as soon as I was able to separate memories from dreams. Bruce spoke as soon as he saw the realization on my face that the previous night had not been a nightmare.

"Ya know, those dudes that crashed last night made their own decisions. When your number is up, your number is up. Ya don't need to beat yourself up about it."

Evidently, Bruce had seen me slip into the thousand-yard stare the night before. I almost immediately lost track of what he was saying again, though I knew he was listing a litany of justifications for my article and was making a strenuous effort to absolve me of any possible reason to feel responsible for their crash. While his words had almost no effect, his intent was much appreciated. In contrast to Bruce's passionate plea for my logic to prevail, Doc sat on the end of my cot and said nothing. I could feel the warm glow of his being; it complemented and deepened the quality of Bruce's plea, and I found I could forgive myself ... barely. Doc wasn't thinking in terms of guilt or innocence; he simply allowed me to feel that he totally accepted the person that I was, beyond any superficial characterization. Looking up from the hole I was staring into the floor, I mustered the courage to wipe the sweat from my brow with the greasy sleeve of my fatigues and looked Doc in the eye. As if oblivious to the drama that Bruce and I were creating, his eyes sparkled with joy and good humor. He smiled at me compassionately, as if I had been a child who had fallen down and skinned his knee. I could see in his eyes that there was no need for me to muck about in gooey, dark emotions, but he knew that it would be for me to come to terms with that realization in my own time.

Leaving my hootch, I felt like a man who had been shot in the leg and was being supported by a buddy on either side. As we made our way across the base camp, I became fiercely determined to walk on my own two feet and demanded that they step aside. Though I walked with a pronounced limp, I knew I'd make it. They had been generous in their support, but the rules we lived by demanded a wholehearted effort on my part. As we approached the aid station, Doc let it be known that he had business to attend to, leaving Bruce and me to continue our trek by ourselves. Nearing a bunker in a remote quarter in the perimeter, Bruce confided in me his concerns about the platoon. I could tell that they were partly to distract me from my own worries, but they were partly genuine.

"Ya gotta talk with Tennessee. You've been around longer than me, and he'll listen to you. We got a newbie named West who wants to walk point. Tennessee always agrees, but when we get in the boonies, he keeps putting him off."

We walked around to the front of the bunker and sat in a narrow band of shade. Bruce pulled a bomber out of his shirt pocket, stuffed it in my mouth, and lit it, laughing.

"Tennessee's getting short, too, ya know, and if he doesn't break somebody in soon, then what? We'll be stickin' some totally green dude up there, and it'll be a fucked deal. Shit, I'd walk point myself if I had to, but we got a guy who wants it. And, ya know, ya pretty much gotta want it, or ya ain't gonna be worth a fuck."

I appreciated Bruce's concern, as well as his semitransparent distraction, and agreed to talk with Tennessee. After my second toke on the bomber, all was well. We both knew that copping a buzz was a temporary fix at best; it reminded me that my state of mind was ultimately a matter of choice. Not that there weren't times when emotions asserted themselves and needed to be experienced, but that one's attitude could either relieve or exacerbate the original problem. A seed popped, and as I jumped about, trying to brush the sparks off my shirt, Bruce was quick on the uptake: "There goes another problem." At that we both cracked up. The well-worn phrase had once again proved its validity. A problem had been solved. The problem of sinking into guilt and self-recrimination popped for a brief moment, long enough for me to once again experience the wonder of the moment.

Through the open door of a moment's levity, Bruce drove his little clown car and unloaded an unbelievable stream of comic characters. Clowning was Bruce's forte; he was without equal. Totally unafraid to make a complete fool of anyone, himself included, he relentlessly attacked me with his humor. I laughed until I could stand it no more, and when at last he had mercy on me, we sat together in a glow of well-being, interrupted only occasionally by a spell of giggling. Had it not been for my stumbling, I might have never known the depths of the concern of my brothers-in-arms.

When we returned to our barracks, I was accosted by half of the platoon. They wanted pictures, and who was I to say no. Like most of the guys in the platoon, I had considered it unlucky and presumptuous to carry a camera in the boonies, so I understood their desire to have at least a few snaps to show the folks back home. My camera, however, was in the drawer of a file cabinet at headquarters, and when I tried to retrieve it, the lieutenant called me over to his desk.

"I want you to take this film down to Phu Cat and develop it for me. It's pictures of my girlfriend at the Red Cross orphanage so — *ya know.*" Yes, I knew — it was unofficial business. Then he continued, "I'll give ya an overnight pass if you want. Just do a good job."

Considering that I'd been completely absent from my job for five days, his request was no problem at all. Besides, I always liked being able to sleep in the air-conditioned enlisted men's quarters — on a bed with real sheets — take in the latest movies, and swim in their pool. I grabbed my camera, the overnight pass, and a roll of film and slipped out of the office before the colonel could appear. After taking pictures of everyone in sight — from the arms-over-each-other's-shoulders group picture of the platoon to a shot of a newbie named Boot-nik, taken down the barrel of his M16 — I split for the air base for the first time with a real pass.

At Phu Cat, I made my way to their photo lab, where I suddenly remembered Neil telling me of the risks involved in developing the negatives. The unexposed film had to be wound on this metal-coil thing in complete darkness without touching itself or it would be ruined. Though he had thoroughly explained the procedure, this was one part of the process I'd never done before by myself. Luckily an air force guy was in the darkroom at the time and he said he'd give me a hand. The guy was a wizard in the darkroom. After successfully making the negatives, we made prints—tons of them. He used filters and a little circle of paper on a wire stick, as well as other exotica unknown to me, to get the prints to come out just right. We made eight-by-tens, five-by-sevens, and a slew of wallet size, and we dried them in both matte and glossy finish. My new friend took to the project with boundless enthusiasm, and when I finally called it quits, I had three bulging manila envelopes of prints of premium quality.

The platoon was delighted with the pictures, but when the lieutenant saw his sweetheart in the near-professional splendor of eight-by-ten glossies, I knew I'd have passes to Phu Cat for the duration. Eventually I bought a huge pink beach towel at the air force PX just to razz the lifers. Whenever they saw me standing on the highway with my towel under my arm, waiting to hitch a ride on a deuce and a half, they knew exactly where I was going but had not a clue as to how I'd pulled it off.

With two weeks left in country and unlimited passes to the air base, things were definitely looking up. After unsuccessfully trying to intimidate me into writing gung ho stuff for the paper by sending me out on a night mission, I had a feeling that the colonel had given up on me. My job was sufficiently nebulous that he would have been hard-pressed to accuse me of not doing it. After all, I could have been writing articles about the Steak House (our enlisted men's club) or the coordination of the air force with our troops on the ground—how was he to know? But I wasn't. And I wasn't about to.

The candle in my hootch was getting shorter along with me, two inches tall and going fast. As I watched its flame flicker, the room once again filled with a golden glow. With the prospect of not only going home but also being discharged from the army at the same time hard on the horizon, I savored the candle's light as a symbol of the now in the face of the unknown. Subtly, progressively, I had learned to trust it and surrender myself to it until there was neither self nor candle. All thoughts, cares, yesterdays, and tomorrows would dissolve into irrelevance as the joy of the moment filled me with wonder. That infinitesimal, silent witness of my existence would acknowledge the steady smile of knowing on my face and retreat into obscurity. Somehow I knew that all that I had learned in Vietnam was brought to bear in the stillness of these moments. The horror, rage, and grief I'd brought to the flame was distilled and transformed. I knew I couldn't think about it or will it, it simply was. Then, as a drop of wax slid down the candle's glassy side, I knew my time was up. It was time to visit with my friends.

As I rose from my cot, I sensed a strange presence in the air. Standing with my feet at shoulder width, my body straightened until it was completely and perfectly erect. In an instant, I realized that my awareness of self had dissolved to near nothingness. When I had arrived in Vietnam, I thought I was a white guy, the son of middle-class parents, with two years of college under my belt. For the next couple of months, I was, for the most part, the pain in my shoulders and legs and the fear in my stomach. Gradually, I became the trail in front of me, each leaf and stone, the sunsets, and the stars at night. In the stillness of my perception, there had been no discernable difference, but now, even that was gone. My awareness of the candle, my room, and my body faded into oblivion. I saw nothing, heard nothing, felt nothing, and had not a single thought. All that was left of "me" was a tiny speck that knew only that I existed.

The room hummed with a low and powerful tone. Energy crackled about me, the way it does in an area where lightning is about to strike, and I knew it would. For a moment, I knew I had the option to run away in fright. I stayed. At the very instant of my decision to stay, my body was completely paralyzed. The lightning struck with such force that I felt sure that my physical body would either disintegrate or explode. It held me transfixed, as if I were between the poles of an inconceivably powerful magnet that was aligning the cells and molecules of my body to its pull. Then, slowly, it wound slowly down and let me go.

For long moments, I just stood there in silence. Stunned, cleansed, empty, yet full. I felt weightless, completely alive. My legs buckled, and I sat on my cot, stupefied by the whole experience. Spontaneously, my stomach convulsed, and I cried with complete abandon, like a child. To this, too, there was no resisting. Tears streamed down my face, as well as mucus from my nose, but I hadn't the will or energy to stop it. Slowly this also came to its natural end, leaving me exhausted. When, at last, I had collected myself enough to make a conscious choice, I stood again and looked out through the rusted screen of my hootch.

There, across the dirt road, was the four-holer outhouse, the enlisted men's latrine, standing in its usual location. It seemed to exist with great authority—as if its seemingly ephemeral, holographic presence had been sanctioned by some divine being. It was neither ugly nor beautiful, but it stood with such an undeniable sense of *being* that it was a wonder in itself. For a time, I marveled at the grain showing through the OD paint on its plywood sides and the simple, ancient weave of the sandbags at its base. Though I could have been content to stare at the outhouse for hours, my gaze drifted to the south and west.

The sky was ablaze with color. Waves of violet rippled over the hint of rose left by the setting sun. Soft, fragile, and exquisitely delicate, the colors filled me with delight. I stared at them without reflection and felt honored by their presence. Again, a wave of overwhelming gratitude crashed over me and brought me to tears. Surely, I was loved and had been loved all along. I sat on my cot and sobbed.

Hours later, in the soothing darkness of my hootch, I awoke. It was late and, for the most part, quiet, so I went for a walk in the cool air to ease my mind. Gradually my vitality returned to some degree. I still felt fragile, but also very high and very much alive. As I looked around the base camp, my view was one from absolute stillness. I felt filled—fulfilled—with a quiet joy. I passed a hootch and heard music. It was Tommy's hootch, and the thought of being with friends suddenly had great appeal. I grabbed the wooden handle on the door and stuck my head in tentatively to see what was going on.

"Baby-san! Baby-san! Come on in!" shouted Bruce from the far corner of the room. "Tommy's got some new tunes from the world, and we're havin' a party. Check it out."

I stepped in the room and sat on a stack of ammo crates just inside the door. At the far end of the room, Bruce, Tennessee, Speed, Orville, and Tommy were checking out the cover of a new album that Tommy's girlfriend had sent him from the States. Doc Mock sat across from me, at the other side of the door. They said it was from some big concert at Woodstock in New York. The light in the room seemed to be blindingly intense and the music a bit too loud, and I felt content to watch them goofing around from across the room. Just as I was beginning to feel almost comfortable, Bruce came over to me with a weird-looking plastic contraption.

"Hey, man, check it out! Tommy's lady sent him this neat bowl. Alls ya do is hold your finger over this hole, and when this tube fills with smoke, ya let go."

"Nah, thanks though," I found myself saying, not wanting to mess with my present state of mind, which was about as high as I could handle.

"What? Ya don't want any smoke?" Bruce was laughing as if I were making some sort of joke. "Don't sweat it, man," he added. "Ya can't OD on grass." It was as if he were trying to cajole some newbie into his first hit.

Seeing that any further resistance was going to make a scene, I took a hit as directed. It had been a usual hit, possibly even amplified by Tommy's new pipe, but I felt nothing at all—and was relieved.

"Great pipe, ain't it?" Bruce asked as if he expected that I'd gone to the moon.

I nodded in the affirmative, exhaling a great cloud of smoke, but still feeling not a thing. Tennessee and Orville gently razzed me for my lack of enthusiasm from across the room, then sensitively and intuitively let me be. I leaned back against the wall and absorbed myself in the music. It was nice, real nice—a cut of Santana's—and when I opened my eyes, I noticed that Doc was studying me from his perch a few feet away. No sooner had our eyes met than he held me, mesmerized, in his gaze. He probed deeply into my eyes and simultaneously revealed himself to me through his. He knew exactly what had happened to me. Not "kind of sort of," but exactly. In the depth, power, and joy in his gaze, I knew that he'd been there all along, or at least for some time. Reflexively, my mind started formulating questions for him, and intuitively, he made some excuse for leaving and split. I took his leaving as my clue to leave also.

"See you dudes later," I said in the wake of Doc's absence. "I gotta go too."

As expected, when I left Tommy's, Doc was nowhere to be found. He wasn't waiting outside the door, and I knew better than to start looking. Unperturbed, I made my way back to my hootch and relaxed on my cot. There was more in what he didn't say than he could have possibly expressed in words. And he knew better than to try.

Against my better instincts, I mused about the nature of my tour. It had been as if each of the guys in the platoon had served as my guide at one point or another. Each had taken me on a tour of that undiscovered part of myself that they knew best. Speed had shown me my primal instincts; Tennessee, my maternal self. Orville had laid open my grief, and Bruce had shown me my long-lost sense of humor. They had all played a critical part in my journey and, by accident or design, had left the last leg of the trip to Doc Mock. Throughout my tour, Doc had badgered and cajoled, berated and amused me with absolutely no conscious intent, and yet with purpose in mind. In the end, he had led me to the source, the edge of an effervescent pool, and he let the water itself draw me in. Though I knew him to be adept, teaching me how to swim had not been part of the deal. The free-flowing, spontaneous nature of his being had only led me to the pool. Whether I waded, learned to swim, or turned tail and ran, denying that the pool had ever existed, was no concern of his. He trusted me and trusted the water. The end. The beginning.

 **HOME**

FOR THE NEXT COUPLE OF DAYS, I FLOATED AROUND CAMP FILLED WITH the joy and enthusiasm of a young child. It was easier than ever for me to turn off my thoughts and enjoy the feeling of freedom and total spontaneity or to flick the switch the other way and listen to the ramblings of my mind. Invariably, my mind would lead me to confusion and drain my energy, so, for the most part, I left it off. Without the chaos of my thoughts, I found that I didn't even need my conscious mind to carry on a coherent conversation. I let another part of myself do the talking. It was "me," but not me — or maybe more me. I would listen with amusement as it described intricate and complex things with a speed I could never approximate. It would ramble far and wide but eventually put a very definitive period at the end of a sentence. Whoever this "me" was, I didn't know and didn't care, except that sometimes it talked to me.

One night, after a very carefree day, it started telling me things I already knew.

"Somebody is going to kill the colonel. You know that already, but are you going to do something about it?"

"Aieeee! Damn. I'd rather not get involved," I said.

"But you know him. He's a human being. What gives you the right to let it happen?"

I tossed and turned and tried to sleep. It was no use. I wheeled around on my cot and fumbled in the dark for my boots. Hair a mess, boots untied, I made a beeline for the chaplain's quarters. It must have been about two in the morning. I pounded on his door, no reply. Maybe he was gone. Maybe I could go back to my hootch and forget it. But then a light went on, and I heard someone getting up and about. Bleary-eyed and disheveled himself, a man whom I'd never met answered the door. He was a youngish man, in his early thirties, pale and untanned, even after living in the tropics. Ill equipped, I thought, to counsel anyone on God's will, particularly since a chaplain's view of God's will was to fight the good fight and die a "hero's" death.

"There must be something troubling you, my son," he said, doing a great impersonation of someone who gave a shit. "Come in, sit down, and tell me about it."

To the best of my recollection, that was the last thing he said. He spent the rest of the next hour or so with his jaw hanging open; I knew he was being ushered into uncharted territory, privy to a reality beyond his wildest imaginings.

"Don't really know how to tell you this," I started, as mildly as possible, "but there's some real trouble brewing here. I'm going to tell you some stuff and trust that the principle of privileged communication applies."

He nodded nervously, so I continued.

"I've been here for almost a year and, up until we got our new colonel, there was an unspoken agreement of sorts between headquarters and the grunts. But the new colonel wants to change things. You see, I'm a grunt—or I was until a few weeks ago—and like the rest of the guys who are risking their asses out in the boonies, I've smoked my share of pot. When I was first introduced to it, it was a when-in-Rome sort of a thing, but later and in retrospect, I can see how it has a survival value. First off, in a war like this, pot lets you know that being still, listening, looking, smelling, and feeling are absolutely essential to anyone who wants to make it through his tour. You see, newbies arrive here with their heads full of bullshit about the superiority of our weapons and themselves as US soldiers. With that frame of mind, they'd be lucky to make it through their first month. So we set 'em down and get 'em ripped. It doesn't do the trick all by itself, but it lets 'em know that there are more sensitive ways to approach the jungle and the VC than thinking you're going to outmuscle or outwit them. Thinking itself is the problem. You *can't* outwit them. By the time you recall your training and respond accordingly, you're singing with the angels. It's too slow. Ya gotta be able to act from instinct and intuition and feel your way around the jungle without making some mind game out of it. A little smoke and some guidance from an old-timer, a survivor, helps the newbies zero in on the moment, but if ya can't get into the moment, ya might as well hang it up.

"Another thing the ol' weed does for us is let us get into each other's head. Believe me, the stuff they got here is so strong that if you can manage to say anything at all, you can bet your rear it's gonna be uncensored. We gotta know each other inside and out to work together well in the boonies. We can't function on guesswork and speculation. When the shit hits the fan, we gotta know what the guy next to us is up to. We gotta know if he's scared to death or if he's gonna sit down and cry. Getting 'em ripped beforehand gives us a pretty good idea. We don't beat each other up for our shortcomings, but we gotta know them. When I was new here, they did the same thing to me, and I gotta tell ya, I've never been treated so tenderly in all my life.

"Last thing, and certainly not the least, is that none of us here believe in this fuckin' war. We're here till we go home — that's it. Most guys think that if they're out there risking their lives, they deserve to get high whenever they want, and I think they're right. If you and the colonel are so gung ho about this shit, get your asses out from under your sandbag bunkers and go fight the son-of-a-bitch war yourselves. I'm tellin' ya — and believe me, I don't know why — if the colonel keeps hassling guys for smokin' dope, that man is dead meat. There is a drug problem, and it's not with pot, but with the heroin that's been introduced here in the last couple of months. If the colonel was really concerned about his men, he'd get them together, ignore the pot thing altogether, and offer amnesty to the heroin junkies. They're being tolerated at present, but everyone knows that they're starting to become a hazard."

Stunned, the chaplain composed himself long enough to thank me for coming in. Having satisfied my nagging conscience, or whatever, I returned to my hootch and slept like a baby. In the morning, I continued ghosting about and hanging out with the guys in my old platoon. I couldn't believe how good I felt. My body felt twenty pounds lighter — strong, supple, and capable of far more than I'd ever tried to do with it. As long as I kept my thoughts at bay, my energy level maintained its level, maybe even ratcheting up a notch or two. Allowing the luxury of a few stray thoughts, I realized that, compared to this, the rest of my life had been a dull, hazy dream, besieged with needless worry, grief, and fear. Although all the self-inflicted suffering of my previous existence had seemed so real and my myriad ways of justifying it had been convincing, I knew now, beyond the shadow of a doubt, I'd been fooling myself for years.

I saw the colonel walking down the path directly toward me. For once, I decided not to try to avoid him, though there was plenty of time and opportunity for me to do it in a completely nonchalant way. As we passed, I gave him the salute that duty required and was astounded when he returned it with great enthusiasm and a big smile. *So much for privileged communication,* I thought. The colonel was obviously glad for the warning, and I knew that even he wasn't so brain-dead that he hadn't realized that he'd been bringing down disaster on himself for quite some time. It just hadn't happened yet. Hopefully, he'd cool down a bit, and everyone would go home in one piece. After running into the chaplain later in the day and receiving an equally pleasant response, I felt assured that my attempt at intervention had been understood in its real intent. The colonel was hard to like, but I was genuinely concerned for everyone involved in the increasingly volatile situation.

Late the following afternoon, when I was returning from a swim at Phu Cat, Bruce and Orville caught me walking through the company area. I could tell even from thirty yards that they were upset.

"Did ya hear what happened?" Bruce asked. "Did ya hear about Doc Cory?"

I shook my head.

"He was wandering around with an M16. I saw him just about here, right here where we're standin'. Hey, the dude was fucked up. Not just stoned, but really, really fucked, man. I tried talkin' to him, but he was gone, babbling like an idiot. He mumbled some shit about the colonel, but he wasn't makin' any sense. I should have stopped him, man. I should have stopped him, but fuck, man, I didn't know. He was so fucked up that I thought he'd fall out — just go somewhere and pass out. So I left. He was a weird dude, ya know? Shit, he was with us for only a month. Then I find out he went down there by the colonel's bunker, got confused, and went into the aid station and wasted the captain and that black dude, ya know? The E-6 medic."

"He killed 'em?" I asked, shocked, but not totally surprised by such an outrageous turn of events.

"Fuck, yes, he killed 'em. Shit, he was firin' on 'em at point-blank range. Caught 'em right across the chest with his 16 on auto." On fully automatic, an M16 fires 650 rounds per minute. "They didn't have a prayer. And those dudes never did nothin' to nobody. They were *medics* — good dudes. All this shit is that fuckin' colonel's fault. If he hadn't started fuckin' with us, none of this would have happened. But, son of a bitch, I should have known; I should have at least taken his weapon away."

I glanced at Orville, and he got the message. When your heart and soul were laid as open as Bruce's were then, you had to be with the guy you felt knew you best. Orville slipped quietly away, leaving Bruce and me to make the trek across the base camp alone. Bruce was on the verge of going into shock. I could see him lapsing in and out of the thousand-yard stare. We walked together silently. Bruce was content to walk without purpose, but I knew where we were going. We made our way to a bunker on a remote quarter of the perimeter. As I had hoped, there wasn't a soul around for at least a hundred yards. No one was likely to disturb us. He followed me around to the front of the bunker and collapsed, looking weary and exhausted, and leaned back against the sandbag wall. He started to say something, but I held up one finger, and he maintained his tortured silence.

I took my old ivory pipe out of my shirt pocket, tapped it on my boot, and packed it with weed. Bruce smiled wanly as I fired it up, and when it was good and lit, I put the bowl in my mouth and aimed the mouthpiece at Bruce. I took a deep breath and blew backward through the bowl while Bruce inhaled the thick stream of smoke.

"Ah," he sighed, exhaling a huge plume of smoke.

I poked around in the pipe, tamped it, and gave him another shotgun. This time, he leaned against the bunker with a grin of relief.

"Remember the last time we were here?" I asked.

His face contorted as he struggled to remember and then calmed when he did. He looked puzzled for a moment, then nodded and smiled. The last time we had been at this bunker was when he had tried to help me with my guilt and grief about the dust-off crew. We were in the same boat. Choices—regrettable choices—were made, and people died, but he hadn't condemned me, and I couldn't place any blame on him. Each of us was being harder on ourselves than anyone else would ever have been on us. When I had been sick with grief and guilt, he had told me stuff that I didn't believe, and now I could tell him the same stuff, but there was no need. We both knew that he wouldn't believe it either. For both of us, it wasn't what was said that helped, but knowing that someone could forgive us or, more importantly, that we were loved all the same. From the look on Bruce's face, I could see that the incredible irony of the situation hadn't been lost on him in the least.

"What can I say, man?" I asked with a smile. "What can I say?"

I held up my hand, and we did a scorching high five. We knew. We knew that we could stand on our heads and spit wooden nickels at each other till the cows came home, and we'd still have to forgive ourselves. We'd make it, we'd survive, and we'd heal—with a little help from our friends.

Bravo Company was gone by the time I woke up the next morning. They'd been sent out on another mission, leaving me to fend for myself.

I was extremely grateful that, by chance or happenstance, they'd been in the rear with me for the last few weeks of my tour. Without them, I would have been lost. But now they had left me to play with the gift they'd given me, my ability to turn off the chaos of my own mind. I no longer needed a candle, a sunset, or the demands of the boonies to keep my crazy-making thoughts at bay. It was now as easy as flipping a switch, and for the most part, I kept the switch off, spending my days in a state of childlike innocence and wonder. Only rarely would I allow myself to reflect on this mysterious new power, and then only when I knew I'd be alone for a while. The slightest conscious reflection on this gift would leave me overwhelmed by an enormous wave of gratitude that would reduce me to sobbing. Though I hadn't a clue of being grateful to what, for what, I knew that the gratitude, joy, and love that overwhelmed me was without beginning or end. Any effort to describe it would diminish it.

Being in no-time time was so wondrous and painless that I didn't bother even keeping track of exactly how short I was. One of the good things about being in the army was that I knew that they'd tell me, but for me, it didn't matter anymore. Here, there, Vietnam, or the States, what was the difference? One evening, I found myself crossing the highway and following the path that led to the top of searchlight hill. I'd been watching the clouds all afternoon, knew they were setting up one spectacular sunset, and wanted a ringside seat. The sky was still light and mostly yellow in the west as I settled in for the show. Even without the colors that were sure to come, the view was tremendous. Waves of lush green hills rolled for miles beneath row upon row of fluffy clouds.

Far in the distance, I saw a tiny curl of white smoke rise from the valley. *No big deal*, I thought. *A white-phosphorous marking round for artillery spotters — happens all the time.* Several curls of gray smoke billowed up from the same general area. *Probably harassment fire*, I mused. *More random shots in the dark by our artillery, trying to impress the NVA.* But the gray clouds kept coming — six, eight, ten, a dozen. Suddenly sober, I asked a REMF who was passing by me on the trail.

"Who's out there, down in that valley?" I asked, pointing to the west.

"Oh," he was unconcerned. "That's Bravo Company."

Having stabbed me in the heart, he continued on his way. More gray clouds rose, and a pair of Huey gunships raced to the scene from the south. Red streaks from their miniguns cut the sky. They didn't fire blindly; they had a target. The shit was hitting the fan. The silent scene filled me with anxiety, but the next event filled me with rage. A chopper rose from the base camp below, then turned, revealing the unmistakable markings on its side. A red cross. The dust-off lifted its tail and raced to the scene. The dust settled, the smoke cleared, and the dust-off returned. I could see it perch on its landing pad, but it didn't shut down. It went back for another load.

Silently watching, I was consumed by a rage so intense, so pure, that it seemed that at any moment, thunderbolts would fly from my eyes, and my body would vaporize from the fire. My mind ran wild. My friends, men whom I loved beyond love, were getting fucked up. Men who had been ground by the war to dazzling perfection and blazing light, and now what? Would the wonder of their overcoming be zipped in a fucking body bag? Was some fucking army chaplain now going to pervert the marvel of their transformation only to have it blasphemed again by some dumb-fuck hometown preacher?

*Be still.*

My mind raged on and on and on. Should I go down to supply, get a rifle, and finish the job that Cory had botched, or should I wait till I got home and pay a visit to Congress?

*Be still.*

I noted that some infinitesimally tiny part of my mind had given me a quiet command. *Be still,* it said. I wrestled and struggled, to no avail. *Be still.* I mustered a Herculean effort and made but a small dent in the rage that so consumed me. With every ounce of energy and will at my command, I struggled to comply with the quiet voice. Slowly, very slowly, the anger wore away. Exhausted and empty, I lifted my head and gazed at the valley below. A trickle of warm, gentle energy filled the void that was me. Once again, I was filled with overwhelming gratitude. Through my tears, I could see a spectacular sunset spreading its arms over the valley. My mind, body, and soul opened to all that was before me. In the depths of silence, I knew much, understood imponderable mysteries, and dared not bring them to mind.

I didn't "know" it, in the usual sense, but rather, I *realized* that death had no meaning. All the power and love that had brought things into being had emerged from a realm beyond time, and thus it was not bound by time, and neither were its creations. Forms changed, their essence did not. I realized that all the suffering on earth was not born of some dark force or curse on humanity but was humankind's own creation. Surveying the valley from a point of utter silence, my awareness sank through layer upon layer of self-deception. I realized with undeniable clarity that I had never for a moment been abandoned, yet all my life I had thought I had been. This had been my bottom-line belief, one that had created so much suffering for myself and others. Though totally responsible for my own actions, this basic belief had allowed me to fall prey to the vultures of religion, society, and, indeed, the military itself, entities that rushed in to offer fulfillment of my own innermost longing. "We," they had proclaimed, "are authorized by seal and sanction to be intermediaries between your lonely soul and the light. All you need to do is surrender to us your time, your energy, and your life, and we will guide you back to your eternal home." Weak and vulnerable, I had capitulated, but no more. My mind had penetrated to the core of their deceptions. My experience itself, in this moment of no-time time, had shattered the final links of the chains of my enslavement. There could be no turning back.

The overwhelming power that had so mercilessly probed the depths of my being now became fine, subtle, and sweet, like the fragrance of a newly opened rose. It eased the pain in every fiber of my being and every cell in my body. It filled me with bliss and revealed to me yet another undeniable realization. Justice was. It had been, was now, and always would be administered with exacting precision. It had no need of my puny intervention. After hours of silence, a single thought slipped into my mind. How could I be worthy of this? Again, out of a sense of total and complete gratitude, I cried.

A staff sergeant from supply was shaking my shoulder. It was morning.

"Get up and get your ass to supply, bud, you're going home."

He efficiently, professionally, led me around the base camp like some lost child to ensure that I hadn't missed any of the important procedures necessary for my departure. We stopped by headquarters for my records, supply for a duffel bag full of stuff I'd left there a year ago, and then to the reenlistment officer to make sure I wanted to be discharged. We stepped in the door, and the officer went into his rap.

"Blah, blah, blah, blah, blah. And if you choose to reenlist right now, I'm authorized to cut you a check for five thousand dollars."

"You gotta be shittin' me. Hey, man, I'm history."

Along the way, I asked, "How did Bravo Company fare last night? It was looking pretty grim."

"Couple of newbies were wasted," he replied, with the callousness of a true rear-echelon motherfucker. "Six other guys were fucked up, but nothin' bad. They still have their arms and legs. A couple of guys from Delta Company got wasted yesterday too. Things are gettin' hot out there; it's a good time for you to be leavin'."

His words and demeanor, which at other times would have thrown me into an uncontrollable rage, had no such effect. My mind stayed clear, calm, and detached, as if his words had no meaning. Perhaps I was in some space so remote and detached that I understood that ultimately it didn't matter—or possibly I was into complete denial. Whichever was the case, I couldn't bring myself to ask about the details of the wasted or wounded men.

In forty-five minutes, I was on a jeep to Phu Cat. From there, a jet to Cam Ranh. At a dizzying pace, my body was hurled from Cam Ranh to Seattle and from Seattle to O'Hare in Chicago.

On the flight from Seattle to Chicago, I spent most of my time either napping or staring at the topside of the clouds out the little window to my left. For me, there was never any comparison between some bland in-flight magazine and the seemingly endless expanse of white, swirling forms sliding beneath and beyond the plane's wing at thirty thousand feet. By the time we landed, the hours of cloud-gazing had eased my mind into the same space it had been during guard duty at night in the jungle — clear, calm, and flow-through open.

The first thing that came to my attention in the concourse was the air. I hadn't realized how accustomed I'd become to the rich, earthy smells of rotting wood and decaying leaves until the first whiff of the stagnant, lifeless, and metallic O'Hare air assaulted my senses. While quietly musing about the effectiveness of the airport's smell in evoking memories of a time eons ago (actually only a year) when I was last at O'Hare, I felt buffeted by turbulence of another sort. Feelings of anxiety, anger, and thinly masked sadness permeated the atmosphere. I knew these emotions were coming from the people around me, as my mind was yet still. Looking around, I saw people carrying skis, luggage, and oranges. Most appeared to be either leaving for or returning from vacation. Occasionally someone would smile, but there was no joy here.

As I exited the gate and entered the main terminal, I found myself in the school-of-fish mob as it made its way through the main concourse toward the baggage area. A small family was slightly ahead of me. The thirtyish parents hurried along as their young daughter, about eight years old, struggled with the net bag of oranges she was carrying. The little girl bobbled a bit and one of the oranges escaped the bag, bounced off her knee, and rolled on the floor ahead of her. Her dad snapped at her in a flash of rage and exasperation as she chased the errant orange. She crumbled, frightened and humiliated, but managed to keep her composure long enough to retrieve the orange. When I looked at him in utter disbelief about his totally disproportional response, he shot back with a mind-your-own-business glare and turned away.

I kept my thoughts on hold and headed for the bar for a Coke. Inner calm prevailed, but as I settled onto the red barstool, my system shifted to a higher intensity level. From experience, I knew that I was either about to experience a premonition of some sort or about to be ambushed.

The place was empty except for the bartender and the three businessmen who sat directly across the fifteen-foot span of the C-shaped bar from me. At a glance, I could tell that two of the three guys, all of whom were in their thirties, were shamelessly sucking up to the third. They were acting as if they were so clever that no one could possibly tell, but it was blatantly obvious. Surprised at the certainty of my impression, I felt like an intruder, so I just stared at the bar, but the scene immediately recreated itself in my mind. The men appeared as mannequins—pithy, lifeless, and hollow—just as in my first impression. It was as if the life in them flickered weakly, the way a bad fluorescent bulb blinks and hums but neither lights nor goes out.

A shot of whiskey appeared on the bar in place of their images, and the barkeep said, "It's from them."

I didn't want to look again but felt compelled to. In one motion, I downed the shot and glanced across the bar. They sat there, for all the world, smiling an acknowledgment to a tanned man just back from Vietnam, but my jungle senses went on overload, telling me to get out of the kill zone. These were extremely dangerous men.

Reeling in confusion, I wandered aimlessly for a time, until a newspaper stand caught my eye. Memories of Sunday morning on my folks' living room floor flooded my mind. I could almost see myself lying on my stomach turning the pulpy pages, feeling at ease and secure. I greedily grabbed a *Chicago Tribune* and was stunned by its headline:

### ONLY FIVE KILLED IN VIETNAM THIS WEEK

My gut wrenched. *Only* five. I remembered that things had heated up before I left. I remembered the bogus report about Heidigger's death. Only five. Sure, right, that's got to be the truth. Only five teenaged kids blown to kingdom-fucking-come, and that's good news? And even if it were true, it meant that there were also *only* two vegetables, three or four one-legged men, a blind guy or two, and *only* a few who were so generally fucked up that they would never regain any semblance of normal physical health. Great, great fucking news.

Taken aback by my own anger, I dropped the paper and stared at my boots. Had to maintain my cool, as my buds in the 'Nam would say. Slowly, as I calmed, I remembered Ski staring at the floor of our hootch, struggling for words to describe his thirty-day R & R in the States. I knew in my bones what he couldn't express — same war, different weapons. In less than an hour, I had been snagged by the wait-a-minute vine of weird emotions on the concourse, ambushed in the bar, and now stood blackened and charred by the booby-trapped newspaper. I remembered Ski being inexplicably jumpy and untrusting when he came back from the States, and now I understood why. He never made it home either. We were destined to lives of alienation, isolation, and loneliness in the place we once called home.

None of us would come home, at least to the home of our imaginings. Rather, we would be exiled to a place where the population had been so thoroughly propagandized by some Immaculate Deception, a deception so seamless and tight that not a pinhole of light was allowed in. Exiled to a place where lies were so prevalent that they were taken for truth, where wonder and delight were snuffed out in a child before the age of five.

I braced myself for a shock before looking up again. I could feel it but couldn't bear to see it. It felt a lot like the feeling that tore at my heart the first time I'd seen a village in Vietnam. Mud huts, cardboard walls, and people wearing slices of truck tires for shoes. The pungent odor of urine, feces, and rice cooking all wafted together, telling of poverty I never knew existed. Now I heard a pop deep in my chest. It was the sound of my heart — breaking.

I dug deep and, to the best of my ability, regained the clarity and detachment necessary to survive the most well-planned ambush I had ever been in. And I looked up — over the sea of the deceived. I looked over the sea of people who had been trained, conditioned to consider themselves to be unworthy of love. The walking wounded. Dressed in expensive clothes, they were the most impoverished people I had ever seen.

But how could they know? No one ever stayed up with them all night when they were scared shitless. No one had ever offered to die for them, except for some dude two thousand years ago—and all that ever amounted to was a sweet story for children and a social club for business connections. If they'd only seen a man dancing his dance of pure joy in the searchlight or Doc Mock risking his life to save a man he barely knew. If they had seen Tennessee kill in their stead or Speed gleefully bear the burden of walking point for thirty men, maybe. But they didn't know, and I couldn't say.

I felt that if I had had one less day in the bush—one less conversation with Doc Mock—I would have sat down and bawled like a baby till the airport security hauled me off, but my system held, if only by a thread. I felt as if I were physically sinking. I knew I had to move and headed for the door.

My jungle senses were keener than ever as I made my way through the crowd. While on patrol, I could feel the emotions of the NVA; here I could sense the thoughts of people. A glance into someone's eyes, and I could tell their intent beyond their conscious thinking.

Sharp glances said, "Hold your tongue! We don't want to hear it."

I blasted out the door and ran across the street from the taxi stand to get a clear view of the sky. Low clouds scudded across my field of vision. It was cold, bitter cold. Icy sleet stung my cheeks. My toes numbed in my jump boots, but as I gazed into the yellow light soaking through the clouds, I could feel the bubble forming deep inside me. It rose slowly through my body and made me smile. The clouds knew. I knew. In that moment, that was all that mattered.

# GLOSSARY

**AFVN (Armed Forces Vietnam Network)** — A radio station set up by the military to provide AM radio to the troops who were serving in Vietnam.

**ARVN** — The Army of the Republic of Vietnam, our allies.

**APC (armored personnel carrier)** — The specific designation for the armored personnel carrier used in Vietnam was the M113 armored personnel carrier. It is a lightly armored tracked vehicle that had been designed to carry a squad of infantry.

**CS Gas** — Also known as tear gas or riot gas. It can be deployed in grenades, bombs, and projectiles for the M79 grenade launcher. The gas causes profuse tearing and profuse discharge from sinus and nasal cavities, acute respiratory distress, blindness, and vomiting.

**Deuce and a Half (M35A2 cargo truck)** — A rugged and powerful 6' × 6' cargo truck capable of hauling a payload of two and a half tons.

**Dust-off** — Emergency removal of a soldier by a medevac helicopter, reserved for cases where the soldier was seriously injured or ill.

**Skycrane (Sikorsky S-64)** — A powerful military helicopter used by the army in Vietnam that was designed for heavy lifting. It has a payload of twenty thousand pounds.

**Frag (M26 fragmentation grenade)** — *n* A sixteen-ounce steel-cased grenade designed for throwing. It was filled with granular or flaked TNT. *v* To toss a grenade toward an enemy position or into an enemy tunnel — or toward an unpopular officer.

**HE (high explosive)**—The abbreviation to designate the type of charge internal to various kinds of ordinance, grenades, artillery shells, and bombs.

**KP (Kitchen Police)**—Duty usually designated to low-ranking enlisted men that required them to help with the most menial tasks in the mess hall, such as washing pots and pans, or peeling potatoes.

**OD (olive drab)**—The standard color used to camouflage equipment used by the army. Also the abbreviation for *overdose* or *officer of the day*.

**MEDCAP (Medical Civic Action Plan)**—A program that allowed the US military to provide medical assistance to Vietnamese civilians. It was part of the attempt of the military to win "hearts and minds."

**Minibase**—A small outpost created in remote areas of Vietnam, usually comprising a dozen or so bunkers arranged in a circle on a hilltop.

**Minigun (M134)**—A six-barreled Gatling gun that was usually mounted on aircraft, including helicopters used in Vietnam. It could fire 7.60 caliber rounds at the rate of four thousand per minute.

**MP (Military Police)**—A policing force specifically designated to enforce laws and regulations that relate to army personnel and property.

**NCO (non-commissioned Officer)**—An enlisted man who made the rank of sergeant or above.

**PX (post exchange)**—A store on a military base, of varying size, depending on the location, that sells civilian-type clothes, food, and goods.

**ROK**—Troops from the Republic of South Korea who were deployed along with the American troops in Vietnam.

**Spec 4**—The army equivalent of a corporal in the marines. The next rank up from private first class.

# ABOUT THE AUTHOR

Gretchen Fawn Photography

Subsequent to his tour of duty, Perry Ulander enrolled in an under-graduate program at the University of Illinois. After three semesters, he left the university due to irreconcilable differences. Prior to work-ing on *Walking Point*, he earned a living as a journeyman carpenter. He is now retired and lives with his wife, Jayne, in a small mountain town east of Seattle.